UNIV... ...INGHAM
W... ...WN
...RAR...

D1634175

CIR... AT... G... ...E FOR RETURN

Class 759.2 No. 2,357 Vol.

ND497.P25.G7

River Series
RE-ORDER
Niger Manilla
No.2004

SAMUEL PALMER

1. A Cow-lodge with a Mossy Roof (72). *c.* 1828-9. *Watercolour, gouache, and pen.* $10\frac{1}{16} \times 14\frac{5}{16}$

[front

SAMUEL PALMER

THE VISIONARY YEARS

By *GEOFFREY GRIGSON*

DEPT. OF EXTRA-MURAL STUDIES
UNIVERSITY OF NOTTINGHAM

KEGAN PAUL LONDON

First published
by Kegan Paul, Trench, Trubner & Co. Ltd.
Broadway House: 68-74 Carter Lane
London, E.C.4
1947

Printed in Great Britain
by T. and A. Constable Ltd., Hopetoun Street,
Printers to the University of Edinburgh

10034771/A-1

If my aspirations are very high, my depressions are very deep, yet my pinions never loved the middle air; yea I will surrender to be shut up among the dead, or in the prison of the deep, so that I may sometimes bound upwards; pierce the clouds; and look over the doors of bliss. . . .   SAMUEL PALMER.

No bird soars too high, if he soars with his own wings.

BLAKE.

Painting as well as music and poetry exists and exults in immortal thoughts.

BLAKE.

. . . the last branch of uninteresting subjects, that kind of landscape which is entirely occupied with the tame delineation of a given spot. . . . The landscape of Titian, of Mola, of Salvator, of the Poussins, Claude, Rubens, Elzheimer, Rembrandt, and Wilson, spurns all relation with this kind of map-work. To them nature disclosed her bosom in the varied light of rising, meridian, setting suns; in twilight, night, and dawn. Height, depth, solitude, strike, terrify, absorb, bewilder, in their scenery. We tread on classic or romantic ground, or wander through the characteristic groups of rich congenial objects. . . .

FUSELI.

Genius may adopt, but never steals.   FUSELI.

. . . Es muss
Beizeiten weg, durch wen der Geist geredet.

HÖLDERLIN.

v

CONTENTS

(A number after every mention of a drawing or picture refers the reader to the chronological catalogue, which includes the known and missing works.)

PREFACE

ADMIRATION of Palmer's early work goes back to F. G. Stephens, the Pre-Raphaelite critic. Five of the Shoreham pictures were exhibited in the memorial exhibition of Samuel Palmer's work at the Fine Art Society in 1881, and in his notes in the catalogue he praises, with some feeling, "The Bright Cloud" and "The Hop Garden," calling them "Keatsian." In 1893 Charles Ricketts and his friend Charles Shannon went to the Burlington House Winter Exhibition and "were greatly moved by six designs in sepia by Samuel Palmer"—an excitement handed on to the late Sturge Moore. All six (Nos. 38 to 43 in my catalogue) were drawn in 1825, when Palmer was twenty; and in them there was much to appeal to the aesthetic of the Nineties. But with our greater knowledge of what Palmer produced in the next ten years, it is not easy to agree with Sturge Moore that they were Palmer's "happiest designs." Indeed, for many years more, Palmer had still to be talked of as a follower of Blake; his painting and draughtsmanship and vision had still to be set free from what I may fairly say was an academic and a literary appreciation. His influence still had to become living and active.

From time to time, more early Palmers came into view, through the sale-room, and at the Blake Exhibition at the Tate Gallery in 1913. Then, in 1926, came the Exhibition at the Victoria and Albert Museum, the bulk of which was given to Palmer. This was a major eye-opener (to which was soon added the Exhibition of British Art at Burlington House, in 1934). For the first time, it was possible to see and feel the power and the individuality, the peculiarity of Palmer's vision, to see, for instance, that his much prized etchings were a reflection only of the fullness of the moonlights of 1830. For making this revelation possible, we owe much to the persistent, if not always well guided, devotion of Palmer's son, the late A. H. Palmer, and to his friend, Mr. Martin Hardie, then on the staff of the Museum. The late F. L. Griggs was also a devotee. But if it is not ungracious to say so, the Exhibition of 1926 was sadly incomplete, and few of the Palmers treasured by the children of George Richmond were included.

Nevertheless, the influence of Palmer began to quicken. Collectors and galleries (notably the Ashmolean through Sir Kenneth Clark) took notice of him. Critics, though still too fond of naming

Palmer a "literary" painter and tieing him heart and head to Blake, began to realize there must be some alteration here in the canon of English art. To younger artists, the revelation of Palmer resembled the revelation of Gerard Hopkins to English poets: here was an artist who had seen the now somewhat jaded and vulgarized world of natural objects, most individually, and at once from the outside and inside of its being and its growth.

But appreciation has outrun analysis and understanding of Palmer; and I have tried in this book, as a result of several years' investigation, to show how and why Palmer painted as he did, to clear his relationship with Blake, and to outline as completely as possible the achievement of his visionary years. He was, indeed, a painter influenced not only by painting, depending not only upon his eyes. His religion, his reading, his politics blend in his work, blend furiously with the clear-sighted unity between himself and nature. And anything but naïf, he was a painter, even at twenty, sharply conscious of what he was about, as open as anyone of his time to precept and to other men's work.

When A. H. Palmer wrote his *Life and Letters of Samuel Palmer*, it was natural for him to think Palmer's middle age and old age the most important. We may have swung a bit too far in our habit of ceasing to admire Palmer abruptly at the point where the admiration of Ruskin and Rossetti began. With ups and downs he always was a sensitive executant; but he was not an extraordinary artist after his early flaming died down to a glow, and there was something in F. G. Stephens' use of "Keatsian" for his early pictures, and "Tennysonian" for his later watercolours—enough to justify me in not carrying this book much beyond Palmer's thirtieth year.

Of course, any new study of Palmer must build on the two chapters or so which A. H. Palmer gave to his early life, and on A. H. Palmer's lifelong absorption in his art and being; but it has been possible to supplement, and in some details correct A. H. Palmer's information, and to draw rather firmer conclusions. Before he migrated to Canada, Palmer's son acted in a way that fills a new study of Palmer, at some points, with conjecture instead of certainty. He burnt his father's early note-books and sketch-books, and much else. So far as I can discover, his records of meeting Blake no longer exist. Nearly all he wrote, his records of his visionary struggles and victories and desolations, which seemed rather embarrassing to A. H. Palmer, were destroyed. But for all that, besides new drawings and pictures, there have been other aids to gaining at any rate a tentative purview of his mind. The interruption of the war has made difficulties, and made it impossible to see a few of the drawings catalogued, and to investigate a few possible sources of documentation. But I have many people to be grateful to.

First of all to various descendants of George Richmond, R.A., especially Mr. Anthony Richmond, who allowed me to see Palmer's long correspondence with his grandfather, Mrs. Medlicott, and other members of the family who own and treasure letters, or drawings and paintings of Samuel Palmer, or portraits of him; various descendants of John Linnell, who have helped freely with documents and information; Mr. Herbert Read, who first stirred me to an interest in Palmer; Mr. Giles Overbury and his sister Mrs. Pilcher; Mr. Martin Hardie, and Mrs. F. L. Griggs, who allowed me to read invaluable correspondence from A. H. Palmer; Miss Wright and Mrs. A. J. Finberg; Sir Kenneth Clark (whose percipient advocacy of Palmer has been invaluable); Mr. Thomas Lowinsky, Col. Buchanan, Mr. Carl Winter, the late Sir Frank Short, R.A., Mr. Leonard Duke, Mr. Graham Sutherland, Dr. and Mrs. Gordon Bottomley, and others who own early works by Palmer.

Mr. K. T. Parker, who has added so well to the Ashmolean Palmers, has been generous and encouraging. Others I must mention are Mr. A. K. Sabin, Mr. Louis Clark, of the Fitzwilliam Museum; Mr. John Piper; Dr. Nikolaus Pevsner; Mr. John Craxton; the photographic staff of the National Gallery; and Mr. Ruthven Todd, who has helped with his knowledge of Blake, with transcripts, with clues, and many hours of sometimes exciting exploration in Somerset House, the British Museum, and elsewhere.

If I may end with a plea, it is this: that more care should be taken to preserve all the various documents which show how and why English artists lived and painted. A terrible destruction must have gone on in the last hundred years, and anyone who knows the MSS. collections of the Victoria and Albert Museum and the British Museum will admit how scantily provided we are with such evidence for the still unwritten history of English art. The sacrosanctitude which preserves all the letters and diaries of authors, does not seem to extend to artists, who are not only creatures with eyes and easels, as even Mr. Clive Bell would admit.

CHAPTER 1

CHILDHOOD

I

THE comfortable, middle-class clan into which Samuel Palmer was born in 1805 was not unlinked with painting and writing. His father was a bookseller, rather because he liked books than because he excelled, or was interested, in trade. His mother, Martha Giles, was the daughter of a well-to-do banker, William Giles, of Walworth—"a man"—so his obituary said—"in whose character were combined so many excellencies, shaded by so few defects, as to command the esteem and admiration of all who knew him. Affable, friendly, affectionate —well-informed—conscientious in all things—most exemplary in his deportment—and in an eminent degree spiritually-minded." [1] William Giles was important in Samuel Palmer's life. It was his death in 1825, and the money which he left to his grandson, which made possible the years at Shoreham. He also wrote poems and books—pious, homiletic books—*A Treatise on Marriage, A Guide to Domestic Happiness, The Refuge,* an answer in letters to Lavinia's question, "What shall I do to be saved?", which, like the *Guide,* was popular enough to go into several editions. The frontispiece —Lavinia gently sitting on a garden-seat under a bower of roses, looking down at some tulips—was engraved from a drawing by Stothard, and the model who sat to him for the drawing was Samuel Palmer's mother.[2] She died in 1817—the first of a series of blows by death which bitterly assaulted Samuel Palmer's extreme sensitivity; and her death no doubt increased his grandfather's influence on Palmer. According to A. H. Palmer, this man of so many excellencies was also "a domestic martinet of the first order." And as he had written books, "he was the pride of his family, who meekly obeyed his orders, and worshipped him (at a very respectful distance) under the title of 'The Author.'" [3] His friends or acquaintances among painters included Thomas Uwins, afterwards R.A.,[4] as well as Stothard; and his relations with them had no doubt made things easier when Samuel Palmer showed signs of being, or wishing to be, an artist. He was a Baptist, and against that his peculiar grandson kicked violently while he was still a child. So Samuel Palmer owed his grandfather these three things: his first contact with artists, the money which gave him seven years' independence, and in part, maybe, the reaction, the impulse, to a high church archaism which made him paint to the glory of God.

The Palmers themselves were mercantile and Church of England. Samuel's grandfather was Christopher Palmer, a hatter of the firm of Moxon, Palmer & Norman, in the City of London, who was in turn the son of a Church of England rector. This grandfather died when he was only three. Of his two uncles, one was a druggist in the City, with an estate in Ireland; the other, Nathaniel Palmer, was a wealthy corn-factor, at a time when corn-factors were among the most powerful of the business-men of London.[5] The Palmers claimed kinship with William Wake, Archbishop of Canterbury, and bore arms—azure, three fleur de lys argent, a border engraved or; with an arm embowed, vested azure, cuffed or, grasping a tilting spear proper, as their crest. Samuel Palmer was very conscious of all of this, and sealed his letters as a young artist at Shoreham with an armorial signet ring.

II

Prudentially, Samuel Palmer the elder did not succeed; he did not acquire money. His marriage to the banker's daughter (though he was married at church) [6] made him into a Baptist. It seems that he did not become a bookseller with his own shop until his son was fifteen, perhaps taking over the business of a William Palmer who was a bookseller till that year in Bermondsey Street. Judging from the sale of his stock in 1827, his business either was not big or else had dwindled; but it was a general stock of good quality: he sold the poets, classics, mathematics, theology, school books, travels, Boccaccio, Rousseau's *Confessions*, books by Hazlitt and Southey.[7]

Samuel Palmer always felt grateful to him for his indulgence and his unworldliness, for the way he allowed him to paint, and encouraged him to his years of vision in London and at Shoreham. "How he loved my childhood's soul and MIND—how he laboured to improve them, sitting in the house and walking in the fields," was Palmer's thought, which he recorded with "the first gush of tears" when his father died in 1848.[8] In an autobiographical letter he wrote for *The Portfolio*, Palmer describes how his father made him learn much of the Bible, and read to him on their walks from "little manuscript books with vellum covers" which he carried in his waistcoat pocket, and in which he transcribed "the essence of whatever he had lately read"; and he dedicated a piece of music he had composed "to my Father, because, not choosing to sacrifice me to Mammon with the mummery all the while of Christian prayers, with an affection rare in this day, he led my erring steps where Faith, Temperance, and Study evermore resort and wait to take the hand of those who love their charming company. And because he supported me, never once murmuring, long after that time when our fathers use to thrust their offspring from their bosom at the first crude opportunity, that they may clutch their gold alone and gorge a richer feast." [9]   One can see the openness of his character, his naïvety, and his sympathy with Samuel Palmer, in spite of their difference in religion, in a letter he wrote, years on, to Palmer during his Italian tour.   It is in a clear, exquisite-shaped handwriting:

"My dear Samuel,—I have read your letter with very great pleasure. 'Bless the Lord, O my soul,' for existing circumstances of such a favourable kind relating to your dear wife and to yourself. I am tolerably well, except a small degree of vertigo; Dr. Thompson has this day written for me; it is the effervescing draught shielded with opium, because of the bladder. . . . Mr. Burns has immersed about 120 & 13 more are ready; how valuable will the fact be when infant sprinkling will be a matter of history & not of practice. But how can an imaginative artist come down to logic; an act of parliament creed will do for such an one. The Pope has prohibited Infant Schools in Rome. William & his wife are well. Give my love to Mrs. Palmer, & best respects to Mr. & Mrs. Richmond. I remain Dear Samuel Your very affectionate Father Samuel Palmer." [10]

III

Palmer was the elder of two surviving children. His brother William inherited his father's fecklessness without his brother's genius, became an attendant in the Antique Gallery at the British Museum, and has his place in history for getting ten shillings out of Rossetti for the document now known as the Rossetti Manuscript of Blake's poems.[11] He had come into contact with Blake at Shoreham and in London. Both children—or at any rate, Samuel—were born in Surrey Square, Walworth,[12] in one of a row of dignified houses, which still exists, and still rises with its ornamental railings and lamp-brackets above the squalor of the Old Kent Road district all around. The square had not been completed in 1805, and looked out towards the open fields of Kent. It was a middle-class square, then, of solicitors and retired soldiers. At the back, a very short distance away, stood Apollo Buildings, in which lived "The Author," and banker, William Giles. Palmer was not robust, and his sensitivity—at any rate in later years—was accompanied by asthma. His son mentioned "his strange liking for shedding 'delicious tears' at performances on the organ." [13]   And he writes himself, as a young man, of "my very early years, in which I distinctly remember I felt the finest scenery and the country in general with a very strong and pure feeling."   He owed much in his Walworth days to his nurse, "who, with little education else, was ripe in that without which so much is often useless or mischievous: deeply read in her Bible and *Paradise Lost*.   A Tonson's *Milton*, which I cherish to this day, was her present.   When less than four years old, as I was standing with her, watching the shadows on the wall from the branches of an elm behind which the moon had risen, she transferred and fixed the fleeting image in my memory by repeating the couplet:

Vain man, the vision of a moment made,
Dream of a dream and shadow of a shade.[14]

I never forgot these shadows, and am often trying to paint them." [15] It was a moment of a kind common enough in the lives of painters and writers and musicians and saints, when a sight or a sound, a glitter on wet leaves or what you will, possessed them and seemed later to symbolize their whole creative existence.   A similar tale was told of Palmer's friend Calvert.   Coleridge, too, built much upon an early experience of the Evening Star.

The loss of his mother is the very next thing that he recalls in his spare account of his own life; and his nurse must have taken her place; she stayed long with the Palmers, afterwards keeping house for them at Shoreham.

Palmer's education seems to have come, classics and all, mainly from his father, who afterwards taught French and Latin and grammar and arithmetic to the children of John Linnell.[16]   An attempt—one attempt—was made to turn him into a schoolboy. This was in 1817, and the Palmers had moved by this time to the less pleasant district of Houndsditch.   He was sent to Merchant Taylors' School, then in its bare, old buildings in Suffolk Lane, in May 1817; to a life, his son declared, "to which he had been carefully unfitted." [17]   He was still there, in the Second Form, in October; [18]   but soon after that was taken away, having endured, apparently, much unhappiness.[19]   He was possibly at school until December, and it was just about now, a little before his thirteenth birthday, on January 18, 1817, that his mother died, after eleven days' illness,[20] and perhaps her death, which "pierced him like a sharp sword," and his removal from Merchant Taylors' were connected.

Long before he went to school he had been busy drawing.   The earliest of his drawings, shown in the Palmer Exhibition at the Victoria and Albert Museum in 1926, was a sketch of a windmill, done when he was nearly eight, and endorsed by his mother "Dec 19 1812" (No. 1); and it is reasonable to think that a mother who had sat as a young girl to so celebrated and virtuous an artist as Stothard, might not be so deterred by the poor social position of artists at that period, and might not object to her son becoming an artist instead of a bookseller like her husband, or a business-man in the City (her brother, the banker's son, dealt in stocks and shares).[21] Soon after her death, wrote Samuel Palmer, "it was thought right that I should attempt painting as a profession. Perhaps this arose from misinterpreting an instinct of another kind, a passionate love— the expression is not too strong,—for the traditions and monuments of the Church; its cloistered abbeys, cathedrals, and minsters, which I was always imagining and trying to draw; spoiling much paper with pencils, crayons and watercolours. It was in the blood: my great-grandfather was a clergyman, and his father, Samuel Palmer, was collated to the living of Wiley [22] in Wiltshire, in 1728." [23] Certainly this love of the Church was something which did not come to him from his father, his mother, or his nurse, who was also, in his words, "a misled Baptist"; [24] but his uncle, Edward Palmer,[25] and his children, and other Palmer relations no doubt kept the Church tradition of the family well polished. And his inclination to draw these objects of his passion, or "the finest scenery and country in general," had been balanced with copying of architectural draw- ings, botanical engravings, and (like the Pre-Raphaelites thirty-five years later) engravings after the Campo Santo frescoes.[26]

When it was thought right that he should paint for a career (after, he says, grammar and arithmetic caused his feeling and taste to leave him) he was sent for instruction to "a Mr. Wate; an obscure artist, but a man whose sterling and unostentatious character, together with his methodical habits, impressed his pupil not a little." [27]

IV

Mr. Wate was no doubt William Wate, then living south of the river in 5 George Street, Blackfriars Road, whose name, with those of Constable and others, appears in the students list of the British Institution for January 25, 1819. I have never seen any of his work, except one lithograph of the new prison at Abingdon, which was cool and mildly pleasant; but from 1815 he had shown, at the Academy and at the British Institution, small landscapes chiefly and studies from nature; and it was no doubt through him that Palmer

came to exhibit for the first time, at the British Institution, when he
was fourteen. Wate that year—in 1819—exhibited "Quarry Wood,
Gt. Morton, Bucks," "Study from Nature, Kent," "Medmenham
Abbey," and "Study from Nature, Bucks." Palmer's exhibits were
"Bridge Scene: Composition" and "Landscape: Composition."

In the Academy, the same year, Palmer showed "Landscape
with Ruins," "Cottage Scene: Banks of the Thames, Battersea,"
and "A Study."

These fourteen-year-old exhibits are now lost, but judging by
Wate's own kind of subject and Palmer's titles and from drawings
of this period, Wate taught him the conventional method of an
Ackermann drawing-book, the antique-house drawing of a De Wint,
or of David Cox as you see it in Cox's *Treatise on Landscape Painting*
—a book which strongly affected Palmer, reminiscences from Cox's
sepia-tinted plates cropping up in some of his boldest work. A note
on the back of one early drawing—a pencil sketch of a pollard willow
on Tottenham Marshes (No. 2)—runs: "This pollard willow was
enriched with a great variety of tints, some of rich olive green and
others where the mosses had not prevailed of a silvery grey. The
foliage was of a light green but very warm." It is early evidence—
though not visible in the drawing (which is perhaps based on one
of Cox's plates)—of Palmer's vision of the embossed, or swelling,
details of nature. Conventional modernity did not entirely swamp
him, even though he did look back on these years as years of decline
from the vision of childhood.

By this time he had got to know two of the artists who were
members of the group he came to dominate in the Shoreham days.
One was Francis Oliver Finch, three years older than Palmer, and
still a pupil of John Varley's; the other, already a man of twenty-
nine, was Henry Walter, the least talented and visionary of his
circle, who painted landscape for himself and drew animals to be
lithographed for Ackermann. Walter made a pencil drawing of
Palmer at fourteen, dated July 20, 1819.[28]

This prodigy, who already had artist friends, and had exhibited
at the two major exhibitions, and had sold a picture from one of
them, and was picking up the way in which the approved moderns
did their work, was also turning round in his mind, and was well
read in religious controversy. He seems to have veered a bit from
his "passionate love" for "the traditions and monuments of the
Church," as well as losing his old vision of natural scenery—at any
rate for the time being, and in several letters written many years
later he talks of himself as being "a free-thinker at fourteen," who
"spent much time in controversial reading which ought to have

been given to painting," [29] and was familiar with "the then stock arguments for infidelity." [30]

V

It was still a good time to the major event of his early life, his contact with Blake during the last of his years, during which Blake walked with him through the fields and showed him "the soul of beauty through the forms of matter." [31] His hand developed quickly from the drawing-book manner of his early exhibits. Turner was one reason for this. In the wonderful year of 1819, the first Academy which he contributed to was also the first he saw. "The first exhibition I saw (in 1819)," he wrote years later to one of his former pupils, "is fixed in my memory by the first Turner, 'The Orange Merchantman on the Bar'; and, being by nature a lover of smudginess, I have revelled in him from that day to this. May not half the Art be learned from the gradations in coffee-grounds?" [32] Palmer and his father also knew George Cooke, the line-engraver, a friend of Stothard, who with his brother was then busy on the *Southern Coast of England*, with its contributions from Turner. Cooke would "sometimes drop in of an evening for a talk about art," and "the engravings of the brothers formed part of the pabulum of my admiration—lunacy I may almost say, before the popular expositors of that wonderful man were born." [33] Cooke, like Blake, had been a pupil of the engraver James Basire, and he may well have been the first to talk about Blake to Palmer. At fifteen, Palmer's precocious and dangerous good luck continued: he had a picture in the Academy—"Wood Scene: A Study from Nature." The year after, at sixteen, the Academy accepted from him one picture—"A Study from Nature: Battersea," and the British Institution two—one with the same name, and probably the same picture unsold—and "Langley Locks, Herts." He had nothing in the Academy when he was seventeen, but three at the British Institution—"A Lane Scene, Battersea," "On the Thames: Evening," and "Hailsham Sussex: Storm Coming On." These, too, have all disappeared; but a watercolour sketch, dated 1821, possibly a study for the Hailsham storm scene, was exhibited in 1926 (No. 18, Plate 6), and I have also seen another version in sepia. Here comes the admiration for Turner. These two sketches of 1821 are directly based on the engraving after Turner of Rye in the *Southern Coast of England*, and there are points which tie them to Turner's *Liber Studiorum*—to such plates, for instance, as the "Peat Bog, Scotland," with its falling sky, the "Martello Towers near Bexhill," or "Inverary

Castle and Town"; and the swirling influence of "The Orange Merchantman" on Palmer is also pretty obvious. Years after, one can see the effect of "The Orange Merchantman," the effect of its swirl of water and its sensationalism. It is not fanciful to see an unconscious repetition of Turner's design in a sketch for the "Wrecked at Home" of 1862 (Plate XII in *V. & A.*, 1926).

But these sketches done at sixteen are an achievement, even though Palmer, within a few years, felt they belonged to that time when he had "entirely lost all feeling for art." What they are born from in existing work and in reality is well enough expressed: they are assured and easy and open; and, in manner, an extraordinary contrast to the work which Palmer would develop four years later after his meeting with Mulready and Linnell and Blake and Edward Calvert. But the elements of Palmer's selection of colour, and his individuality, are discernible in the typical lead-blue of the clouds, in the fresh combining of lead-blue, yellow, and white, green and dark green, in the 1821 watercolour. The steps forward are all pretty clear, and they were healthier perhaps than Palmer realized afterwards, or A. H. Palmer conceded. He lacked what A. H. Palmer seems to think would have done him good, "the healthy emulation of the schools where he might"—(and he might not)—"have profited by seeing the workmanship of those more experienced than himself." [34] The schools, when he had developed only so far, might have confirmed him still more in the small talk of a descriptive manner. He did better as he was, "floundering into the deep waters of his profession," getting advice (if A. H. Palmer's statement is trustworthy) from Stothard as well as tickets to Flaxman's academy lectures on sculpture. [35] Flaxman's preaching of the ideal made weight against the fashion of transcribing from nature. "I once saw, and have since endeavoured to trace it, but in vain, a small bas-relief by Flaxman, a flock of sheep, and nothing more; *ideal* sheep, of course—let drovers laugh! its matter and detail were as nothing; yet it has lain in memory some thirty years, without losing a certain savour" [36]—and he recalls, as though he had heard Flaxman's lecture on Composition, the dictum that "Sentiment is the life and soul of fine art! without it all is a dead letter! sentiment gives a sterling value, an irresistible charm, to the rudest imagery or most unpractised scrawl. . . ." [37] "Sentiment" meant to Palmer not just nature, but the double vision, the soul of beauty through the forms of matter, and "sentiment" was to be a Shoreham battle-cry. And "So, at a time when he should have contented himself with the alphabet of art, he was full of theories and speculations more suitable to the most learned professors; and full also of a boyish certainty about things of which he knew very little." [38]   But the theories, speculations, as far as they were Flaxman's, inclined him the right way, and certainly made the process easier for John Linnell and for Palmer himself, when, as Palmer described it, "it pleased God to send Mr. Linnell as a good angel from Heaven to pluck me from the pit of modern art."

He felt afterwards that he had sunk pretty deep into that pit. "As it seems reasonable," he wrote in his note-book for 1824, "to divide the soul's journey into stages and starting-points, and to stop and look back at certain intervals, and at each fresh stage to go back to the primitive and infantine feeling with which we set out; and to lay in such a store of humility, simple anxiety to get on, and diligence in the great, nay stupendous pursuit of grand art as may stand us in stead for a year's journey or so, I divide my life with respect to art into two parts.   First, my very early years, in which I distinctly remember that I felt the finest scenery and the country in general with a very strong and pure feeling; so that had I then seen the works of the very ancient Italian and German masters I should have admired and imitated them, and wondered what the moderns could mean by what they call their 'effects.'   Then, when I gradually learnt arithmetic and grammar, my feeling and taste left me, but I was not then completely spoilt for art.   But when I had learnt to paint a little, by the time I had practised for about five years I entirely lost all feeling for art, nor did I see the greatest beauties of even the Dutch masters, Cuyp, Ruysdael etc.; so that I not only learnt nothing in this space of time that related to high art, but I was nearly disqualified from ever learning to paint." [39]

Then came the plucking from the pit, and the casting into darkness of Mr. Wate, and the drawing-school manner, and—for the time being—the sweep and naturalism of Turner.   On the edge of the pit stands the good angel dusting Palmer's jacket and introducing him to Dürer with one hand and Michelangelo with the other.

CHAPTER II

THE MEETING WITH LINNELL

I

MR. GLOSS CRIMSON, R.A., wrote Lord Lytton, "is one of those who measure all art" by the Royal Academy exhibition. "He ekes out his talk from Sir Joshua Reynolds' discourse. . . . He is intensely jealous, and more exclusive than a second-rate countess; he laments the decay of patronage in this country; he believes everything in art depends upon lords; he bows to the ground when he sees an earl; and thinks of Pericles and Leo X. His colours are as bright and gaudy as a Dutchman's flower-garden, for they are put on with an eye to the Exhibition where everything goes by glare." [1] Gloss crimson glare—that superficially was the nature of the pit of modern art at this time. "The low and the mercantile creep over the national character and the more spiritual and noble faculties are little encouraged and lightly esteemed," Lytton wrote; and another of his characters was Snap, the academical philosopherling who has studied Locke at Cambridge and "looks down if you utter the word 'soul' and laughs in his sleeve."

It was a modern art of "effects" supplanting "sentiment," and getting ready to replace noblemen with manufacturing patrons from the North. There was a new world of difference between Sir George Beaumont as a patron, and Sir Robert Peel with his dealer's collection of Dutch exteriors and interiors; and what Palmer felt as the pit of modern art was an art of nature without spiritual meaning. Still, Blake and Fuseli and Coleridge were alive. There were still fortresses in painting, and in letters, of the romantic, the primitive, or the mystical.

John Linnell, Palmer's good angel, had known Blake since 1818. He was a small, energetic, sharp-eyed, self-opinionated man, son of a frame-maker, who at this time painted both men and landscape as though they had something divine about them. He belonged to the generation of Keats, De Quincey and Delacroix, Shelley and John Martin—he and Shelley were born in the same year; and he should not be estimated by the diffuse, less "inspired" landscapes and scripture subjects of his middle age and old age which made his great Victorian name and wealth. His power and individuality are in the compact glow of his early landscapes and portraits, such as the portrait of Richard Trevithick, the engineer, with its vista of dark satanic clouds, which is now in the Science Museum at South Kensington. He liked artists of the sixteenth century, who had a vision of two worlds at once. He liked the energy of the muscles and heroism of the later figures of Michelangelo, of Giulio Romano's fallen Titans; he liked the particularity of Dürer, as well as fullness and excess; and he disliked Constable for being too close to nature and Haydon for being too far from it. Yet he was fanatic rather than visionary: he had a tendency towards hard malice, which comes out in his one recorded story of Haydon, his early friend who "had a remarkably conceited manner of laughing in sound something like the short cry of a sheep or goat with the consonant B taken away and the a-a-a left." [2] Many years later Palmer had to suffer from that ruthlessness of tongue and steeliness of heart.

In the days of his friendship with Blake, Linnell's character still had not tightened and closed. He had not, and never could have had, the child-like and "primitive" innocence at the centre of Blake or Palmer; but he felt Blake's serenity and power and glow, not only enough to help him, but to take him round, for example, to see such powerful friends as Sir Thomas Lawrence; and Blake found enough good in Linnell to go with him to galleries and to the theatre, and to begin at least one letter to him "My dearest friend." [3] Linnell met Palmer, it seems, and began the process of plucking him from the pit and the slime of modern art towards the end of 1822, in September. He had seen and admired some of Palmer's drawings in sepia, and Palmer was introduced to him.

They liked each other. Linnell was thirty, Palmer was seventeen. Linnell knew every artist of worldly importance, and Blake as well. But it was nearly two years before he introduced Blake and Palmer, and so ousted himself as the main influence on Palmer's thought and feeling. Through Linnell, Palmer straight away got to know Mulready, with whom Linnell was intimate, and Varley, who had been Linnell's master.[4] It has been stated that Palmer had some lessons from Varley, "the fat astrologer," as W. B. Scott called him, in a dressing-gown, with "a black skull cap on his small head." He had reduced romantic landscape to an easy formula, and was not the kind of man who could have given Palmer much except advice in technique. From Mulready he certainly had advice, and he always remembered him with respect. Many years later he supplied the vague Pre-Raphaelite critic, F. G. Stephens, with recollections for his book about Mulready, for whom, and for whose strong, lively drawing, the Pre-Raphaelites had a justified regard.

II

There is scanty evidence for these years surviving in the fragments from a note-book and sketch-book or two, which were published
by Samuel Palmer's son; but this evidence needs sorting out and
rearranging.   He filled oblong Whatman books [5] with "all that was
noteworthy—picked passages from favourite poems, poems and
essays of his own, long lists of uncommon or old-fashioned words
met with in his reading, rough designs in black and white." [6]   But
all these books except one, which he started in the late summer of
1824, have now been destroyed, and with them an incomparable
record of the nourishing and budding of an artist's mind.[7]   The
earliest note-book from which A. H. Palmer quoted, was filled with
consequences of his meeting with John Linnell.   It is clear that
Linnell above all made him look at engravings by Dürer and Van
Leyden, made him think about Raphael's landscape, and encouraged
him to draw the human figure.   His sensible advice that Palmer
should immediately "begin a course of figure drawing" was less
sensibly carried out by doing it in the antique galleries of the British
Museum,[8] where he started in November 1822.   Drawing from
the marbles in the Elgin and Towneley Galleries at the Museum
was the usual stage before trying for admission into the Royal
Academy schools, especially for poor students.   Solomon Hart, R.A.,
who also worked in the Museum, describes in his autobiography the
happy-go-lucky methods of studentship.   "A picturesque old German
kept watch over the priceless relics.   There was no-one to instruct
nor to give information.   Left to ourselves, everyone did that which
seemed good in his own eyes.   Great diffuseness and delay arose
from this want of direction." [9]   Other students who were there
with Palmer—George Richmond, for one, Sidney Cooper, R.A.,
J. R. Knight, R.A., George Lance, Catterson Smith, P.R.H.A.,
and Solomon Hart, R.A.—all passed the test with their drawings
from the antique and gained entry to the Academy schools, where
they came under the caustic tuition of the now ancient Fuseli.
Palmer did not go with them, there is no knowing why.   It is the
more curious, because he much admired Fuseli (who was one, not
merely of the English, but of the European pioneers in the Romantic).
At the Museum, he wrote, "sedulous efforts to render the marbles
exactly, even to their granulation, led me too much aside from the
study of organization and structure"; [10] and he implies that this
was due to advice that he had from Mulready, or advice, perhaps,
that he misinterpreted.   "No one," Mulready remarked to him,

"had done much who had not begun with niggling." He already liked the jewelling of nature, and Mulready's "discipline of exactness" which was "the copying sometimes objects which were not beautiful, to cut away the adventitious aid of association," [11] his advice to "do everything as well as you can," and his remark that "to get one quality of flesh is comparatively easy; to get two is difficult; to unite three is very difficult," [12] and his praise of niggling, all seem to have prevailed against his injunction that "The painter cannot take a step without anatomy." Mulready's precept to work hard, and long, and well seems to have affected Palmer more than the rhythmical and unromantic brilliance of Mulready's drawing, which was not an expression of ideas or ideals. An entry in his note-book, written in 1823, after much of this Museum drawing, shows how he realized this lack of the study of organization and structure: "N.B. in my attempts to copy the Antique statues to try and draw most severely, and to cry out for more and more form; and then I shall find in the Antique more than I can copy, if I look and pry into it earnestly for form. I shall not be easy till I have drawn one Antique statue *most severely*." [13] One experience he had in the British Museum which ripened in him and remained in him through life: he met and drew and worshipped the Graeco-Roman figure—he miscalled it "The Sleeping Mercury"—of "Endymion the Shepherd Boy Asleep on Mt. Latmos." "One of the very deepest sayings I have met with in Lord Bacon," he wrote in 1834 to George Richmond, "seems to me to be 'There is no excellent beauty that hath not some strangeness in the proportion.' The Sleeping Mercury in the British Museum has this hard-to-be-defined, but most delicious quality to perfection." [14] And again, thirty years on: "Below, in the Townley Gallery, is the sure test of our imaginative faculty—the sleeping Mercury. More than two thousand years ago the sculptor bade that marble live. It lived but slept, and it is living still. Bend over it. Look at those delicate eyelids; that mouth a little open. He is dreaming. Dream on, marble shepherd; few will disturb your slumber." [15]

Palmer took the sleeping shepherd in his mind from the Museum into his Kentish country of divine shepherds and laid him asleep again, slightly altered, in the doorway of a Kentish barn, in his panel picture of "The Sleeping Shepherd," painted at Shoreham (No. 140, Plate 64); and the shepherd can be seen once more in his later etching of the same title (1857).

III

To return to the first note-book. He wrote much in it of the
things he saw with or by the advice of Linnell. A passage from it
I have already quoted—"Had I then" (in his very early years) "seen
the works of the very ancient Italian and German masters I should
have admired and imitated them, and wondered what the moderns
could mean by what they call their effects"—suggests to me that
by the end of June 1824—the probable date of this entry—Linnell
had already taken Palmer to see the celebrated collection of the
German merchant and insurance broker, Charles Aders, in his house
in Euston Square. Years later Palmer told Crabb Robinson he had
seen it. It was a collection famous both in Germany and England,
brought together under the romantic and mediaevalizing influence
of such Germans as Wackenroder, and Tieck, and the Schlegels.
The pictures, which covered the walls and the staircases, did not
always fit the names they were ascribed to; but there were paintings
in the collection given to Jan van Eyck, Petrus Christopherus,
Memling, Dürer, van der Weyden, Schongauer, and others; and it
must have seemed to Palmer at eighteen or nineteen, as it seemed
to Charles Lamb, that the Aders house was not simply a house, but
a chapel or an oratory.[16] Lamb, who went to the Aderses for whist,
felt the holiness around the walls strongly enough to write a poem
which seems to me to have in it much of what Palmer was now
feeling about the holiness of art in general:

> Friendliest of men, ADERS, I never come
> Within the precincts of this sacred Room,
> But I am struck with a religious fear,
> Which says "Let no profane eye enter here."
> With imagery from Heav'n the walls are clothed,
> Making the things of Time seem vile and loathed.
> Spare Saints whose bodies seem sustain'd by Love,
> With Martyrs old in meek procession move.
> Here kneels a weeping Magdalene, less bright
> To human sense for her blurr'd cheeks; in sight
> Of eyes, new-touch'd by Heav'n, more winning fair
> Than when her beauty was her only care.
> A Hermit here strange mysteries doth unlock
> In desart sole, his knees worn by the rock.
> There Angel harps are sounding, while below
> Palm-bearing Virgins in white order go.
> Madonnas, varied with chaste design,
> While all are different, each seems genuine,
> And hers the only Jesus: hard outline,

And rigid form, by DURER's hand subdued
To matchless grace, and sacro-sanctitude;
DURER, who makes thy slighted Germany
Vie with the praise of paint-proud Italy.

Whoever enter'st here, no more presume
To name a Parlour, or a Drawing Room;
But, bending lowly to each holy Story,
Make this thy Chapel, and thine Oratory.

Aders, who knew the Schlegels,[17] and almost certainly Tieck, must have read Wackenroder's famous essay on Dürer, and Tieck's novel, *Franz Sternbalds Wanderungen*, of the young artist who works under Dürer and Lucas van Leyden, and then goes off to Raphael in Rome. Tieck's novel taught "that the highest achievement in art is an allegorical Christian landscape, which in and through nature best reveals the ideology of the Christian religion." Such ideas, inspiration, humility, and the child-like heart, must have been discussed at Aders's house, whether they came to Palmer first hand, or second hand through the Aderses' friend Linnell, who not long before (1822) had been making a copy on ivory of one of Lord Cowper's celebrated Raphaels.[18] In the note-book, Palmer made his "first attempt at figure designing," no doubt after his busy prying in the British Museum; but it was no classical subject, it was a Christian one—St. Christopher, apparently, with the infant Christ on his shoulder.[19] There are entries about Van Leyden, Dürer, and Raphael: "Look for Van Leydenish qualities in real landscape, and look hard, long and continually. Look for picturesque combinations of buildings, and elegant spires and turrets for backgrounds."[20] And though Linnell had not yet taken him to see Blake, he had introduced him to Blake's drawings [21] and no doubt given him some idea of Blake's purity and power and character.

He went much to the Dulwich Gallery, and entered in his note-book comments on one visit made with Linnell:

"Memoranda, day after going to Dulwich. Cox is pretty—is sweet, but not grand, not profound. Carefully avoid getting into that style which is elegant and beautiful but too light and superficial; not learned enough—like Barret. He has a beautiful sentiment and it is derived from Nature; but Nature has properties which lie still deeper, and when they are brought out the picture must be most elaborate and full of matter even if only one object be represented, yet it will be most simple of style, and be what would have pleased men in the early ages, when poetry was at its acme, and yet men lived in a simple, pastoral way.

"Girtin's twilight, beautiful, but did he know the grand old men? Let me remember always, and may I not slumber in the possession of it, Mr. Linnell's injunction (delightful in the performance), 'Look at Albert Durer.' In what a simple way Landscape impressed the mind of Raffaelle; yet his little bits make me despair.

"How superior is Mr. Linnell's style of colouring to that of any other modern landscape painter, and yet not half so captivating to an ignorant eye as others.

"Look at Mr. Blake's way of relieving objects, and at his colour. The copy of Leonardo da Vinci at Dulwich is merely a head and shoulders. How amazingly superior it is in style to any portrait there. The tone of the flat blueish sky is wonderful, though it is nothing of itself. It is the colour of the soul, not vulgar paint.[22] Ruysdael, Hobbema, Paul Potter, and Cuyp—how intense, how pure, how profound, how wonderful!" [23]

The note on Cox signifies how he was freeing himself from a most powerful influence. The effect of the *Treatise on Landscape Painting and Effect* shows itself not only in early Palmer drawings such as his "Pollard Willow" (No. 2) and his "Old Cottage and Elms" (No. 16); it is still there in "The Haunted Stream" (No. 44, Plate 17), based on Cox's "Morning, Eton College"; and Cox's landscape plate with tufted trees and sheep and a bright cloud with horizontal bars of stratus—his Plate 24—seems to me a seed for Palmer's drawings and landscape of "The Bright Cloud"—yet Cox "is sweet, but not grand, not profound." "Carefully avoid getting into that style which is elegant and beautiful but too light and superficial."

His business was to deepen and round out David Cox; and he was looking already at Blake's colour and manner, and fastening in the Dulwich picture on that "flat blueish sky," which he repeats again and again. He was still able to admire the Dutch, but his eyes were already fixed deeper into such things as Dürer's "Flight into Egypt" from the *Marienleben*; and an earlier entry of late 1823 shows how much religion and the beginnings of mysticism were already affecting his views about painting, even before his friendship with Blake. It follows straight on from his talk of drawing "one Antique statue *most severely*":

"I cannot execute at all. The least bit of natural scenery reflected from one of my spectacle-glasses laughs me to scorn, and hisses at me. I feel ten minutes a day, the most ardent love for art, and spend the rest of my time in stupid apathy, negligence, ignorance, and restless despondency; *without any of those delicious visions which are the only joys of my life—such as Christ at Emmaus; the repenting thief on the cross; the promise to Abraham; and secondary visions of the ages of chivalry, which are toned down with deep gold to distinguish them from the flashy and distracted present."* [24]

All of which, the part I have emphasized, can only mean what it says, that, like a mystic in the elementary stages of his way, Palmer had had visionary scenes in front of his eyes. Either at the end of this early note-book or at the beginning of the next, he urges himself to ask Christ to show him the visions that he needs. He looks back over his "first struggle" now concluded—his struggle with figure-drawing; and ends up in the spirit of the twilight sepias which he began to draw within two years:

"*November*, 1822 to *June* 9 1824.—Now it is twenty months since you began to draw. Your second trial begins. Make a new experiment. Draw near to Christ, and see what is to be done with Him to back you. Your indolent moments rise up, each as a devil and as a thorn at the quick. Keep company with the friends of Publicans and sinners, and see if, in such society, you are not ashamed to be idle. Ask Christ to manifest to you these things; Christ looking upon Peter (called *Repentance*) and Peter's countenance. Christ's promise to the dying thief—the looks of both. Christ leading His blessed to fountains of living waters (which being the union of all vision, should be done as the artist's Prince); Jesus weeping at Lazarus' tomb. The three first are the chief, and are almost unpaintable—quite, without Christ. Lay up silently and patiently, materials for them in your sketch-book, and copy the prints to learn such nicety in pen sketching, or rather making careful studies, as may enable you to give the expressions. But smaller subjects of separate glories of Heaven might be tried—hymns sung among the hills of Paradise at eventide; . . . a martyr, having painted his murder, laughing, or rather smiling at his torments. A family met in Heaven. . . ." [25]

He was nineteen when he wrote this, a person rapidly fitting himself to meet Blake.

CHAPTER III

PALMER AND WILLIAM BLAKE

I

IT was in October 1824 that Linnell took Palmer to see Blake at Blake's lodgings in Fountain Court, and Blake, unforgettably, "fixed his grey eyes" [1] upon him. But before trying to discover the way and the degree of Blake's effect on Palmer as a man and as an artist (the two effects were not altogether the same), one thing may be emphasized. Palmer, frequently and too glibly, has been called a "follower of Blake." Tacked on to Blake, in books on English painting, comes a paragraph, or two, on his "followers," Palmer, Calvert, and Richmond.[2] But their painting, their vision, Blake's and Palmer's, even when it is most like, is never like enough for such a label. And what I have said already shows, how at nineteen, before he met Blake, Palmer was already a Christian, a visionary, and a mediaevalist. He learned from Blake, he profited from Blake's bigness and nobleness of nature, his own tastes—some of them—were deepened and made more powerful by Blake; but, as we shall see, what he did was in many ways the opposite of following. The opposite: remember Blake on Raphael, in answer to Sir Joshua Reynolds: "I do not believe Rafael taught Mich. Angelo, or that Mich. Angelo taught Rafael, any more than I believe that the Rose teaches the Lilly how to grow, or the Apple Tree teaches the Pear tree how to bear Fruit. I do not believe the tales of Anecdote writers when they militate against Individual Character." [3] It is safe to go ahead remembering that; because Palmer's Individual Character was, before and after Blake, very much his own.

The actual meeting, according to Palmer's note, was in the morning of October 9. Palmer's celebrated description must be quoted again:

"On Saturday, 9th October, 1824, Mr. Linnell called and went with me to Mr. Blake" (they would have walked down from the bookshop in Broad Street, now part of High Holborn, to the Temple). "We found him lame in bed, of a scalded foot (or leg). There, not inactive, though sixty-seven years old, but hard-working on a bed covered with books sat he up like one of the Antique patriarchs, or a dying Michael Angelo. Thus and thus was he making in the leaves of a great book (folio) the sublimest designs from his (not superior) Dante.[4] He said he began them with fear and trembling. I said 'O! I have enough of fear and trembling.' 'Then,' said he, 'you'll do.' He designed them (100 I think) during a fortnight's illness in bed! And there, first, with fearfulness (which had been the more, but that his designs from Dante had wound me up to forget myself), did I show him some of my first essays in design; and the sweet encouragement he gave me (for Christ blessed little children) did not tend basely to presumption and idleness, but made me work harder and better that afternoon and night. And, after visiting him, the scene recurs to me afterwards in a kind of vision; and in this most false, corrupt, and genteelly stupid town my spirit sees his dwelling (the chariot of the sun), as it were an island in the midst of the sea—such a place is it for primitive grandeur, whether in the persons of Mr. and Mrs. Blake, or in the things hanging on the walls." [5]

This note, written not so very long [6] after that October morning, shows that Palmer found what he had expected in Fountain Court, and he had expected much, and had heard much, and probably seen much to feed that expectation. Linnell already owned a good many things by Blake. The Linnell-Blake account book (now in Yale University Library) shows that Linnell had bought of Blake several years before a *Songs of Innocence and Experience*, *Jerusalem* (Chapter II), and a *Marriage of Heaven and Hell*, all three likely enough to excite Samuel Palmer; it was in these no doubt that Palmer had examined Blake's colour and his way of relieving objects. And though Blake was nearly sixty-seven, and had a little less than three years to live, and was gradually becoming a sick man, he was still strong in hand and mind, and full of an assured, passionate serenity—and meeting him, whom it would have been so easy not to meet, not to hear of, meeting one of the rarest living men, was an extraordinary stroke of luck, a fortunate stimulus for someone who, at nineteen, in such a time as 1824, had Palmer's nature, youth, and exhilaration.

Palmer and his friends, as they got to know Blake in those three years, came to know his rooms as "The House of The Interpreter." [7] In *Pilgrim's Progress*, Christian came to the House of The Interpreter and knocked: "Sir, said Christian, I am a Man that am come from the City of *Destruction*, and am going to the Mount *Zion*, and I was told by the Man that stands at the Gate, at the head of this way; that if I called here, you would shew me excellent things. Such as would be a help to me in my Journey." How exactly that describes how Palmer came, knocked, and saw, and felt about the things—

the excellent things which he was shown, things which would be a help on the journey of the next few years.

II

In middle age, when he was fifty, the letter which Palmer wrote to Alexander Gilchrist, full of the essence of his memory of Blake, shows exactly how the Interpreter helped him and strengthened his tastes.[8] He gave him the confidence which a boy, even such a precocious, intuitive, enthusiastic boy, required in his own preferences and his own ability. It was not only that Blake's conversation was "nervous and brilliant," that he was "the Maker, the Inventor; one of the few in any age: a fitting companion for Dante." Not only his grandeur and energy, his wide sympathies, his power to inform and instruct. "His eye was the finest I ever saw: brilliant, but not roving, clear and intent yet susceptible; it flushed with genius, or melted in tenderness. It could also be terrible." It was the contact with a man wholly, unreservedly, purely devoted to the things which Palmer already felt were alone the essence of life. He was already in debt to Linnell, and he was to owe still more to Linnell's advice, when Linnell impressed on him in the year after Blake's death that the rock of the ideal was the world of objects. But there were defects, narrownesses, and contortions in Linnell's character for which other artists (Constable, for one) detested him and of which Palmer must already have had an inkling. Twelve years later, Crabb Robinson asked Palmer one day in Wales, "whether Linnell is not a man of worldly wisdom."— "He understood the insinuation, and said, only *defensively*." [9] But Blake had no need for such defences. "He was a man without a mask," wrote Palmer, "his aim single, his path straightforward, and his wants few; so he was free, noble, and happy." He shed round himself "an atmosphere of life, full of the ideal." He declined "like Socrates . . . the common objects of ambition," and pitied "the scuffle to obtain them." John Stuart Mill burst into tears and could go no further when he read Shelley's *Ode to Liberty* to Lord and Lady Amberley: Blake read the parable of the Prodigal Son to Palmer, "but at the words, 'when he was yet a great way off, his father saw him' could go no further; his voice faltered and he was in tears."

"Such," Palmer concluded, "was Blake as I remember him. He was one of the few to be met with in our passage through life, who are not in some way or other, 'double-minded' and inconsistent with themselves; one of the very few who cannot be depressed by neglect, and to whose name, rank and station could add no lustre. Moving apart, in a sphere above the attraction of worldly honours, he did not accept greatness, but confer it."

This overwhelming example, a revelation of the possibilities of a man, gave Palmer the additional strength that he needed to resist the world for the few authentically creative years of his life, adding flame to a boy already on fire.

Blake certainly quickened toward the signs of vision in Samuel Palmer, and gave much of his time to Palmer, Richmond, and Calvert and Frederick Tatham. He would call for Palmer at his father's bookshop in Broad Street on the way up to join the Linnells in their farmhouse lodgings on Hampstead Heath, behind the Bull and Bush. After the move to Shoreham, he came down once at least to the valley.[10] In London, Palmer went with him to the Academy, where Blake praised a picture by Wainwright (whom they both knew, and who was a pupil of Linnell's): "While so many moments better worthy to remain are fled, the caprice of memory presents me with the image of Blake looking up at Wainwright's picture; Blake in his plain black suit and *rather* broad-brimmed, but not Quakerish hat, standing so quietly among all the dressed-up, rustling, swelling people, and myself thinking 'How little you know *who* is among you.'" [11] (Wainwright, Palmer recalled years after, after preparing a poisoned supper for his sister-in-law, "went forth with his paint-box and sketched a fine sunset from Waterloo Bridge.")[12] Together, at the Academy, Palmer and Blake examined the copy of Leonardo's "Last Supper"; and looking at the heads of the Apostles, Blake "remarked of all but Judas: 'Everyone looks as if he had conquered the natural man.'" Blake visited Calvert and his wife at Brixton, where Palmer frequently stayed and worked; and it is probable that some of Calvert's engraved variations of themes by Blake were done with Blake alongside.[13] Blake, too, had promised to take Palmer to see Thomas Butts and all the Blakes he had amassed; but he never lived to do so.[14]

At the very end, Richmond and Calvert and Frederick and Arthur Tatham arranged and attended Blake's funeral. Palmer, down at Shoreham, was told of the funeral by Richmond, but did not attend. He was the victim of his sensitivity, so moved by the death of those he loved that he could not harden himself to seeing them buried. Perhaps this inability to face the ceremonials of death originated in the loss of his mother during his childhood. He was prostrate in the same way years later and unable to endure the funeral of his son.[15]

What did Palmer get from Blake in knowledge of painting, and

poetry and life beyond the broad and powerful effect of Blake's
singleness of heart? What direct trace of Blake's own practice can
be seen in Palmer's painting? The first question is more important.
He talked to Palmer of Dürer, Michelangelo, Raphael, Giulio
Romano, Caravaggio, of Fra Angelico and "the early Christian art,"
and of Fuseli's imagination. They looked together over Italian
prints of the fifteen-hundreds, and examined antique gems (from
which Palmer, like Calvert, probably derived some of his figures).
They talked of Ovid, and of Milton, whose poems moved Palmer
more than anything else in literature, and of the Bible. "He was
fond," Palmer wrote, "of the works of St. Theresa, and often quoted
them with other writers on the interior life," [16] a significant recollection, because it suggests that Palmer added to his own visionary
experiences a knowledge of the greater visionaries—St. Teresa in
her autobiography, and almost certainly Jakob Boehme, a favourite
of Blake's. Blake spoke much of Gothic architecture. "Everything
connected with Gothic art and churches and their builders, was a
passion with him"; [17] he spoke of his "earliest and most sacred
recollections" in Westminster Abbey. "I asked him how he would
like to paint on glass, for the great west window, his *Sons of God
shouting for Joy*, from his designs in the *Job*. He said, after a pause,
'I could do it!' kindling at the thought." [18] Talking of the English
eye resting in Italian cities from the right angles and straight
lines of London, Palmer recalled, in old age, "presuming to demur
to an assertion of Mr. Blake's that our old cathedrals were not built
to rule and compass; but I now see that, like many of his art statements, although literally a stretch or violation of truth, it contained
or suggested a greater truth." [19]

Blake thought "that no one could be truly great who had not
humbled himself 'even as a little child,'" [20] and reinforced in Palmer
this attitude so common to the great romantics from Goethe and
Wackenroder to Wordsworth—and for which there is so much
warrant in such a mystic as Boehme.

Discussion between them went as far as the ideas in *The Marriage
of Heaven and Hell*,[21] even if Palmer (why should he have done,
as an artist and one of between nineteen and twenty-two?) little
understood their profundity. Advice on the central springs of
painting cut deeper: "You have only to work up imagination to the
state of vision, and the thing is done," he advised a young painter,
almost certainly Palmer.[22] But what may at first seem surprising
is Blake's advice on nature, and on the paintings of Claude. "*Talent*
thinks, Genius *sees*; and what organ so accurate as sight. Blake
held this strongly. His word was 'precision.'" [23] Nature, very

reasonably, may have put him out; but, advised Blake, "We should draw anything we want to master a hundred times from nature, till we have learned it by heart," [24] advice which deepened all that Palmer had felt in his earliest years, and advice which was to be supplemented by Linnell's harder-headed precepts after Blake's death.   Add to this his imparted admiration for Claude: "Among spurious old pictures, he had met with many 'Claudes,' but spoke of a few which he had seen really untouched and unscrubbed, with the greatest delight; and mentioned, as a peculiar charm, that in these, when minutely examined, there were, upon the focal lights of the foliage, small specks of pure white which made them appear to be glittering with dew which the morning sun had not yet dried up. . . . His description of these genuine Claudes, I shall never forget.   He warmed with his subject, and it continued through an evening walk. The sun was set; but Blake's Claudes made sunshine in that shady place." [25]   Milton in poetry—especially the pastoral Milton of moon-light and tufted trees—and Claude in painting are parallel as two prime influences on Palmer, in his moonlights and twilights; and Blake's praise of Claude suggests that he did not see in Claude's landscapes "the Natural Man rising up against the Spiritual Man continually": [26] he saw in them the spiritual imaged by the visible, and he also advised Palmer that "he who does not imagine in stronger and better lineaments, and in stronger and better light, than his perishing mortal eye can see, does not imagine at all." [27]

Nature, Precision, Spirit—those are the steps, and no wonder Palmer wrote that "to walk with him in the country was to perceive the soul of beauty through the forms of matter."

IV

All the same, where, in after years, did Palmer keep the four pictures he owned by Blake?   He kept Blake's memory clear and warm enough in his mind, but he kept the pictures—"The Bard," "Satan Calling Up His Legions," "The Spiritual Form of Napoleon" (now lost), and "The Spiritual Form of Pitt"—or at any rate three of them, in the cellar of his house at Redhill.[28]

In his painting-room, in his portfolio of things especially loved, he did, it is true, preserve proofs of Blake's Virgil wood-engravings which Blake had printed for him before his eyes, and then signed; and with them perhaps some of his Blake drawings.   He spoke warmly enough at times of Blake as an artist, but for one mention of anything particular by Blake in his correspondence, there are three or four of engravings by Bonasone, pictures by Claude, or Michel-

angelo, or Fuseli.   And this is valid evidence of his earlier states of
mind, because through middle age and old age, even to the use of
the same words and phrases, Palmer looked back to the flush and
splendour of his early imaginative life to a big, a surprisingly big
degree.

The Virgil engravings mattered to him especially.   He, and
Calvert, were moved by them above their worth, if "moved" is
not to say it too feebly.   In his sketch-book for 1825, after describing
Michelangelo as "The Salt of Art," and speaking enthusiastically of
the old German and Italian masters as compared with the "Venetian
Heresy," Palmer wrote, "I sat down with Mr. Blake's Thornton's
Virgil woodcuts before me, thinking to give to their merits my very
feeble testimony.   They are visions of little dells, and nooks, and
corners of Paradise;   models of the exquisitest pitch of intense
poetry.   I thought of their light and shade, and looking upon them
I found no word to describe it.   Intense depth, solemnity, and vivid
brilliancy only coldly and partially describe them.   There is in all
such a mistic and dreamy glimmer as penetrates and kindles the
inmost soul, and give complete and unreserved delight, unlike the
gaudy daylight of this world.   They are like all that wonderful
artist's work the drawing aside of the fleshly curtain, and the glimpse
which all the most holy studious saints and sages have enjoyed, of
that rest which remaineth to the people of God.   The figures of
Mr. Blake have that intense, soul-evidencing attitude and action;
and that elastic, nervous spring which belongs to uncaged immortal
spirits." [29]

He goes on about the supremacy of excess; and for believing in
that Blake and Milton alike supported him: "Excess is the essential
vivifying spirit, vital spark, embalming spice . . . of the finest art.
Be ever saying to yourself 'labour after the excess of excellence.' . . .
There are many mediums in the *means*—none, O! not a jot, not a
shadow of a jot, in the *end* of great art.   In a picture whose merit
is to be excessively brilliant, it can't be too brilliant; but individual
tints may be too brilliant . . . we must not begin with medium, but
think always on excess, and only use medium to make excess more
abundantly excessive."

It is worth quoting a piece more before thinking of the chief
surviving Palmers of this same year: "Though I hope we shall all
be severe outlinists, I hope our styles of outline may all be different
as the design of Michel Angelo from his equal, Blake, and the outline
of Albert Dürer from that of Andrea Mantegna.   There is no line
in nature, though excessive sharpness.   The visions of the soul,
being perfect are the only true standard by which nature must be

tried. The corporeal executive is no good thing to the painter, but a bane. In proportion as we enjoy and improve in imaginative art we shall love the material works of God more and more. Sometimes landscape is seen as a vision, and then seems as fine as art; but this is seldom, and bits of nature are generally much improved by being received into the soul, when she thinks on such supernatural works as Mr. Linnell's picture by Lucas van Leyden. . . . Often, and I think generally, at Dulwich, the distant hills seem the most powerful objects in colour, and clear force of line: we are not troubled with aerial perspective in the valley of vision. . . . Genius is the unreserved devotion of the whole soul to the divine, poetic arts, and through them to God; deeming all else, even to our daily bread, only valuable as it helps us to unveil the heavenly face of Beauty." [30]

"Excess" and "excessive sharpness" and a visionary clearness are the qualities of the six highly finished drawings of 1825, the "Rustic Scene," "Valley with a Bright Cloud," "Early Morning," "Late Twilight," "The Skirts of a Wood," and "The Valley Thick with Corn" (Nos. 38-43, Plates 11-16). These are "bits of nature . . . improved by being received into the soul"; but they are surprisingly unlike Blake, except in being consonant with the ideas of vision imparted by Blake—surprisingly unlike, in spite of Palmer having taken some of the detail and design from Blake. The man and the oxen in the "Rustic Scene" come, much translated, from the last wood-engraving in the Thornton *Virgil*. In "The Skirts of a Wood" it is more obvious that all the design, from tree, shepherdess and shepherd, to the shepherd, with his flock, leaning on the edge of the cliff, is based on the drawing of "Homer and the Ancient Poets" in the Dante series (on which Blake was already working when Palmer first called on him at Fountain Court). Details of foliage come from the same drawing. But these are small borrowings; and there are as many traces in these six of an attraction to Breughel, or engravings after Breughel, and to Lucas van Leyden.

V

The three years in which influence in the form of borrowing from Blake are visible, as distinct from an enlargement and energizing of spirit, are 1824, 1825, and 1826—naturally enough. There are Blake derivations in the surviving pages of the 1824 sketch-book— the vast rayed sun, for instance, sinking down in Page 9. "Strange, sometimes grotesque," A. H. Palmer wrote in describing this sketch-book, "is the purview of this 1824 workmanship. . . . From careful studies of a cheap bedroom window-curtain on its rod, and a leaf

of cottager's kale, we turn to a wild flight of spirits across the disc
of a planet. There are thirty-three moons in this one volume, and
vast flaming suns; but never a cast shadow from beginning to end.
There are noble abbeys and palaces and, as backgrounds for figures,
lofty lancet windows; but, above all these, the designer glories in
'The Primitive Cottage' as he calls it; nestling with its dove-cote
and its mighty thatch, by brooks, in dells, and sometimes by a
rumbling watermill." [31]

Already, before knowing Blake in person, there is the visual
effect upon him of reading Milton: "So exquisite is the glistering
of the stars through loop holes in the thick woven canopy of ancient
elm trees—of stars differing in glory, & one of prime lustre piercing
the gloom—and all dancing with instant change as the leaves play in
the wind that I cannot help thinking that Milton intended his
'Shady roof, Of branching elm *star proof*' as a double stroke—as he
tells of the impervious leafy gloom, glancing at its beautiful opposite
—'Loop holes cut through thickest shade' and in them socketed the
gems which sparkle on the Ethiopic forehead of the night." [32]

Milton is discernible in the only serious poem of Palmer's early
years which has been preserved—also from this 1824 sketch-book:

TWILIGHT TIME

And now the trembling light
Glimmers behind the little hills, and corn,
Ling'ring as loth to part: yet part thou must
And though than open day far pleasing more
(Ere yet the fields and pearled cups of flowers
   twinkle in the parting light);
Thee night shall hide, sweet visionary gleam
That softly lookest through the rising dew;
    Till all like silver bright,
    The faithful Witness, pure and white
    Shall look o'er yonder grassy hill,
    At this village, safe and still.
    All is safe and all is still,
    Save what noise the watch-dog makes
    Or the shrill cock the silence breaks
    Now and then—
    And now and then—
    Hark!—once again,
    The wether's bell
    To us doth tell
Some little stirring in the fold.
Methinks the ling'ring, dying ray
Of twilight time, doth seem more fair,
And lights the soul up more than day,
When wide-spread, sultry sunshines are.

Yet all is right, and all most fair
For thou, dear God, hast formèd all;
Thou deckest ev'ry little flower,
Thou girdest every planet ball—
And mark'st when sparrows fall.[33]

A poem which suggests, by the way, that Palmer was making excursions to Shoreham (a sketching-ground well enough known to artists) long before his migration there.

He was feeling an identity with the landscape that he saw. For example, under a delicate drawing of a valley and church spire, cornfields and trees (No. 24 (7)), he observed, "These streaks were as when one throws a stone into the water which spreads out in circles. They were caused (? thus) heaps of reaped corn were laid on lines across the field—I think Titian felt streaked fields"; and "The colour of ripe corn gives to the green trees about it increased depth and transparent richness." On the reverse is a sketch of ploughed land sloping to a hedge, and under it Palmer wrote:

"Opposite the cottage was (across a little valley where they were cutting corn) a range of hills: you walk up, the sheep bells going all the while, through several fields (of different sorts, rye, hops, fallow, meadow) of colour and form and texture various—then you come to the line of thick wood which runs all along the summit very close wild & intricate yet such as you would wish to explore guided by one that knows its mazes, to a shaded cottage and garden of sweet herbs & flowers in the midst, where you might forget the wretched moderns and their spiders' webs—& their feasts on empty wind, thistles & dung—its a dog refusing plum pudding would lap up a vomit." [34]

Deepened from childhood, and renewed, his Gothic delight is already full-formed before its confirmation by Blake. Here are two 1824 notes:

"Seen in Midsummer, 15th July 9 o'clock p.m. At that time of twilight, when the azure behind a high spired turret was very cool but almost blueless, the chastened glow of the light tower against it was very beautiful, the sky being textureless and without a cloud, but what I write this for is to remark that though all was low in tone as preparing to receive the still and solemn night, yet the tower on which the last light glimmered, seemed luminous in itself and rather sending out light from itself than reflecting it, and I noticed it on other stone buildings, going along, that it was as if they had inherent light reminding one of mother-of-pearl it was luminous, though pale, faint, and glimmering. Nothing but melting

in the many gradations in the lights opposed to elaborate . . . the
sharpness of the cool shadows against the cool sky could I should
think give that mild glimmering poetical light of eventide."

"A monastic figure with much background of Gothic cathedral,
the time twilight. The pinnacles and enrichments in light painted
with silver and toned down into the many gradations of colour &
shadow. Warmish tones, and elaborate feeling of that time in
summer evenings when venerable buildings seem no longer to be
brute matter but with a subdued solemn light which seems their
own & not reflected, send out a lustre into the heart of him who
looks—a mystical and spiritual more than a material light. And
with what a richness does it beam out from the neutral coolness of
the quiet flat sky behind it—it is indeed such a precious luminous
tone that though it is not perhaps really lighter than the sky and
only as light in the very highest lights, yet it shows as a mass light
from the sky." [35]

Not merely latent here are all the developed preferences he
carried with him to Blake, with specklings of Blake among them
already.

VI

Little more of Palmer's extant work belongs certainly to these
last years of Blake's life. "A Hilly Scene" (No. 53, Plate 21), I think,
was painted in 1826, or perhaps in 1825, obviously near to the series
of 1825 monochromes; and it is one of the most enchanted of his
visions of divine serenity and fertility—"the earth is full of thy
richness." Earlier than "A Hilly Scene," no doubt, is "The Repose
of the Holy Family" (No. 30, Plate 9), probably the "Family" which
Palmer "laid by . . . in much distress, anxiety, and fear", about
July 15, 1824.[36] Here again is one of his few direct borrowings from
Blake—the donkey (which Blake himself had already borrowed),
which occurs in Blake's "Flight into Egypt" and his colour-printed
drawing "Triple Hecate." [37] The "Joseph's Dream" of 1824 has
disappeared; and not much is visible now of the Gothic excess of
1826. By the early summer of 1826 he had taken courage to obey
his visions. About disobedience to his visions, or at any rate about
falling short of them for worldly reasons, he had pulled himself up
the autumn before. He had done just over £30's worth of drawings
on commission for a "Mr. Bennett"—probably the Hon. Henry Gray
Bennett, M.P., who was a patron of Linnell's (Linnell painted him
and gave his sister lessons).[38] When the work had been finished

he had written to Mr. Bennett, begging to state that "the pictures and drawings now delivered" were "somewhat different in style from those he used to paint when Mr. Bennett gave the commission," and saying that he would take any back that Mr. Bennett disliked.[39] Soon after he recorded that "It was given me this morning (16th October, 1825), to see that I had done wrong in seeking for Mr. Bennett's pictures, visions more consonant with common nature than those I received, at my first regeneration, from the Lord. I will no more, by God's grace, seek to moderate for the sake of pleasing men." [40] Probably the 1825 series of monochromes, which he had ready to send to the 1826 Academy, followed the Bennett drawings, and he made in them less compromise. Just after this October memorandum, it seems, he had put down that "the artist who knows art, ere he bring his work forward to the envious world, or hope for the admiration of the few select discerners, will elaborate it to his utmost thought" (cf. "A Hilly Scene"); "if indeed, material tablet can receive the perfect tracings of celestial beauty." [41] He had already shown "A Rustic Scene" and "A Scene from Kent" at the 1825 Academy—"so amazing," according to an Academy notice, "that we feel the most intense curiosity to see what manner of man it was who produced such performances. We think if he would show himself with a label round his neck, 'The Painter of *A View in Kent*,' he would make something of it at a shilling a-head"; [42] but discretion had evidently been swept away by 1826. Excess, preached by Blake, and now practised by Palmer had also, as I have said, warrant in Milton whom both Blake and Palmer so revered; and the Milton text shows exactly how Palmer, at twenty-one, justified excess against Academy critics or desire to satisfy patrons

> . . . thy desire, which tends to know
> The works of God, thereby to glorify
> The great Work-master, leads to no excess
> That reaches blame, but rather merits praise
> The more it seems excess . . .[43]

There was visionary excess, as well as Gothic extravagance, in two works of 1826, now missing, but well described by A. H. Palmer, and in two drawings probably of the same year. In "Naomi before Bethlehem" and "A Biblical Subject," Palmer must certainly have been at his most excessive, blending hints from Blake and Fuseli and Bonasone and Michelangelo. We know that he wrote down projected subjects "from the books of *Ruth, Daniel*, and *Jonah*," that he put down in his sketch-book, "Young as I am, I know—I am certain and positive that God answers the prayers of them that believe, and hope in His mercy. I sometimes doubt this through the temptation of the Devil, and while I doubt I am miserable; but when my eyes are open again, I see what God has done to me, and I now tell you, I *know* that my Redeemer liveth." [44]

We know that he wrote down a prayer in the spring of 1826 "On going to Shoreham, Kent, to design from *Ruth*," and that he went to Shoreham for his first preliminary sojourn in company with Frederick Tatham.[45] This date is usually given as the beginning of his "Shoreham period," but, as I shall argue, his most typical Shoreham pictures do not begin until 1827, until he turned away somewhat from Blake to an intensified scrutiny of nature, until, in fact, Blake's death. Until 1827 he was a lodger in Shoreham, rather than an artist living there in devoted seclusion.

About his biblical pictures of excess in the name of God, conceived and carried out in this Shoreham stay, these notes survive from "a short, fragmentary journal," now destroyed:

"At Shoreham, Kent, August 30, 1826. God worked in great love with my spirit last night, giving me a founded hope that I might finish my *Naomi before Bethlehem*, and (to me) in a short time. . . . That night, when I hoped and sighed to complete the above subject well (it will be my maiden finished figure drawing), I hoped only in God, and determined next morning to attempt working on it in God's strength. . . . Now I go out to draw some hops that their fruitful sentiment may be infused into my figures.

"August 31. We do or think nothing good but it has its reward. I worked with but little faith on my *Naomi before Bethlehem* this morning and succeeded just in proportion. After dinner I was helped against the enemy so that I thought one good thought. I immediately drew on my cartoon much quicker and better. . . . Satan tries violently to make me leave reading the Bible and praying. . . . O artful enemy, to keep me, who devote myself entirely to poetic things, from the best of books and the finest, perhaps, of all poetry. . . . I will endeavour, God helping, to begin the day by dwelling on some short piece of scripture, and praying for the Holy Ghost thro' the day to inspire my art. Now, in the twilight, let Him come that at evening-time it may be light. God bless my father and brother and poor dear old nurse; who, though a misled Baptist, shall sing among the redeemed for ever.

"The last 4 or 5 mornings I thank God that He has mercifully taken off the load of horror which was wont so cruelly to scare my spirits on awaking. Be His great name ever blest; He persists to do me good, spite of myself, and sometimes puts into my mind the unchangeableness of His promise, the reality of future things. Then I *know* that faith is the *substance* of things hoped for, the *evidence* of things not seen.

"Wednesday. Read scripture. In morning, ill and incapable, in afternoon really dreadful gloom; toward evening the dawn of some beautiful imaginations, and then some of those strong thoughts given that push the mind a great progress at once, and strengthen it, and bank it in on the right road to TRUTH. I had believed and prayed as much or more than my wretched usual, and was near saying 'what matter my faith and prayer?', for all day I could do nothing; but at evening-time it was light; and at night, such blessed help and inspiration!! O Lord grant me, I beseech Thee grant, that I may remember what THOU only showedst me about my *Ruth*.

"Thursday. Rose without much horror. This day, I believe, I took out my *Artist's Home*, having through a change in my visions got displeased with it; but I saw that in it which resolved me to finish it. Began this day with scripture.

"Friday. So inspired in the morning that I worked on the *Naomi before Bethlehem*, which had caused me just before such dreadful suffering, as confidently and certainly as ever did M. Angelo I believe." [46]

"The Artist's Home" is no more than a name. The "Naomi before Bethlehem" still existed in the eighties—that is, if A. H. Palmer's identification was correct. "The wildest conceptions of Blake and Fuseli combined with the most extravagant symbolism of early art could not be more wild and extravagant than this," A. H. Palmer wrote. "There are crowded into it seven or eight figures. Upon the right, staring fearfully and fixedly at the spectator, stands a woman. She points towards a kind of symbolic city which is half concealed by the flaming rays of a portentous sun, and her extended arms separate a heavy, shroud-like cloak. Leaning on her bosom in a somewhat graceful attitude is a girl in classical drapery. On the left and also in the foreground are two old men with limbs so huge, attitudes so contorted, and countenances so forbidding, that it is difficult to associate them in any way with the story of Ruth. They are reapers, and one holds in his hand an archaic sickle, his foot resting on bundles of corn. Behind them walks another reaper, and behind him again appear the grotesque heads of two oxen. In the middle background a sleeper pillows his head upon the abundant grain, while over him seems to hover a female spirit possessed by some great emotion. Close to the sun and just rising above the horizon, a crescent moon and six stars of astounding size blaze in the sky." [47]

Similar, though without the symbolic Gothicism of the city, must have been the biblical subject which A. H. Palmer also described. In this "two inordinately brawny female figures, one young, the other older, are crammed into the opposite sides of a design. . . . Between them is a low table bearing some small fruits, and on the sward just beyond the barn or cottage where they sit, dance four men and women in a measure which would do honour to the orgies of any savages correspondingly muscular. A few sheep (in the conventional rows affected by Blake) browse behind, and behind them again is a cottage bosomed in rugged but abnormally fertile country. On one side, an open manuscript shows certain biblical writings. Parts of the figures, such as the extremities, are elaborated with evident pains and show some knowledge." [48]

"Naomi before Bethlehem" sounds the most Blake-like of his finished drawings; and there is a building of enjewelled fairy-land, Gothic in the sepia drawing, now in an American collection, known as "The Haunted Stream" (No. 44, Plate 17)—a blend of a Miltonic text and a reminiscence, as I have mentioned, of a plate in David Cox's *Treatise.* "The Haunted Stream" probably belongs to this time. So does "A Shepherd and His Flock under the Moon and Stars" (No. 46, Plate 18), with its castle and its Gothic building.

I have talked of Palmer's admiration of the Virgil wood-engravings. Deriving from them directly, though the subject is Palmer's own, is the wood-engraving "Harvest with a Crescent Moon" (No. 50, Plate 19), which he perhaps cut direct on the wood in 1826. To understand its genesis, it is necessary to go back to Palmer's first meeting with Blake. Blake was at work on *Dante.* But "at my-never-to-be-forgotten first interview," wrote Palmer, "the copper of the first plate (of the *Job* engravings)—'Thus did *Job* continually'—was lying on the table where he had been working at it. How lovely it looked by the lamplight, strained through the tissue paper!" [49]

What Palmer saw in that plate was not only the shepherd sons and daughters of Job, the serried sheep, the Gothic cathedral and the last curve of a flaming sun, but a dark hill, lit from behind, at the sharp end of which a crescent moon hung in a darker sky. Other plates in the *Book of Job* have in them dark hills against an afterglow, and from this early wood-engraving such hills dark against light were imagined by Palmer again and again, and several times with a crescent moon in attendance. Blake's moon and hill Palmer saw for himself in the Kentish hills, Blake reinforcing what he saw for himself no doubt before, and still more intensely afterwards.

Blake helped Palmer not only to see, but to see religiously. So did Milton, and Bunyan, and much else which Palmer read. It was because they only saw that Palmer so denounced the modernists of his day, had so longed, as he wrote in his 1824 sketch-book, to explore the mazes of a wood till he reached "a shaded cottage and garden of sweet herbs and flowers in the midst where you might forget the wretched moderns and their spiders' webs—and their feasts on empty wind, thistles and dung." [50]   There was plenty of pastoralism in the eighteen-twenties, in varied degrees of homeliness or insipidity. There were plenty of shepherds in poems and in frames. But for Palmer, as for Blake, a shepherd was not merely pastoral, or Virgilian. Palmer's shepherds are the shepherds of *Pilgrim's Progress*, shepherds in the Delectable Mountains, with their gardens, and orchards, and vineyards, and streams—the mountains from which the Celestial City was visible.

Blake elaborated Bunyan's image of the land of Beulah, and no doubt talked of it to Palmer.[51] A Blake-like moon of love and inno- cence hangs in Palmer's twilights for several years after Blake's death, but as far as these twilights are symbolic, they derive more from the original straightforwardness and simplicity of Bunyan: "Now I saw in my Dream, that by this time the Pilgrims were got over the Inchanted Ground, and entering into the Countrey of *Beulah*, whose air was very sweet and pleasant, the way lying directly through it, they solaced themselves there for a season. Yes, here they heard continually the singing of Birds, and saw every day the flowers appear in the earth: and heard the voice of the Turtle in the land. In this Countrey the Sun shineth night and day; wherefore this was beyond the Valley of the *shadow of death*, and also out of the reach of the Giant *Despair*; neither could they from this place so much as see *Doubting-Castle*. Here they were within sight of the City they were going to: also here met them some of the inhabitants thereof. For in this Land the shining Ones com- monly walked, because it was upon the Borders of Heaven."

That is the text to remember in looking over Palmer's moon- lights; and his shepherds are not silly shepherds or shepherds of the popular wood-engraving, but Bunyan's, in Bunyan's near-heavenly land:

> Thus by the Shepherds, Secrets are reveal'd,
> Which from all other men are kept conceal'd:
> Come to the Shepherds then, if you would see
> Things deep, things hid, and that mysterious be.[52]

It was Palmer's strength that he worked in both worlds at once. He could absorb all this from Blake and Bunyan, and his favourite

c

poets, and still not allow it to glaze his eyes. He saw inward and outward at the same time, even while the living Blake glowed all around him. And in his drawings of 1825 there is one very curious proof of this outward vision. I think I am right in saying that Palmer and Tennyson (who was born five years later than Palmer) were the first to paint and to describe what by their early days had long been famliar in the English landscape—the horse-chestnut tree. But the horse-chestnut had not been part of the painter's or writer's tradition. Gilpin, for example, had condemned it as ugly and unpicturesque.[53] Wordsworth never wrote a word about horse-chestnuts—though he made plenty of reference to the classical sweet chestnut, which had made its way into painting and into landscape approval via Salvator Rosa. But Tennyson, like Ruskin and the Pre-Raphaelites, and Gerard Hopkins, was devoted to the horse-chestnut; and even when Palmer was closest to Blake, even at the height of his devotion to sixteenth-century art, to Milton and to Bunyan, Palmer was free enough in his own vision to draw the horse-chestnut trees in front of his own eyes. Even in his "Skirts of a Wood" of 1825 (No. 42, Plate 15), with its direct derivations from Blake, Palmer puts in, large and bold, and patterned, the horse-chestnut he has seen, and goes further and puts his shepherd and shepherdess underneath its wide branches and leaves. So, too, in the "Pastoral with Horse-Chestnut" (No. 96); and in his "Hilly Scene (No. 53, Plate 21), he uses the horse-chestnut to make a Gothic arch to the picture, and loves it so much that the horse-chestnut is there most unbotanically in flower, when the autumn has filled out the ears of corn.[54]

CHAPTER IV

THE PALMER CIRCLE

I

THE clues to Palmer's inner life in these early years are not as full as one would like them to be. His life and his painting circle around religion, and if most of his papers had not been destroyed, we might know more of how Palmer separated himself from the Baptist atmosphere of his childhood and his family, a separation in which he must have had some support. It is pretty certain that he was never baptized, when he grew up, into the Baptist communion, in spite of his father (who became a Baptist preacher when he retired from bookselling and went to live at Shoreham), in spite of his Baptist nurse, and all his Baptist cousins of the Giles family, with whom he was intimate all through his early years. He may have been baptized into the Church of England as a baby—seeing that his father began as a churchman and married his Baptist wife in church. But it is just as likely that he finally separated from the Baptists when he was eighteen or so, round about 1823; and was baptized into the Church of England in some London church. But there is no record of such a crisis and such an event, which would accord with his access of religious and creative fervour. By 1826, as we have seen, he was calling his nurse, Mary Ward, "a misled Baptist"; and the year before he had stated baldly that "Genius is the unreserved devotion of the whole soul to the divine, poetic arts, and through them to God; deeming all else, even to our daily bread, only valuable as it helps us to unveil the heavenly face of Beauty." [1]

His first figure drawing in 1823 had been St. Christopher carrying the infant Christ, and even in that year, even when he was eighteen, he had been so convinced of his *mission* as an artist, that he conceived he was doing wrong to give so much time to music, and accordingly gave up his membership of an amateur musical society, to concentrate upon being an artist. [2]

So it was natural that the group of artists which his personality, by its force and glow, gathered around itself, should also share much of his own religious enthusiasm. The Palmer circle consisted of six artists, Henry Walter, F. O. Finch, George Richmond, Edward Calvert, Frederick Tatham, and Welby Sherman; and of two, who were deeply concerned with art, though not artists themselves.

35

These were Tatham's brother Arthur, an undergraduate, and
Palmer's Baptist first cousin—John Giles—a double first cousin,
Palmer's mother having been a Giles and Giles's mother a Palmer.[3]

Like Palmer, Giles developed leanings toward the Oxford Movement; he went still further, and lent towards Rome—so much so
that he was hurried off by his friends to be baptized into the Church
of England by Manning, in Cardinal Manning's pre-Roman days.[4]
He was a stockbroker, who looked after Palmer's money affairs, a
devoted mediaevalist with a love of sixteenth-century Catholic
books of devotion, and a habit of pronouncing the -ed at the end of
words, as in "mincèd pies."[5] He much admired Palmer's visionary
paintings long after the Shoreham years, and bit by bit he built up
a good Palmer collection. He, too, was bound by personal veneration
for Blake.

Welby Sherman made the least mark of the circle. He was
younger than the rest, had little talent as an artist, and wished to
become an engraver. He has left an inept drawing or two, an
engraving, and a few engravings after Calvert and Palmer. And
there is a drawing of him by Richmond, who painted him several
times. The circle tried hard to launch him, he was patronized—or
at least tried out for a little—by the celebrated Dr. Monro in Monro's
old age; he was with Palmer at the very close of his Shoreham stay.
But his beginnings and his end are mysterious. He appears to have
become the black sheep of the pasture, going off to France eventually
with money belonging either to Richmond or Henry Walter.[6]
Henry Walter was more considerable; he was older than Palmer,
a hard-working professional artist of mediocre skill, who painted
animals and, as I have said, did animal plates for Ackermann
drawing-books. I have seen many of his pictures, but none with any
scrap of the inward vision of his friends. But he was one of the first
artists—younger artists, at least—who were known to Palmer, although
his work suggests only an easy straightforwardness in religion. The
Tathams, Finch, Calvert, and Richmond came much closer in spirit.

To begin with Finch. Palmer called him "my earliest friend."
As an artist—and his watercolours are still in and out of the sale-
rooms—his ideal was not strengthened enough by observation. He
was three years older than Palmer, and painted in a careful idiom
derived from Claude, or the less intense kind of Turner, via John
Varley. Now and again I have seen an oil by Finch, or a solemn
low-toned and less fanciful watercolour, which explains Palmer's
respect for him. His letters and papers and poems are as commonplace and unimaginative as much of his painting (from which it is
only an inch to Birket Foster). But, though in his output he was

the least influenced by Blake (Walter excepted), he knew Blake
before the others. With exaggeration Palmer wrote of him as a
"*very* old friend of Blake." He had heard much of Blake from
Varley when he was still one of Varley's pupils; but though their
painting was so different, though he was the least excited, the
calmest, and most balanced of the circle, yet, wrote Palmer, Finch
of all of them "was most inclined to believe in Blake's spiritual
intercourse." He was religious, came across a Swedenborg volume
in the British Museum Library, and joined the Swedenborgians.
On the evidence, he meant more as a living man than as an artist.[7]

The Tathams were also religious, one orthodox, one unorthodox.
Their father was a friend of John Linnell's—an architect with a
pretty fair connection at one period. According to Linnell, he found
it expedient, as an architect with patrons in the aristocracy, to come
over from dissent to the Church of England.[8] Of his sons, Frederick
revolted to a new religious eccentricity. Probably he deserves the
strictures that have been passed on him for destroying Blake manuscripts, but if he did destroy them it was in obedience to his own
beliefs as a member of the new Irvingite church.

He drew and did sculpture with at any rate enough talent to
earn Palmer's respect, but not enough to prevent himself being
quickly discouraged as an artist. John Linnell introduced him to
Blake (though Blake had known his father, C. H. Tatham, since as far
back as 1799), and probably also to Palmer, and he was certainly as
close to Blake as any of them, eventually looking after Blake's funeral,
and taking care of his widow. He says in his short MS. life of Blake
that Blake bequeathed him his unsold writings, paintings, and plates
and that Blake had commended him to his wife, as he lay dying, as
the manager of her affairs.[9] I do not think myself that there is any
reason to doubt Tatham's word, as several have done. Palmer, in
his letters, years after,—and Palmer's respect was always well founded
and worth having—gives the impression that Tatham could have
been nothing but an upright and good man—a grave, charitable
young man (who taught him that it was his duty to have a daily
bath). Palmer not only went first of all to Shoreham in his company, but wrote to his sister when he died in 1878, that "I seldom
think of Shoreham without recalling his persistent and self-denying
kindness to a poor cottager whose sores he daily dressed with his
own hands, and that for months together; nor did I ever witness
such ardour of continuous study as that which at one time he devoted
to a branch of art-study; .& happily, with commensurate results in
the opinion of some of the best artists. During this time there were
three consecutive weeks in which all regularities of food & repose

were slighted." And he writes on of the powerful effect upon him of a pen-and-ink or chalk design of Gideon, which Tatham drew at Shoreham.[10]

It is inconceivable to me that Palmer would not at once have broken with Tatham had there been any illegality about his control of Blake's property, inconceivable, that Tatham was such a man, or that Tatham did anything for Mrs. Blake without the most decent and kindly intentions. It may be worth pointing to a note, signed J. H. and written in a copy of *Nollekens and His Times,* which was published a few years ago: "Mrs. Blake was hardly the passive creature here described—at all events Tatham did not find her so, for she was opposed to everything he did for her benefit & when she submitted to his views it was always with the words she 'Had not help for it'—that at last Tatham tired with her opposition threw the will behind the fire & burnt it saying There you can do as you like for the will no longer exists and left her. Early the following morning she called upon him saying William had been with her all night & required her to come to him & renew the Will which was done & never after did she offer any opposition to Tatham's proceeding." [11]

That sounds likely enough; and it seems to me likely that Palmer and Richmond (who had a shallow knowledge of Blake's systematic ideas) would have agreed to the destruction of any Blake MSS. making religious statements that seemed to them likely to harm Blake's reputation; or, at any rate, that they would not have disapproved.

Calvert, apparently, did disapprove, but Calvert by this time had departed from orthodox Christianity into a Greek pantheism.[12]

Tatham probably had dealings with Samuel Palmer's brother William in disposing of things left by Blake; [13] and no doubt it was through Tatham that Palmer received his Blake pictures, books, and drawings.

At any rate, Tatham was another member of the circle with a deep and an unusual religious fervour, who had probably heard, and been possessed by, some of the addresses—the wild addresses— of Edward Irving, preaching, with fanatic eyes and long black hair to the shoulders, of the second coming of Christ. Irving's celebrity was at its height during the years in which the Palmer circle was formed and was most strong.

Arthur Tatham, his brother, also felt his religion deep. "I was with him," wrote Palmer, "on the eve of his ordination, and remember his saying that it would probably cost him his life in testimony to the truth; so stormy were the prospects at that time" [14] (just before the Reform Bill); but Arthur Tatham passed out of his life into the peaceful cure of the Cornish living of Boconnoc.

The Tathams were still more closely integrated into the circle through George Richmond's Gretna Green elopement (aided by Palmer) with one of the Tatham daughters; and it is probable that Palmer himself was in love with another of the daughters, who turned him down during his years at Shoreham.

This leaves on the roll the two artists who, besides Palmer, were also men of distinction—Edward Calvert and George Richmond.

II

W. B. Yeats at one time had planned to write a book on Calvert, whom he called "a fragmentary symbolist." Such a symbolist "evokes in his persons and his landscapes an infinite emotion, a perfected emotion, a part of the Divine Essence"; but "he does not set his symbols in the great procession as Blake would have him, 'in a certain order, suited to his imaginative energy.'" [15] And Calvert did not equal Palmer in his power to invent and to sustain his vision. Blake and Palmer increased the youthful fire in him which caused his brief flare; and then he slowly frittered away his life with much less result, and more uncertainty of purpose. He was six years older than Palmer and had seen active service in the Navy before he came to London and met Palmer and Blake.[16] He inherited a livelihood, and came of a family which seems to have had something to do with painting. His father is said to have patronized Girtin. After a childhood in the Fowey valley at Lostwithiel, and his naval service, he began to paint at Plymouth, mainly under A. B. Johns. Johns painted landscape in the haze of Ideal light. His oils of "sentiment" were akin to Turner without fire, or J. B. Pyne; and he sent Calvert up to London with a letter of introduction to Fuseli. Palmer met him first at the Academy exhibition in 1826, looking like "a prosperous, stalwart country gentleman," who was "redolent of the sea, and in white trousers." [17] He had just settled, in May, in a small house in Brixton; and he had brought stocks up with him to sell through John Giles. At the Academy, the year before, he had exhibited a painting of nymphs, one of them "opening a way for herself through a nut-tree copse," which had brought Alfred Chalon to call upon him in admiration.[18]

One can discover much of his early tastes. Leaving aside Blake for a moment, he loved Schiavone and Claude. With Linnell and Palmer and Wainwright, he admired Bonasone's broad engravings; and also (I should say) Aldegraver. "Claude and Bonasone," he

wrote in his old age, "frequently present us with forms of childlike
grace and innocence seated in recesses of woodland growth—the
freshness of an early age—midst seeming pathways, threading the
mysteries of retreat to seclusions of blessedness, that make one laugh
outright from very joyfulness of soul." [19] Wordsworth's poetry, as
a young man, "he read aloud exquisitely." [20]

The effect on him of Blake's Virgil blocks anyone can trace
in detail by comparing with them his own set of engravings. He
worked on some of them under Blake's eye; and he also adopted
in them figure groupings from the antique gems which Blake so
much admired (the figure, for instance, in "The Chamber Idyll").
But there was a serpent—or so it seemed to Palmer and Richmond,
and Calvert's widowed mother down at Lostwithiel—twined round
the tree of Calvert's paradise, a Greek serpent. Discreetly disguised,
it is still visible in Richmond's reminiscences of him as a young man,
for besides Wordsworth and Byron "He was a very great lover of
Plato, and admired W. Savage Landor very much. . . . Chapman's
Homer and some of his hymns, especially that to Pan, I have often
heard him read." [21] He started off, in fact, with a vague aspiration
towards Pan; then, in tune with Palmer and Blake, changed to a
brief period of mystical Christianity, and finally backslid into a
curious, developing and devitalizing paganism. Blake was not the
only odd man in London, and to Richmond's phrase "a very great
lover of Plato" might be added, I think, that he was also a very great
reader of Thomas Taylor the Platonist. But the story is apparent
enough in the texts around the engravings, and in some sentences
in letters from Palmer and from Calvert's mother.[22]

"My poetic loves," Calvert wrote at some date or another to
Richmond, "have been associated more fondly, first and earliest,
with Pan and the rustic deities—elemental natures." [23] His Academy
picture, the "Nymphs" of 1825, was no doubt a product of this early
fondness, and so was the little drawing of the Hamadryad. Then, as
he settled in London, and came under the spell of Blake and Palmer,
he was turned from the rustic deities. The earliest result of this
that we know is the wood-engraving "The Ploughman" or "Christian
Ploughing the Last Furrow of Life," completed and published in
September 1827. The block was inscribed, "Seen in the Kingdom
of Heaven by vision through Jesus Christ our saviour." But he
was not completely converted. There was wavering between Christ
and the elemental natures. In 1828, Calvert cut the wood-engraving
now called, I believe incorrectly, "The Bacchante." Palmer knew
this figure with a lyre as "The Prophet," and it is perhaps a somewhat androgynous Apollo, based on a common enough representa-

tion of Apollo in antique gems. In a letter of June 24, 1828, Palmer wrote to Richmond (and Richmond endorsed the letter "Calvert's mysticism"): "I dare say Mr. Calvert has got his print of the Prophet into a fine state by this time, and that his naughty disobedient heresies are falling away from about him like the scales of leprosy, & melting as the morning vapours melt from the sun." [24] Calvert's mother was also worried. In letters written before the end of 1828, she warned him: "I certainly think that with your stimulated feelings you should compose yourself to less inquisitive study. It seems to me, whether on poetry, philosophy, or religion, all that you read tends to a dangerous disquiet." And more tartly: "You also ask 'And is your heaven in futurity?' which question I can only answer by inquiring if your heaven is now in possession." [25]

Then, in September 1828 Palmer told Richmond: "Mr. Calvert I found as I prognosticated in a former letter, risen from temptation, and finishing with surprising rapidity, the effect of prayer, a beautiful and luxuriant design of the cider pressing." [26] It was published on October 10, inscribed "Edwd. Calvert inven. et sculp. by the Gift of God in Christ." "The Sheep of His Pasture" was probably done in 1828 as well. By November 17 he finished and published "The Bride," inscribing it with a confession of his own return to God "A stray lamb is led to thy folds." He seems to have stayed in the fold, engraving more variations on the theme of the Divine marriage, between the autumn of 1828 and the autumn of 1831. He inscribed one of these—"The Brook"—with the words "The waters of this brook shall never fail to the married wife of the Lord God." But he fell away once more, till Palmer, writing certainly of Calvert, tells Richmond: "I cannot help daily anxiety for a dear friend of yours & mine who though the most amiable & conscientious of men—if he knew what was right & true—we have beheld now for years remaining in deliberate hostility to the gospel of Christ— do let us pray for him & at all seasonable opportunities not contend with, but 'perswade' him, 'knowing the terrors' as well as the unspeakable mercies of our Lord." [27] (Shoreham, October 14, 1834.) His wavering back to Pan may explain why, in their third states, he cut away the religious sentences from "The Ploughman," "The Cyder Feast," and "The Brook."

Plato and the Greeks were holding him, and he became the dreamer of pagan ideals chasing perfection and exploring harmonies in colour. He had enough money to preserve him in his dreams. His poetic loves began in the "elemental natures," and "thence" —to continue the quotation from his letter to Richmond—"thence upward through impulsive and Dionysiac energies. I have been busied with the beautiful Antique myths; ever in an upward course of purpose, and in vows to the Muses and Apollo."

Probably both Calvert and Palmer read the writings and Platonic translations of Taylor, which were well known to John Linnell, and certainly to Blake; [28] but Palmer went no further than a Christian neo-platonism: earthly objects to him were to be admired as hints of the perfections of Heaven. Earthly objects for Calvert were to be very much second to the divine ideas after which they were modelled.

"I have a fondness for the earth, and rather a Phrygian mood of regarding it," he wrote. "I feel a yearning to see the glades and the nooks receding like vistas into the gardens of Heaven." [29] But as the earth dimmed for him, so his painting grew steadily more vapid. Palmer differs from Calvert and excels him because of his delight and absorption in natural objects as glorious images of a greater glory beyond nature. And when Palmer as a man was enthusiastic, open, richly observant, positive, a curious compound of gravity and fun, Calvert was detached, aloof, and solemn. Palmer once teased his somewhat unreal heaviness by singing the British Grenadiers to him without stopping.[30] And his writings have a heavy and rather pretentious touch.

Many people, artists and writers as well, had been touched by a similar taste and yearning. Coleridge had read Giordano Bruno when he was himself "intoxicated with the vernal fragrance and effluvia from the flowers and first-fruits of Pantheism, unaware of its bitter root." [31] But Calvert went almost as far as Pagan Taylor. Isaac D'Israeli represents Taylor in his novel, *Vaurien, or Sketches of the Time*, as "abstracted from all things and all men," in a watch-tower at the end of his garden, where "he reads Plato and Homer, and views nothing but the skies." Taylor believed in sacrifice, and held that animals which are sacrificed represent "the irrational life of our souls." [32] He is said to have "sacrificed lambs in his lodgings to the 'immortal gods' and poured out libations to Jupiter, until his landlord threatened to turn him out"; and in the 1820's it was gossip that he sacrificed a piece of every rumpsteak or chop on his plate to Jupiter.[33]

Much the same kind of thing was said about Calvert in his narrower circle. A. H. Palmer remembered stories of back garden sacrifices, and Samuel Palmer's godson, Sir William Blake Richmond, stayed with him as a boy: "it was not without a thrill that I saw in his little back garden an altar erected to the honour of the great god Pan." [34]

There is a pathos in Calvert's career. He had one of the qualities most scarce in the lives of English painters—a truth to himself, an indifference to the extraneous demands made upon a man's art by fashion and society. He felt there would be no one after Ingres "to arrest the rapid decadence of painting in Europe," that painting tended "toward the rankest materialism," that "amid a feverish production of trifles, there is not even time to remember that there is such a thing as the BEAUTIFUL IDEAL, much less to *meditate upon it*" (1855).[35] He wrote to his son: "I coveted the mastery over colour, and it has eaten up the bulk of my life." [36] But if he was true to himself, the self was faulty; and for a painter, that self was never securely enough footed upon earth, to be able to rise with safety into an ideal heaven. He had, while his years were still fresh, his few moments of intercourse between himself and Nature, himself and Blake, himself and Palmer, and then thinned away into his idea.

III

George Richmond was a much simpler case. He was born four years after Palmer, the son of a miniature painter who made no particular mark, but knew other artists well enough to simplify his son's early progress. Richmond met Blake first of all at the Tathams' house in St. John's Wood. "Upon leaving late in the evening," according to his son, Sir William Blake Richmond, "my father asked Blake to permit him to escort him on the way home. . . . The walk continued till my father had made the whole journey from the Regent's Park to the Strand. Upon giving an account of it later, my father said: 'I felt walking on air, and as if I had been talking to the Prophet Isaiah.'" [37] Through the Tathams and their friend Linnell, no doubt, he met Palmer. Round about 1821 he began his drawing from the antique in the Elgin and Towneley Galleries at the British Museum, where Palmer, as we have seen, started work in November 1822. Knowing several R.A.s, he had no difficulty in getting a letter of recommendation to send in with his drawing when he wished to go on to the Royal Academy schools; and there he met with friendship from Fuseli, now very old, "a small man with a great head covered with a mass of shaggy grey hair, wearing spectacles, and wrapped in a thick blanket," and shuffling about in slippers; and also from the President, Sir Thomas Lawrence. Fuseli invited Richmond and Sidney Cooper and Catterson Smith to his studio to see "The Lazar House." Lawrence "shewed very great favour" to the three of them, and had them round to his house "to see the drawings that he possessed of Michael Angelo, and other great masters"; [38] but as the Palmer circle gradually established itself, Frederick Tatham, Calvert, and Palmer

became his intimates, and Blake their source of light and interpretation. "Never did he enter Blake's house," he confessed, "without
imprinting a reverent kiss upon the bell-handle which the seer had
touched; nor was he alone in this homage, which was practised by
all the band of friends"; and Richmond told his friend Joseph
Severn, "I used constantly to go to see Mr. and Mrs. Blake when they
lived near Blackfriars Bridge, and never have I known an artist so
spiritual, so devoted, so single-minded, or so full of vivid imagination
as he. Before Blake began a picture he used to fall on his knees
and pray that his work might be successful." [39] Richmond showed
his own things to Blake, and asked for Blake's advice (which was
prayer) when he was seized with depression.

Yet, in a sense, George Richmond was scarcely an artist at all,
through all his long and successful life. His relations with Palmer
were not unlike the relations between Gerard Hopkins and Robert
Bridges, who was scarcely a poet at all; although he succeeded
publicly, where Hopkins remained obscure. Richmond was a
natural Academician: there is no style about his art, early or late.
A thinness of drawing and a hardness of colour mark his religious
pictures, his drawings from nature, his landscapes, and his portraits.
Entirely without fire (like Robert Bridges), there is in his painting
no strong conjunction of belief and observation; and if his early
work is liveliest, it is still a repository of other men's ideas and
manners, and remains interesting, really, on that account. Historic-
ally, if not intrinsically, it deserves exploration and record. His
"Creation of Light" (reproduced in Binyon's *Followers of William
Blake*) combines Milton and Blake and John Martin. The text is
Milton:

> Again the Almighty spake, Let there be lights
> High in the expanse of Heaven, to divide
> The day from night.

The plan is altered from John Martin's mezzotint in his *Paradise Lost*
—a plate which was published in 1825. Richmond has reversed the
position of the sun and the crescent moon; and in place of Martin's
sun inserted a vast rayed orb out of Blake; and in place of Martin's
creator, he has borrowed the Adversary from Blake's drawing "The
Baptism," in the *Paradise Regained* series (which Linnell had
acquired in 1825). Blake's figure had been taken from Michelangelo's
"Last Judgement." But all this, in its lavish blue and green and
black, with its moon disc a raised ridge of pigment and its flames
from the sun not merely red and gold, but red and real gold,—in all
this there is only an assembly of elements, not their re-creation. In
"Christ and the Woman of Samaria" in the Tate Gallery, Richmond

has combined sheep from Blake, corn from Palmer, a Gothic City from Blake, and delicate plants and tree simplifications from Palmer again. He was very young when these pictures were painted, but he matured only into a conventional thinness. The magic of Blake, of dawns and twilights with Palmer and Calvert and Tatham, the ecstasies and prayers, died out of him soon enough. Richmond was not a mystic; and he had sense enough to realize how he could live and prosper. He was at Blake's deathbed, and actually closed Blake's eyes, and then soon enough started off towards the year 1868: "Total earned this year £3469 14s 6d, the largest income I have ever made." He became friendly with the right friends at the right early time —Gladstone was one of them. He painted everybody—Wilberforce, Macaulay, Darwin, Thackeray, Harriet Martineau, Cardinal Manning, one portrait differing little in quality from the next. He became a somewhat gloomy slave to principles, a Victorian moralist and "a pre-Adamite Tory," with a fixed and severe countenance, who never mentioned to his children the fact that he and his wife had eloped, with Samuel Palmer's help, to Gretna Green. And there is a world of social history in comparing a black photograph of him in his Victorian fame with the miniature he painted for his marriage to Julia Tatham in 1831—a miniature of a handsome, large-eyed, dreamy face touched with the delicacy and incompleteness of youth, a miniature of the lips which had kissed Blake's bell-handle— perhaps the most authentic of all his paintings.[40]

He and Palmer kept fairly close all through their lives, but Palmer was strained now and then by fitting ill into the social proprieties of the household of a wealthy mid-Victorian painter—a painter who buttressed the weakness of his imagination by the grim weight of his morality. A. H. Palmer was frequently bitter about Richmond, and stated that he had gone so far as to say to his father that all the years at Shoreham were a waste of time.[41] Richmond, with his little talent, prospered by compromise; but he was not altogether unfaithful to his youth. After all, he named one of his sons William Blake; and even if he made Palmer feel that he was a success and Palmer a failure, even if he grimly and woodenly rebuked John Giles for leaning over towards Rome, he was at Palmer's bedside when he died, and then wrote down, when he was seventy-five, of Palmer and of Mrs. Richmond: "Among all the many mercies of my now long life, the friendship of Samuel Palmer and then this early love were, to my poor seeming, the greatest that ever were given to me. God grant that I may never lose the blessedness of acknowledging and remembering them. All Saints Day 1884." [42] And it is only through the piety of his many descend-

ants that much of the very best of Palmer's work has come down to
us at all, as if Richmond had obscurely felt, after all, that Shoreham
genius was more important than Royal Academy success, and had
taken care to hand down a family tradition of the visionary excellence
of his friend.

IV

The thing which distinguishes Palmer is not that he belonged
to a group of artists, or that he led that group, or that he knew Blake,
or that the group had certain peculiarities and tastes, or that it
reacted against the movement of the age. All these things and these
facts were adjuncts to a unique personality, which they helped to
shape and develop. The tastes and nature of Palmer's circle were
not at all unique. These young men had grown up in the hard
period after the wars, in years of unsettlement, and fear—machine
breaking, agitation for reform, the "Manchester Massacre," the
Cato Street Conspiracy, the scandal of Queen Caroline, a season of
"reciprocal distrust" between rich and poor, cruel laws and filth
and vile poverty, of an opening breach not only between industrial
workers and employers, but between farmers and their men. It
has been called "an age of economic revolution and anarchy," in
which "the complications of industrial phenomena were such as to
bewilder the strongest mind." [43] It was an age of speculation and
collapse, of earthquakes actual and social, of "years of elemental
turmoil," in which "men felt as singular a sense of precariousness
—with the globe groaning and heaving under their feet, and meteors
flashing and storms rushing about their heads—as we may suppose
a race of ants to feel, when man comes with his candle and gunpowder to blow up their settlement. Amidst the conflicting forces
of nature, men felt as powerless as they." [44]

And so it was a period in which many good men looked for
security either in religion or fanaticism or reaction—the period of
Joanna Southcott, of the Holy Land Pilgrims, who sold up their
property to go to Jerusalem to meet the Lord, the period of Edward
Irving, "the shrill unearthly sound from the lips of the 'gifted'
in the grey chapel in Newman Street," of the wild universal dooms
of the pictures of John Martin, the period of the Reform Bill, and
eventually of the Oxford Movement, whose leaders "believed they
were fighting against the spirit of the age." [45]

In this medley there were plenty of parallels to the primitivism
and Gothicism and intense religious feeling—the "excess"—of
Palmer and his friends. Other artists—James Ward, for example—

were touched by Edward Irving's prophecies of the end of the world and the second coming, by which Tatham was finally swallowed up and which led him to destroy manuscripts by Blake. "God is not to be mocked! The vivid lightnings are gone forth! Farm house conflagrations. York Minster conflagration, Senate House of Kings, Lords and Commons burnt—'I will overturn! overturn! overturn!' Ezek. xxi. 27. King, Church, Government, and people beware!" cried James Ward in his pamphlet, *The New Trial of the Spirits*. ". . . We have witnessed the morning, noon and evening, of a gloomy and tempestuous era. We have seen the reign, the triumph, and the downfall of the Great Beast with seven heads and ten horns. . . ."

Palmer reacted violently against the Reform Bill and disapproved of the abolition of the restraints upon Catholics and Dissenters, and this reaction was all of a piece with the tastes and peculiarities which helped to form and direct his vision as an artist. Finch, it will be recalled, became a Swedenborgian as Tatham became an Irvingite, and when one thinks of all this in connection with Palmer's circle, one must think too of the Gothicism of Pugin, of such men as Kenelm Digby and Ambrose Lisle March Phillips de Lisle. De Lisle was born in the same year as George Richmond, a Leicestershire squire's son who mediaevalized his name by adding "de Lisle," saw Christ in a dream, and joined the Church of Rome in answer to his rebuke (he was fifteen), and was carried by his guardian angel "to old ruined abbeys and churches, where once the praises of God had been sung and souls saved." Pugin enlarged and ornamented his chapel at Grace-Dieu in which "the cantors wore copes of cloth of gold with crimson hoods richly foliated from Pugin's best designs; the women, mediaeval hoods or cloaks . . . whilst the acolytes were clothed in scarlet saches and skull-caps." [46] De Lisle's friend was the fantastic mediaevalist Kenelm Digby, whose *Broad Stone of Honour, or Rules For the Gentlemen of England* (1822), a mediaevalized hand-book to chivalry and duty, drawing on Malory, Froissart, Plato, Wordsworth, Coleridge, Cudworth, Fénelon, etc., went into many editions, influenced the young Disraelian Tories, and is said to be explored still by members of the "English Mistery." "The question," Digby says in the prologue, "is not, whether mankind ought to be influenced by feeling and imagination, but whether these are to be enlisted on the side of religion or against it." [47]

Such was the atmosphere in which Palmer and his friends became, in Calvert's words, "brothers in Art, brothers in Love, and brothers in all that for which Love and Art subsist—the Ideal—the Kingdom within" [48]—the atmosphere, in which they wandered in country walks around Sydenham and Dulwich (before Palmer moved to Shoreham), began their monthly meetings, visited the House of the Interpreter, read Milton and Wordsworth and Keats, made their watchword "Poetry and Sentiment," sketched Gothic buildings, drew each other's portraits, shared a sense of religious awe, meditated upon a pastoral, primitive innocence, and felt with Fuseli, that the pale hands stretching from the tomb in Lieven's "Raising of Lazarus" were one of the sublimest movements in all the art of mankind.[49]

CHAPTER V

LIFE AT SHOREHAM

I

THIS is Palmer's own brief account of the move to Shoreham, from the autobiographical letter in *The Portfolio*: "Forced into the country by illness, I lived afterwards" (after his association with Blake) "for about seven years at Shoreham, in Kent, with my father, who was inseparable from his books, unless when still better engaged in works of kindness. There, sometimes by ourselves, sometimes visited by friends of congenial taste, literature, and art and ancient music wiled away the hours, and a small independence made me heedless, for the time, of further gain; the beautiful was loved for itself. . . ."

The illness was probably bronchitis, coupled with asthma; and the real move, I think, was not made in 1826—the usual assumption —but in 1827, from which the "Shoreham period" (a term which has been too loosely used for all Palmer's visionary work) really begins. Probably Palmer had visited Shoreham before 1826. There may have been some family connection with the village—since a cousin of the Palmers, Charles Wake, had been vicar there thirty years before. And when he went to Shoreham in the spring of 1826, "to design from Ruth," in company with Frederick Tatham, he may have remained for the best part of a year.

In January 1827 he was staying with Calvert in North Brixton. Almost certainly he had visited Shoreham in 1824 and 1825—the sepia drawings of 1825 are suggestive of the Shoreham scenery, and at the 1825 Academy he had shown "A Scene from Kent." Richmond, moreover, had been at Shoreham, according to one of his two note-books, in 1825, though his first prolonged stay there did not take place until the June of 1827. Palmer's grandfather had died in 1825, but his will was not proved until the end of September, and it would have been some considerable time, no doubt, before his affairs were settled, and Samuel Palmer and his brother William received their fifth share each of his estate. His other legacies were inconsiderable, and it would be reasonable to hazard that the debts of such a man would not come to very much. The will (Somerset House) was proved at £18,000; so Palmer and his brother probably received some £3000 apiece.

In addition to Palmer's state of health, there was, if A. H. Palmer's account is to be trusted, another reason for the move. His father does not seem to have been dependent so much on his bookselling as on his well-to-do brother Nathaniel, the corn-factor, who made him an allowance, and seems also to have disliked his activities as a tradesman. "At last," says A. H. Palmer, "my father's austerely business-like 'Uncle Nat' lost his patience with his brother. Samuel, the bookseller, must either live once more the life of a gentleman of leisure, and live a widower, or forfeit his allowance." [1] In any event, he gave up, and the stock was sold. The sale, according to a marked copy of the catalogue in the British Museum, brought no more than £133, 6s. as a contribution to the new life; [2] and it is unlikely that the move was made until just before or after the sale, which took place in the first fortnight of March 1827. By May, the family, Mary Ward included, were in Shoreham, though not, I think, in anything so spacious yet as Waterhouse, to which they shifted later on. At any rate, they had no room for George Richmond, to whom Palmer was writing early in May about engaging lodgings for his "descent into 'that stinking hole Shoreham' which indeed is now highly scented with the buds of spring." [3] Welby Sherman was also there in lodgings.

Shoreham today only differs from the Shoreham in which they settled by the presence of a few extra houses, and a busy main road, and a railway, well away from the village. Hasted's *History of Kent* (1797) says: "The high road from Dartford through Farningham and Eynsford, towards Sevenoke, runs along the hills, on the eastern side of this parish, about a quarter of a mile from the village of Shoreham; which having no high road of any public intercourse through it, is but little frequented by travellers, nor does the nearness of the turnpike-road above mentioned contribute much towards it; the soil of which being wholly chalk and very stony, renders it not very pleasant to travel on at any time." A Shoreham carrier and fruit-waggons and hop-waggons went between the village and London; but it was a secluded village, fit for the nursing of primitive ideas, tucked between tall green hills, with a green valley floor cut, through alders and pollarded willows, by the inlaid silver thread of the Darenth; which gave Palmer that "glint of water," without which he held that no landscape was perfect, however lovely it might be.[4] Here (until the rick burnings began) Palmer could believe in sylvan and pastoral innocence, romanticize the farm workers who wore smocks and stamped in with hob-nail boots to eat with their masters, listen to the sheep in their folds—"in that genuine village," he wrote when he was seventy-four, "where I mused away some of my best years, designing what no body would care for, and contracting, among good books, a fastidious & unpopular taste." The river, "that translucent current," which shines again and again in his designs, was "rich with trout," and there "were all the village appurtenances—the wise-woman behind the age, still resorted to; the shoemaker always before it, such virtue is in the smell of leather; the rumbling mill, and haunted mansion in a shadowy paddock, where sceptics had seen more than they could account for; the vicarage with its learned traditions; and Wordsworth brought to memory every three hours, by

> . . . the crazy old church clock
> And the bewilder'd chimes.

Byron would have stuffed his ears with cotton had he been forced to live there." [5]

The great round hills of the valley and the surrounding country gave exquisite feelings of exuberance and richness. There were yew trees, great horse-chestnuts; as well as vast oaks (still existing) and beeches and chestnuts next door in the Park at Lullingstone; there were churches with spires, vistas not far off from the line of the Kentish Weald which suggested infinity and God's eternity to Palmer; there were walled gardens enriched with well-kept fruit trees; and the north-south run of the valley caused excellent effects of glow after the sun had disappeared, or before the moon rose, behind the black slopes.

II

Blake died in the year of the move, though not before he had once visited Shoreham. Palmer, as we have seen, did not go to his funeral in Bunhill Fields, and was not at Blake's deathbed. Blake continued very much in his mind and as one of the treasures held in common which joined the circle of artists together. Their Monthly Meetings continued, at each other's homes, and Palmer did not completely shut himself off; London was in easy reach, and there was plenty of toing and froing. But at any rate for the next three years or so, Palmer deepened and heightened his visionary explorations, mingling them with reading widely and observing intently. However solitary in his depth, he was a sociable creature, relishing company and argument and fun, and profiting by them; and his friends, Linnell included, came to visit him and stay at Shoreham. They bathed in the river, walked to farms, read poetry in the evenings—Shakespeare, Milton, and Keats especially—and delighted in the novels of Mrs. Radcliffe—Palmer and others of them once starting out to Sevenoaks at ten o'clock at night to get hold of a copy of the *Mysteries of Udolpho*.[6]

Welby Sherman was with Palmer at Shoreham in May 1827, and in the summer George Richmond, Henry Walter, and Frederick Tatham were there—Richmond making his first independent stay in the country and living in a room Palmer engaged for him at two shillings a week rent. His note-books show that he was there from June 8th for about five weeks—and during that time he finished his engraving of "Christ the Good Shepherd" and worked on his engraving from "Macbeth." [7] Palmer's drawing of him (No. 56, Plate 23) shows him at work on "The Shepherd." Richmond was in London for Blake's death and funeral early in August, then back again at Shoreham. His note-books are scattered with prayers and invocations, as well as bits of drawing by Calvert and Tatham. He had begun his portrait work, but early drawings and pictures show the taste of the group well enough—"a drawing of Angelo's Night," "a sketch of Samson carrying the Gates of Gaza," "a drawing from *Midsummer Night's Dream*," "a sketch of a figure cast on an island," "a study of Michelangelo's Thief on the Cross"—and so on. Tatham was up to the same kind of work, the design of Gideon (which Palmer treasured afterwards for many years), a design from *Job*; and Calvert was already at work on his mystical engravings. Palmer's state of temper about now is visible enough in the notes he made in his copy of the connoisseur Payne Knight's *Analytical Enquiry into the Principles of Taste* (1805), to which he reacted much as a younger painter now might react to the pronouncements of Roger Fry on Blake, or the pronouncements of Mr. Clive Bell. He attacked Payne Knight's lukewarm appreciation of Michelangelo—"When he made his knowledge subservient to his art, and not his art to his knowledge," wrote Payne Knight, "he produced some compositions of real excellence"; to which Palmer added, "He produced some compositions of real excellence!! Michelangiolo produced some compositions of real excellence!!!!! O! Knight, had you spent your time in making works yourself instead of writing about other people's, you might have known better." He rebutted Payne Knight's hits at the grand style, in which he saw an attack on Fuseli, and commented on his elevation of Salvator Rosa as against "the vast and turgid compositions" of the Sistine Chapel. "Those artists who are so base that they do not attempt grandeur of form and yet lyingly pretend to grand effect are now called modest; but those who, as William Blake, do attempt and achieve both will, with him, by blind cunning and stupid wilfulness be set down impudent madmen: for our taste is Dutch; Rembrandt is our Da Vinci, and Rubens our

Michelangiolo! This is not an oversounding of the depth of our degradation," and he goes for "the miserable varieties of imitation, spiritless and castrated, blind wanderings and glaring impudence" of Venetian and Flemish pictures, setting against Rembrandt Da Vinci's "Last Supper" (he had seen the Academy copy of this), and against his etchings "the *Illustrations of Job* by our most lamented William Blake." [8]

There are not many works which one can be sure were done in this summer and winter of 1827, though I think the delicate and mysterious "Moonlight: The Winding River" (No. 55, Plate 22), with its touches reminding one of the 1825 drawings, and its Dürer-like palm tree, cannot be much later. I have mentioned his drawing of Richmond engraving "The Shepherd"; his lost "Young Man in a Landscape," on ivory (No. 57), was evidently an attempt at grandeur of form; with its "long black locks," its intensely coloured flesh, its hair "heightened with real gold," its solemn twilight, church, castle, windmill, and brilliantly lit "Druidic remains," and its thick paint, it was probably done, on the evidence of a letter, between November 1827 and early in 1828; [9] more puzzling, since they fit in with the phase of grandeur and Michelangelo, are his sketches "Ruth Returned from the Gleaning" (No. 69, Plate 29) and "The Deluge," both in the Academy for 1829. "The Deluge" has vanished, but it had an ark under a dark sky, and on the rocks in the foreground a beautiful naked woman lying "dead or dying at full length," with an arm on her dead child and the other arm falling with her hair into the flood. [10] Both aimed at "the eternal style," as Palmer called it, at "the great edifice of the divine human form" —the great edifices being based—certainly in the "Ruth"—on the forms of Michelangelo and the brawny sweeping figures of Palmer's "great copper-master of shadows," Bonasone. [11] Seeing the nature of the datable work of 1828 to 1829, the studies from nature and the natural "excesses" which followed them, I should say that they were conceived either early in 1828 or late in 1827, and worked up later for the Academy.

III

Palmer has been called (under the white light of pure painting) a "literary painter," so we may as well see what the relation between his reading and his painting really was. It was close; even if the bulk of his best designs never belong to a text, say, in the Pre-Raphaelite manner. Writing of his etchings in 1872, he spoke of "great needles sharpened three-corner-wise like bayonets; opodeldoc rubbed into the forehead to wake the brain up; and a Great Gorge of old poetry to get up the dreaming; for, after all, *that's* 'the seasoning as does it'"; [12] and it is certain that that Great Gorge was an old habit stretching back into these early days at Shoreham, which formed the pattern of behaviour, even of references, and words and images he repeated in his old age.

What are some of the books he read at Shoreham—the vital, central books? Milton, but more needs to be said of Milton whose early poems and much of *Paradise Lost* he knew by heart, when we get to the moon drawings of 1829 and 1830; Fletcher's *Faithful Shepherdess*; Barrow's *Sermons on the Creed*. Milton he is always talking of, the *Faithful Shepherdess* he found "pure gold," and he recalls it in a letter he wrote to L. R. Valpy, the patron of his old age: "I can remember nothing which so agreeably disturbed my male lethargy, except perhaps my first reading of Fletcher's *Faithful Shepherdess*. But when there I found, in black and white, all my dearest landscape longings embodied, my poor mind kicked out and turned two or three somersaults." [13] And writing to another friend, also in 1880, he declares that he "can never forget reading through Barrow's folio on the Creed in the recess of a Kentish village"; [14] he read much else, from Shakespeare and Spenser, to Keats and the pseudo-Chaucerian *Flower and the Leaf* (a favourite also of Coleridge's) for its delicious sense of spring and the red tinge of the young oak leaves; and Lydgate's *Complaint of the Black Knight* (given in his day to Chaucer), from which he took the text of his 1825 drawing "Early Morning" (No. 40, Plate 13). But Barrow, Fletcher (whom he had read by 1828), and Milton are worth considering in detail in relation to his vision. It is easier enough to detect the things which Palmer owed *visually* to Milton and to Fletcher. Palmer's warmth and sensuality, his passion for the round, the luxuriant, the velvet solidity of shadow (Keats's "embalmed darkness" was a favourite quotation with Finch,[15] and no doubt with Palmer as well), the rich contrast of light and dark, as in the glow from behind a hill, or the inlay of shining water between trees in twilight—all this warmth, sensuality, and passion found descriptions in Milton and Fletcher which made him look for the things described, or see them with more possessive, more innocent vision. The principle is well put in one of the popular books of the day, Archibald Alison's engaging and well-written *Essays on the Nature and Principles of Taste* (which was reprinted in 1825). He argues the importance of "the influence of an acquaintance with Poetry in our earlier years, in increasing our sensibility to the beauties of Nature." To such people as have read their poets "it is

not common nature that appears to surround them. It is nature
embellished and made sacred by the memory of Theocritus and
Virgil, and Milton and Tasso; their genius seems still to linger among
the scenes which inspired it, and to irradiate every object where it
dwells. . . . Even the familiar circumstances of general nature,
which pass unheeded by a common eye, the cottage, the sheepfold,
the curfew, all have expressions to them; because, in the compositions to which they have been accustomed, these all are associated
with peculiar characters, or rendered expressive of them; and,
leading them to the remembrance of such associations, enable them
to behold, with corresponding dispositions, the scenes which are
before them." Blake was not the only advocate of Milton who may
have influenced Palmer. Flaxman had ended his Tenth Lecture
on Modern Sculpture (which Palmer may well have heard) with an
invitation to artists to work from Milton. "Is it to be believed, that
this Poet, abounding in subjects and characters of the most extraordinary kind," he asked, "has been almost entirely neglected in
the Arts of his own country, whilst his merits have been vindicated
and illustrated by the liberal mind and genius of a foreigner!" [16]
—the foreigner, one presumes, being the other living idol of Palmer's
admiration—Fuseli.

And in Milton it was not only the moonlights Palmer fed upon,
but fruit and corn and shade and *tufts* of foliage—

> Under a tuft of shade that on a green
> Stood whispering soft,

or "Thick shelter of black shades" in a wood—or:

> . . . There does a sable cloud
> Turn forth her silver lining on the night
> And casts a gleam over this tufted grove.

A description of a tree in Milton was enough to start him noticing
such a tree and drawing it; so, too, with "The Faithful Shepherdess,"
which is full of dells, thick woods, moonlight, the sense of May,
water, sheep and shepherd and shepherdesses—"The nightingale
among the thick-leaved spring" or (the lines stand well enough for
the Darenth):

> I am this fountain's God: below,
> My waters to a river grow,
> And 'twixt two banks with osiers set,
> That only prosper in the wet,
> Through the meadows do they glide,
> Wheeling still on every side,
> Sometimes winding round about
> To find the evenest channel out—

There is one passage, which Palmer, I think, may directly have used for a drawing (No. 81, Plate 37)—a moonlight, in which

> No way is trodden; all the verdant grass
> The spring shot up stands yet unbruisèd here
> Of any foot; only the dappled deer,
> Far from the fearèd sound of crookèd horn,
> Dwells in this fastness . . .

And if Palmer had that in mind in this drawing, and if, as I think, he also profited by the memory of a drawing of deer in David Cox's treatise, therein you can see some of the mixed sources of his vision; and see, also, how personally and individually he filled out and created from such hints.

But about Fletcher, pure gold or not, there is a somewhat suggestive and doubtful innocence. Palmer, as an artist mystically inclined, wanted (and this is particularly true of the early years at Shoreham) a mystical sanction for admiring the natural world; he had Psalm LXV; and he had St. Paul to tell him that "the invisible things of God by the making of the world are clearly seen, being understood by things that are made"—but he had also Milton—

> What if earth
> Be but the shadow of heaven, and things therein
> Each to each other like, more than on earth is thought—

and that constant sense in Milton's descriptions that nature is more than nature. Just that double nature is in his own best drawings, and as he found it in Milton, so he found it in his favourite Dürer wood-engraving, the "Flight into Egypt," still more in Claude, in Elsheimer, in the fruitfulness of the engravings after Breughel, in the earlier Florentines; and so he deplored its absence, by comparison, in Rembrandt and in Rubens and the Venetians, in the English Dutch taste.

And certainly, having known Blake, his mysticism never ended at Milton. Knowing Blake and Calvert, he read Plato: Pagan Taylor and the *Timaeus* were there to be quarried, and to correct Platonism (writing of Florence, in 1838, he called it "full of the gems of those divine and divinely inspired arts which, three centuries ago, lived there in wedded love with the old Platonic philosophy"),[17] and Calvert's naughty heresies, there were not only Milton and the New Testament, but St. Teresa and Jakob Boehme. How great the influence of Boehme, "a generative thinker" as F. D. Maurice called him, has been in English poetry and painting no one yet seems to have calculated to the full. The emotional rediscovery of Boehme worked in the German romantic painters—in Runge, for example (there are affinities between Runge and Palmer)—and Blake, as I have said, must have talked of Boehme, of the purity and sweetness and child-like innocence of his spirit: all on this earth, repeats Boehme as a mystic, "all is a type of the heavenly pomp," and angels in heaven are like children on earth picking flowers in the May meadows; and he speaks of the eternal "May of Heaven." He developed "a mysticism of life, which seeks both nature and God," and held that nature must not be made an end instead of a means, "the one sin is to subordinate yourself to natural objects and serve them. The one virtue is to subordinate natural objects to the spirit and make them serve it and you." [18] It is this virtue precisely that Palmer tried to achieve. He makes, as far as I know, only one possible reference to Boehme, writing to George Richmond, on June 24, 1828, from Shoreham, of "a German mystic" to whom "it was reveal'd that by the prayer of faith he might have whatever he chose"; [19] but Boehme fits him close.

Of St. Teresa's autobiography there were seventeenth-century English versions to draw upon: "But now, let us goe back to our Orchard, or Garden, and see, how these Trees beginne to button, and budd out towards flowring, that they may yeild fruit; and how these Gillieflowers, and other odoriferous Plants, dispose themselves, to give delightfull Sent to the Owner. I confesse, that this Comparison regales, and pleases me much; for, manie times, in my beginnings . . . it was of much delight to me, to consider, that my Soule was a Garden, and that our Lord walked it, up, and downe." [20]

Is it fanciful to see such influences of the bud and the flower working to make Palmer welcome explosive visions in nature, as in his watercolour of the Shoreham apple tree (No. 78, Plate 34)? For the truth is, that whatever he read, with his nature and tastes, and with his friendship and discussions with Blake, and with the temper of the 1820's, he cannot have avoided mystical literature.[21] One could quote for ever—from John Smith, the Cambridge Platonist: "Thus may a man walk up and down the world as in a garden of spices, and suck a Divine sweetness out of every flower. There is a twofold meaning in every creature, a literal and a mystical, and the one is but the ground of the other"; [22] from Blake himself; or from the translation published in 1817 of von Eckartshausen's fascinating *God is My Love* [23]—in which God is Love, love of flowers, scented fruits, waterfalls, trees, the song of birds, "the majestic lion" who "exalts his hoarser voice," and which ends with a litany in which all things—from "The host of stars, so brilliant in the obscurity of the night" to "the rivulets which meander through the 'verdant meadows" and "The fresh mornings of spring time" and "the rich fertility and mellow tints of autumn"—all things "Announce to us thy love." One could quote from John Flavel's *Husbandry Spiritualised* (1669), a book referred to by Palmer [24] and on sale in his father's shop—"the World below, is a Glass to discover the World above: Seculum est Speculum" or "To make a ladder out of earthly materials, for the raising of ourselves in spirit up to Heaven, is *the Art of Arts*"; and the deep effect on Palmer of Barrow's *Sermons on the Creed* fits in well enough. Isaac Barrow (1630-1677) was a mathematician as well as a divine—he taught Isaac Newton; he liked "a good perspicacity of apprehension, a penetrancy of judgement, a vigour and quickness of mind, grounded in the purity of our faculties"; but this reasonable man who talks of the world as "this great machine" and of God as its architect, also finds the world good; and Palmer at Shoreham, either starting a discipline of vision and observation or trying to find a balance later after his most fanatic extremes, no doubt valued Barrow—valued the reading of the sixth sermon, on "The Being of God proved from the Frame of the World"; for here was reason controlling, but not contradicting, his inclinations:

"Whence comes it to pass, that ordinarily in nature nothing occurs noisome or troublesome to any sense; but all things wholesome or comfortable, at least innocent and inoffensive? that we may wander all about without being urged to shut our eyes, to stop our ears, our mouths, our noses; but rather invited to open all the avenues of our soul, for admission of the kind entertainments set before us? Doth she not everywhere present spectacles of delight (somewhat of lively picture, somewhat of gay embroidery, somewhat of elegant symmetry) to our eyes, however seldom any thing appears horrid or ugly to them? Where is it that we meet with noises so violent, or so jarring, as to offend our ears? is not there rather provided for us, wherever we go, some kind of harmony grateful to them; not only in fields and woods the sweet chirping of birds; by rivers the soft warbling of the streams; but even the rude winds whistle not unpleasant, the tossing seas yield a kind of solemn and graver melody? All the air about us, is it not (not only not noisome to our smell, but) very comfortable and refreshing? And doth not even the dirty earth yield a wholesome and medicinal scent? So many, so plain, so exactly congruous are the relations of things here about us each to other; which surely could not otherwise come than from one admirable wisdom and power conspiring thus to adapt and connect them together."

Barrow held that "the attentive observation of this world, or visible frame, is not only in itself a most worthy employment of our thoughts, (much more noble than any of those petty cares which commonly possess or distract our minds) but . . . even a considerable duty not to be neglected by us"; and how Palmer would have welcomed his eulogies of God's nature, for instance, of "the rude and boisterous winds" which "fulfil God's word . . . in gathering together, in scattering, in spreading abroad the clouds; the clouds, those paths of God, which *drop fatness* upon our fields and pastures."

But if we do not acknowledge Palmer's mystical tasting of nature, of art, and of reading, his reasons for "opening all the avenues of his soul," if we do not realize that a painter, a beginner in mysticism, cannot meet a great mystic and consort with other beginners in mysticism, in such a time as the 1820's, without painting mystically —we shall blankly misunderstand what Palmer of the "Shoreham period" was up to. A German painter like Runge could more easily put his notions systematically: that was not so easy for an Englishman of the time, more or less isolated; but if the notions are obscured, they are still there to be tracked down.

IV

The Palmers settled down at Shoreham, gradually coming to know and be liked by the people whom Palmer idealized so much. Richmond's lodgings in 1827 had been with "a nice old labourer who had a bright and busy wife with 2 daughters," and he adds, "The people of the Village could not make out what we were after, for we walked much in the deep Twilight, and into the Night, so 'Astrologers' seemed the most likely, and so I believed we were dubbed, but in time they knew better, and came to know us, and we to love them." [25] And there are other recollections of their twilight excursions, of Palmer's tenor voice ringing from one side of the valley to the other, of "that first flush of summer splendour which entranced me at Shoreham," [26] of the "nooks and dells of Paradise," of the splendour of the Shoreham apple trees in blossom. [27] For the rest of his life, Palmer hankered after that feeling of harmony and unity with nature he was now enjoying. "Thoughts on RISING MOON," he put down on the outside of a portfolio in 1860, "with raving-mad splendour of orange twilight glow on landscape. I saw that at Shoreham." [28]

There were the occasional feastings upon goose, evenings of vivid green tea, visits to London, walkings back through the night, when old Palmer, the circumambient Baptist preacher whom the village called "The Man of God," would get up and welcome Palmer and Richmond and Giles with tea, even after midnight.[29]

Not asking himself, prudentially, whether his visions of divine nature were likely to go down well with the Academy hanging committee, or appeal to a buyer even if they were hung, Palmer slogged away year by year, preparing his full quota of eight pictures or drawings for the summer exhibition.

At first, at Shoreham, he seems to have been poorly enough housed and straitened for room. Not till the autumn of 1828, it seems, did the Palmers establish themselves comfortably enough in Waterhouse, then a fairly modern building, which still stands close by the bridge in Shoreham village.[30] "The Bridge at Shoreham" (No. 68, Plate 28) shows what could be seen from the front windows.

By the time of the establishment in Waterhouse, when Blake had been dead just over a year, the great change in Palmer's practice was taking place—he was in his period of closest, realistic contact with nature. But before that, we may go back to the autumn of 1827—to a long, and till now unpublished, letter written to George Richmond, in his curious blend of a language vigorously individual and strongly Jacobean, a species of late and more literary Sturm und Drang, yet original like that of Fuseli or of the young Goethe's *Von Deutscher Baukunst* fifty years before. As usual in his early life, the letter is religiously flavoured, and was sealed with an imprint of the Palmer coat of arms, a tribute less to "family" in our sense, than to tradition and the past.

"Shoreham, Kent, Novr. 14 1827.

My dear Sir

Winter, shorn of the pleasure and instruction of your society which brighten'd my summer—a Shoreham midsummer, is a very emission of loss; and this gasping hiatus sucks in many dank and acrid crudities of the gloomiest month: I mean in the jaded halts of intellect tugging up the hill of truth with the sun on her head & this excrescent wen of flesh broiling on her back: for tho' the eclipses of thought are to me a living inhumement & equal to the dead throes of suffocation, turning this valley of vision into a fen of scorpions & stripes and agonies, yet I protest, & glory in it for the sake of its evidence of the strength of spirit that when inspir'd for art I am quite insensible to cold, hunger & bodily fatigue, & have often been surprised, on turning from work to find the fingers aching & nearly motionless with intense cold. Nor can the outward sense govern thus in turn; it is a tyranny of those brothers cruelty & weakness for whom the *rear* of spiritual thoughts is found too much; the recollections of happy enlighten'd hours, spiriting up to resistance the whole territory of man, till all his energies & desires break chains—march out & rush to prevent half way, with hymns, triumphs, acclamations, the majesty of their returning Freedom.

I want so much to be talking with you that you see I cannot wait till next coming to town, but use (would I could as it deserves) that choice device, that wing of lovers' thoughts which 'Wafts a sigh from Indus to the Pole'; but not to baulk Montesquieu's too true notion of an Englishman—he says had he been British he had been a merchant—head & shoulders will I shove in mine own secular interest, & beg the favour that if in your ivory researches, you meet with 3 or 4 morsels of very fine ivory, size & proportion not very particular so they be from about 1 inch by 1½ inch up to about 3 inches by 2 inches, you would buy them for me. Some thoughts have concocted & condensed in my mind of what I have seen walking about in midsummer eves & I should not care if I got a few of the subjects on ivory now, to study upon with fresh recollections of similar appearances next midsumer if God spare me; I prefer doing them very small, for they are not things by themselves, but wings, terraces or outbuildings to the great edifice of the divine human form— otherwise snares. But I have beheld as in the spirit, such nooks, caught such glimpses of the perfumed & enchanted twilight—of natural midsummer, as well as, at some other times of day, other scenes, as passed thro' the intense purifying separating transmuting heat of the soul's infabulous alchimy, would divinely consist with the severe & stately port of the human, as with the moon thron'd among constellations, & varieties of lesser glories, the regal pomp and glistening brilliance & solemn attendance of her starry train. Remembering me kindly to all friends you may see, if you think of it, would you, Sir, do me this kindness in particular to present Mrs. Blake with my most affectionate & respectful remembrances; only the having nothing to shew prevented my going to Mr. Linnell's when I was last in town. You will perhaps also, giving the same to Mr. Frederick Tatham & best respects to Mr. and Mrs. Tatham & Mr. Waters if he be there, most adoringly, vehemently & kissingly present my quaint but true knightly devotion to the young ladies One and All, collectively ador'd & individually belov'd—telling them, imploring them sometimes to think on me (for is it not an honour for fair ladies to think on me, tho'd it be only to set their pretty mouths a-giggle at the remembrance of my spectacles?)

Tell them that herein is my disadvantage—whereas mine eyes are dim save when I look at lady fair—& whereas I can only see their lustre thro' my goggles; those said unlucky goggles are so scratch'd & spoil'd that all the fire of the love darting artillery of my eyes is lost upon *them* & redounds not to my advantage, the ladies seeing only two huge misty spheres of light scratched & scribbled over like the sun in a fog or dirty dish in a dark pantry, as lustre lacking, as leaden & as lifeless as a lad without a lady. But tell them sometimes to think on me, as I very often think of them, & as in sullen twilight rambles, sweet visions of (their) lovely bright eyes suddenly sparkle round me, (and il)lume my dusky path—double the vigour (of my) pace, rebuild my manhood & renew my y(outh). You see the perfections of the ladies are unsp(arihg?)—that is the reason that no sooner do I begin (to) write of *them* than lo! I scribble nonsense—arrant nonsense. Hervey's Meditations & the heath's of Fingal & the vapours of the hill of storms.

Ought I to send you such a scribble? but I will send it for the ivories' sake, & to speak my hope that you may have the blessing & presence of the Almighty for ever, & that absence has not yet rased from the tables of your memory, dear Sir,

Your affectionate & Humble Servant
Samuel Palmer.

If you are so kind as to get me the ivories, pray, Sir, make no hurry, but let it be, till you go about materials for yourself & bring the ivories in your pocket when you do us the favour of a visit, when you will perhaps come in the coat you mention'd. Be pleas'd to present my best respects to Mr. & Mrs. Richmond. I wish I could add '*& to Mrs. Richmond Junr.*'

I must let this note go unpointed, uncorrected, with all its orthographic blunders whether of negligence or ignorance, for if I begin to revise I shall sentence it to the flames very speedily. I am looking for a wife." [31]

None of the ivories painted at this time are known. "A Young Man in a Landscape," already mentioned, and described by A. H. Palmer,[32] was no doubt painted after this letter, having in it not only "the great edifice of the divine human form," but "perfumed and enchanted twilight." Richmond's father was a miniaturist, and Richmond himself was doing a number of miniatures in these years.

Things to be noticed in the letter, beside the general tone and style, are the evidence of Palmer's continued alternation between aridity—the "eclipses of thought" which turn "this valley of vision into a fen of scorpions & stripes and agonies"—and the presence of inspiration for art which filled him to the point of insensibility to his own physical being; the midsummer eves beheld "as in the spirit," the scenes which must pass through "the intense purifying separating transmuting heat of the soul's infabulous alchimy." [33] "Montesquieu's too true notion of an Englishman" is perhaps a backward kick at his own family, and his uncle in particular; and the letter, the greetings for the Tatham girls (with one of whom Richmond was already in love), and the postscript "I am looking for a wife," show the limitations of Palmer's other-worldliness: the normal man in this wild creature, with a sense of fun, and a gusto for company and good food, was too strong, or the abnormal man in him was too weak, to allow him thrust beyond a certain point on the path of mysticism.

There are so few documents about this stage in Palmer's unfolding that what there are need giving in full. The next comes late in February 1828, from Richmond, to "Mr. S. Palmer junr." :

My dear Friend,   "Wednesday night, 2 o'clock almost.

As I thought it would be a pity to let the Parcel go without an accompanying line & knowing that you would glad to hear how the little Knot of artists were going on, must plead as my excuses for sending this wretched morsel—Walter & I began drawings of M[ichel] A[ngelo's] Thief on the Cross tonight and we worked with spirit for above 3 hours. But

1

Mr. Walter has gone to his nest
Mr. Tatham is now in Edgeware,
While Sherman in Hackney doth rest
And Hackney'd He is I dare swear.

2

Should this rhyming your pity create
Should you think it as foolish as bad,
The only excuse I can make
Is—you know very well *I am mad.*

3

But tis time to give over this joke
And a very good reason d'ye see
For my bacca's all ended in smoke
And the smoke gave the rhyming to me.

Forgive it all.   Forgive it all
BURN THIS or use it any other way you like best   I am in one of my fits tonight therefore you must impute this (not) to me *but* to the fit.   I shall be better by & by.   It is not my fault
Yrs aff^y
G. Richmond

Uncle was sick the other night over my [*paper torn*]   Tatham is concocting a design from Job.   Sherman goes on well and I will go to bed." [34]

Down the margin, the letter is ornamented with little caricatures of Walter, Tatham, and Sherman; drawings of a pair of spectacles and a coat, of Richmond himself in the tasselled cap he wears in Palmer's drawing (No. 56, Plate 23), and of Walter and Richmond working with spirit on their Michelangelo. The mention of Walter shows that he was at any rate touched with the prevailing taste of the group, though I have never seen any such studies by him.

This note must have been written not long after a meeting, between Palmer and Richmond, probably in London. In possession of the Richmond family there is one of Richmond's many drawings of Palmer, dated February 3, 1828. It is a fair drawing, a good likeness in Richmond's slightly dry and scratchy manner, and it dates for certain the remarkable self-portrait of Samuel Palmer (No. 58, Plate 24), now in the Ashmolean. Both have the same pose, the same white stock, the same untidy hair, and slight moustache, one achieves, the other tries after, the same look of worried intensity. Palmer's own drawing of himself at twenty-three is a feat of extraordinary self-record. The bristling hair, the full bright lips with the face swelling a little to each side of them, the shadow of a moustache above, the big, intent, disturbed dark eyes, which stare at the spectator as if keeping him, gazing outward but thinking and tranced inwardly, the slight puzzlement in the forehead which does not contradict the obsessed, rebellious, almost sullen, powerful, clenched expression of an exploding, brooding nature. Here is the deepest Palmer, not the young man of goose feasts and humour, but the painter who becomes part of nature, in order to go beyond it, who shifts from pit to height and height to pit, who becomes insensible when "inspir'd for art" to "cold, hunger & bodily fatigue." And what this self-portrait says is well enough confirmed, if slightly coarsened by George Richmond, who gives him, by means of frowning brow and larger eyes, a look of an intensity altogether more decisive and self-assured than it was. It wonderfully shows his increasing grasp of nature, the increased adequacy of his means for his ends.

From Shoreham comes next a note to George Richmond, then staying with Frederick Tatham, a note of little significance:

"Shoreham   Kent   St. Patricks day 1828
(17 Mar.)

My Dear Sir

Because you were so kind I am so troublesome—but as what I want you to do for me has relation to painting it would ill compliment you to apologise.

Would you then order for me in time to use about a week before the Royal Academy takes in a gilt flat two inches broad: *Sight measure eight inches and one eighth by five inches and three eights?*

I believe it is better not to get the glass of a frame maker but at the glass warehouses—I will get it when I come to town unless you should happen to go to the glass-maker's for yourself.

I beg pardon for sending only this morsel of self interest, but I have been very hard at work and have quite work'd out my stock of ideas for this evening;—therefore with sincerest wishes for your victorious consummation of whatever you may be engaged in now or hereafter by the Divine Blessing overshadowing, which make one prayer that I also may enjoy

I will subscribe
My Dear Sir
Your affectionate & obt. Sert.
Samuel Palmer.

Please to present my best respects to Mr. & Mrs. Richmond & love to Mr. Tatham's sweet Sisters." [35]

The letter which follows is more notable, coming when the twilights of another summer have begun, and after another spring in the Valley of Vision. George Richmond, in his old age, has pencilled an abstract across the top: "Procrastination—Mr. Linnell's & G. R.'s visit to Shoreham postponed—Sherman's print of Mr. P's 'Shepherd' to be published immediately—The Impressions of Samson—Prayer and Effort—Council of the 'Blessed'—G. R. housing S. P.'s moons—Tatham's Gideon—Calvert's mysticism— Tatham's dissent—True churchmanship—Christian commendation." It may be one of Palmer's more sententious letters, less revelatory, but it mentions an engraving after him, a copy of which still has to be found; it mentions this paganism of Calvert's (which I have talked about already); and what we may suppose was the first wavering of Frederick Tatham from a Church of England ortho- doxy; and here too is that "German mystic" on the power of faith:

"Shoreham, Kent   June 24th. 1828.
My dear Sir
I beg your pardon for not having sooner answer'd your favour of the 11th inst. Though I read it over and over and over, I strangely missed or forgot that you desir'd an answer on its receipt: till, now, having intended to reply in two or three days, the date of your letter tells me the time is come when we were to have had the great pleasure of your company with Mr. Linnell. I am ashamed and

E

should be surprised at my negligence were this my first experience of the stealthy and swift escape of time thro' the loose boundary of undefin'd intentions. Say to yourself, 'By frequent prayer and the Divine blessing I will have finished such and such a work in three days ' and most likely you will get thro' it; but *a day or two*, too often the language of indecision or listlessness, is, alas, well English'd by *a fortnight or a month*. Who is there that looks with a true eye on prospective opportunity? To us who are young it is lengthen'd like the tube of a perspective when you look into the wrong end of it; to the old, no longer prospective, it is the brevity of a dream. The mist of uncertain purpose magnifies the spaces of futurity into a wide and ample scope which hope and fancy throng with rich succession of schemes and projects that distend each one their dimensions in the execution as the time for their accomplishment grows less, and the vision of many years is vanishing away: and the aged man, bringing in review before him the speculations of his life, beholds in what he has completed that incompleteness with which conquest & the richest possession fall short of hope, remembers many gay hopes and many industrious endeavours which remind him of blighted springs and blasted autumns, and grieves upon a huger heap of futile hints and fond imaginations and belated enterprises, which must remain among forgotten things and be buried along with him in his grave. He has known the conception of a day—a month's amusement swell almost into the labour of a year, and seeing the favorite, the nurs'd desire, the mediated achievement, the task of honour which bound up the victory and the crown, stretch out beyond the last cape and jutting promontory of this existence, sits down too late to the bitter stimulant of Hippocrites. Art is long and life is short; confesses that few and evil have been the days of his pilgrimage; that all this sublunary existence is a succession of changes and decay, full of wind and vanity and vexation of spirit.

The weather here has been for some time fogg'd and cloudy, the landscape a sickly white or gray, *especially the hills*: now, as we should wish the valley and the village to smile when Mr. Linnell first looks upon them, would it not be better to defer coming for a few days, when we may expect a change, with the full glory of Summer? I *must* come to town in 8 or 10 days to stay one day, and will then, if convenient arrange by word of mouth (the surer and pleasanter way) about meeting you with Mr. Linnell. But if yourself or Mr L cannot come, unless immediately, will you please to let me know exactly when and where to meet you: either way it will be perfectly convenient to us; only if you come now you will be drench'd in hot white mist. If you determine to wait till I come to town *I shall not expect to hear from you.* Will you offer my best remembrances to Mr. & Mrs. Linnell, & if you happen to see them, to Mrs. Blake, Mr. Walter, Mr. Tatham, Mr. & Mrs. Calvert and Mr. Sherman. If Mr. Sherman have finish'd his print, he needs not wait till I see it, but may bring it out directly if he please, as the more copies are sold the sooner the plate will be his own. Both with respect to finishing the shepherd and selling the impressions of the Samson, I am sure he may freely apply to Mr. Linnell's kindness for advice. Could not some means be devised among the 'Blessed' in council assembled for selling some impressions of Samson? Could Mr. Tiffin be of use or Mr. Clay. It is wonderful what good th(ings?) may be suggested where nothing offers at first by the laying together of two or three (heads?) and hearts; and at all events there remains mighty prayer, which is better and more *sub (lime?)* than all; tho' not to supersede use of means, but to be their vanguard & flank and rear. I am at present two pounds behind the half year & therefore cannot possibly do anything at this instant; but shall take a dividend next month & if I can wring a little out of it, shall be very glad if Mr. Sherman will begin another little job for me. Our Blessed Lord teaches us not to be anxious about the morrow; spiritual difficulties should be the only serious trouble of a bright intellectual essence: other disturbances are for the most part terrific phantoms which vanish on approach; unshapely reflections of the light of worldly wisdom & prudence from the dusk & misty vapours of futurity. This, for brevity, comprehension & general usefulness, may be call'd an aphorism—*He most effectually makes provision for the morrow who best performs the duty of today*—or familiarly 'Take care of today, & tomorrow will take care of itself.' I hope while there is a Saviour, a Comforter, a throne of grace, a very present help in trouble, a sure answer to prayer & the command of Jesus to pray for our daily bread, Mr. Sherman will not suffer the devil to make him doubt & waver and falter any more about money, for if there were no other right way of getting it, we should find it dropp'd for us in the street & other peoples' eyes would be holden from seeing it till we came and pick'd it up. ONLY BELIEVE. I am very glad the young ladies got home safely (give my love to them) & very sorry you cannot yet come to Shoreham for the season, but we know not the morrow; a German mystic says it was reveal'd to him that by the prayer of faith he might have whatever he chose & St. James, who was neither mystic, fanatic, nor sectary, but Bishop of Jerusalem, tells us that if we ask and have not it is because we ask amiss—'but ask' says he 'in faith, nothing wavering.' I am much obliged to you, Sir, for housing my pictures, but fear they gave you trouble, however so many moons in your apartment ought to save the trouble of lighting candles. When I come to town I hope you will favour me with a sight of what you may have on the stocks for next exhibition. Why do Mr. Walter & Mr. Calvert fancy Shoreham a hundred miles off? let them get on the road by chance & walk a bit & ride a bit & they will soon look down into the valley. I am very glad Mr. Tatham gets on well with Gideon & long to see it. I daresay Mr. Calvert has got his print of the Prophet into a fine state by this time and that his naughty disobedient heresies are falling away from about him like the scales of leprosy, & melting as the morning vapours melt from the sun. I hope the same of Gideon's droll affectation of dissent, for I will not do Gideon's good sense the injustice to suppose that he is a puritan at heart: he has taken it up in spite & will lay it down in silence. I hope, Sir, that the Lord will confirm you & comfort you in true and sweet affiliation to the Apostolic Church which only has Bishops and pastors (tho' many drones & wolves), in which only are the efficacies of the holy sacraments, the authority of absolution & blessing, the delegated power of Jesus Christ, the eternal shield against the gates of Hell, the chief corner stone which was set at naught of the builders; the rock St. Peter, the indissoluble foundation of the apostles & prophets, stronger than the pillars of the world & the fabric of the universe, & the gift of the Holy Ghost. Tho' I believe the free & sovereign Spirit doth shed forth some glimmering of his beams on those who, thro' ignorance or perverse education, are without the fold & who half averted from that healing light, half giv'n over to their own imaginations, have yet not giv'n up to seek & to feel after the God of their fathers tho' shock'd & stumbled among the dark mountains in a dim & twilight hemisphere of wanderings & doubts. Let us pray for each other that we may have grace to pass thro' this wicked world without losing suddenly or slowly our souls & understandings among its treacheries & wonderfully deceiptful snares.

Be pleas'd to offer my best respects to Mr. & Mrs. Richmond. Praying that the Heavenly benediction may rest upon you forever

I remain Dr: Sir

Your affectionate & obt. Sert:

Samuel Palmer." [36]

Linnell's visits to Shoreham in the summer and autumn of 1828 much affected Palmer. Though it was through Linnell that he met Blake, though Linnell guided him, for instance, to the study of Dürer and Bonasone and Van Leyden, yet Linnell was never of

Blake's persuasion: in a deep way, he was not an imaginative painter; skilful, and versatile, energetic, dominating, able to appreciate imagination, yet there was in him a persistent prosiness, which he escaped only in relatively few early pictures and drawings, judged against the great bulk of his work. He shows often the tricks of imagination without the substance. His especial friends, after all, had been Wilkie and Mulready. He had been close with Constable for a time; and, in spite of his religious leanings towards the puritan and the primitive, he and Palmer looked upon religion (as Palmer was to find) very divergently. He was a "naturalist," and his naturalism tempered Palmer's idealism.

Palmer wrote to him from Shoreham in a letter postmarked September 17, 1828:

> "Shoreham near Dartford Kent
> Tuesday   September
>
> My Dear Sir,
> The unsettled state of the weather which has now happily taken another turn & is perfectly fine will have prevented you from wondering that I did not come to town.
> The hop picking began yesterday & I think as the days are glorious you had better come *directly*—The picking will last a month so if you sieze (*sic*) the fine weather & begin immediately you can if you feel disposed spend a day at Bayswater between whiles & still have time left to come back & finish your sketches. You will find some boy at Morant's Court Hill who will let me know your arrival there when I will immediately put forward with horse & cart. If you see Mr. Tatham will you be so kind to tell him the picking is begun & that I hope he will make a point of coming before it is over, & the sooner the better Pray Sir do not defer coming for if you put it off to the end of the picking & it should then turn out rainy you will be vex'd.
> I have just received a letter from Mr. Richmond, he is at Calais & in good health & desires to be remember'd to yourself Mrs. Linnell & family.
> My Father presents best respects uniting with whom I re(main) in great haste as the post is g(oing)
>
> Dear Sir
> You obligd humble Sert.
> Sam'l Palmer." [37]

It was on the visit following this letter that Linnell commissioned Palmer to make a number of studies from nature; and there is little enough doubt that Linnell argued with Palmer against too mystical a view of nature. "That asses bridge of superstition built with nothing but the rubbish of human tradition," [38] was Linnell's summary some years later of much of the belief in which Palmer was rooted; but there was still much in common between them; and Palmer much respected the grasp and energy of his mind, the width of his knowledge, and the keenness of his taste. In this same month—though he did not finish it until October (the post-mark is October 17)—Palmer wrote a vast letter to Richmond, still working in Calais before going on to study the pictures in the Louvre, and possibly going further, Palmer thought, to Italy. It pictures his relations with Linnell, the degree and the limits of Linnell's influence with him, and gives the news of this sharper study of natural scenery to which he was persuaded by Linnell:

> "Please to direct, Water House, Shoreham, near Dartford, Kent.
> Shoreham, Kent : Sept. 1828.

My dear Sir:

I had not forgotten you, but was silent because I had nothing to say, or send but such good wishes as I hope are always under-stood. However, as you desired a letter, both on your departure, and again from across the sea, it were churlish to be mute, tho' my head were ever so little in an exporting capacity. But, there *is* one thing I would enjoin, if you cross the Alps, about which, if it had occurred to me sooner, I should have sent you a line, even had you not by your kind soliciting compelled me to a scribble. It is, that from the time you set forward, you punctually devote half an hour every evening to the setting down the prominent circumstances of the day; particularly anything pictorial or intellectual: and that you never miss, thinking to make it up by writing for two or three days at once; for so the task will soon look too formidable and per-haps the journal be discontinued altogether. The characteristic of an ephemeris is slight, vivid sketching from transient occurrences and *first impressions*; not finished periods nor elaborate diction. I should like to know how the Giants of the Sistine Vault strike first upon your soul, in words as near as possible like those you would break forth into on entering the chapel—such words are those you w^d put down the same evening at your inn; unless indeed, your spirits were rather bound up; and expression itself lock'd in chains of golden rapture; for there are works which wise men admire and fools approve. To be technical, you know that a grand corrusca-tion of sudden light is imitated, either by immediately dashing in the masses on a paper the size of your hand, or by nursing the image in your meditation thro' the slow stages of a picture. Now a traveller's diary is just parallel to the former;—a laboured volume I do not expect you to compose: tho' the daily detail of an artist's pilgrimage to the works of the giants would soon swell into a pretty pamphlet that would amuse his friends at home in the winter evenings, and revive in his own mind as by a magic recall of transpired existence, those precious moments which first brought before his sight the inspirations of the two or three great geniuses of Italy; as Donatello, Da Vinci, Buonaroti: it not being the *number* of pictures that feeds a designer, but he grows most as he eats and drinks with nice, selecting appetite, and draws into a hungry soul of digestive and assimilating function the pure and condensed, insuperfluous aliment of those abstracted, essential, fiery, & eternal conceptions known by few in any age, and embodied, not by the learning of man, but by the wisdom of God. I could wish, also, that you put down a memorandum of any disappointment, whole or partial, from works of which your expectation has been much raised; nor does this imply censure: if you say that you expected more brilliance of colour or force of shade in any man's work than you found; still you assert not whether you expected what was extraneous or inconsistent, or whether *he* omitted or neglected. I suppose, with most young men that go to Rome, you will disagree with me when I suggest that it is not most useful to spend the time in copying one or two pictures elaborately in colours: in a shorter stay how well might you serve the arts in your country by making small drawings for engravings, of a few of the very finest sculptures (not antiques; we have casts enough of them here; good, bad, & indifferent) and of some of the most precious single figures & groups of in (*sic*) the frescoes of the 14th., 15th., and 16., centuries. I fancy myself working intensely hard for a week on grey paper; the quickest way of copying statues; to give my country a true version of the divine St. George of Donatello: the thought of bringing home a true & lively transcript of those intense lineaments, and of only a few other such works, would, if I had extra money, surprise you with a waking vision of me and my round spectacles some evening at Calais, ready, with canvas jacket & trowsers, club and knapsack, to start next morning for the South. By both working hard together for only one month, we might bring home between us a dozen faithful transcripts of true gems of art; which engrav'd with decent care, would make a drawing book for young students of other kind than the execrable trash with which their first appetite is gorg'd, their taste perverted, their intellectual eyes jaundiced, and their very fingers tortured almost out of the power of drawing a single line or shape of real beauty. But I must not indulge this pleasing dream; rather I must kiss the inoppressive links of lenient penury which tie me to this pleasant valley & to humility, & school & purify the soul;

and while they check me in from taking flight over seas & continents
yet let me lift up my mind to those altitudes of her own unbounded
hemisphere, whence she may serenely muse and contemplate,
beyond the waters of the extremest ocean, and last cape & promontory of this transitory world; and far above those noises, of scrambling
ambition; wars, tumults, envyings, murders, devastations, gather to
the consimilating attraction of her divine regenerate nature such
beauty and wisdom, as, fixt by high art, in humility, tribulation, and
self-abasement on the canvas or the page may perhaps be heard of
even across a continent or an ocean when the hand that work'd is
moulder'd, & the eye that saw is blinded in the dust, the spirit then
happily beyond the corrupting touch of gold; a base, deject, dirty,
& shameful barter for the treasures of the soul; which, only by
despising it could attain to do anything truly worthy of their remembrance whose notice is commendation & glory. But how I ramble!
believe me, I am in a humble and chasten'd mood; yet will great
hopes betray themselves—those trembling hopes which are O how
different, how much more self suspicious & apprehensive than the
calm assurance of lesser expectations. The high & hoary majesty
of the oak wrestles with many a gust & gale that howl innoxious
above the trainling of the wall. Great hopes mount high above
the shelter of the probable & the proper; know many a disastrous
cross wind & cloud; and are sometimes dazzled & overwhelmed as
they approach the sun; sometimes, vext & baffled, they beat about
under a swooping pall of confounding darkness; and sometimes
struggle in the meshes, or grope under the doleful wings of temptation or despair: but shall escape again & once more sing in the eye
of morning thro' Him who is the mightiness of the feeble, & the
solace of the broken-hearted. Forgive my spirits; they sometimes
haunt the caves of melancholy; ofttimes are bound in the dungeon,
ofttimes in the darkness; when the chain is snapt they rush upward
& revel in the temerity of their flight. What I have whisper'd in
your ears I should not blaze to vulgar apprehensions: if my aspirations are very high, my depressions are very deep, yet my pinions
never loved the middle air; yea I will surrender to be shut up among
the dead, or in the prison of the deep, so I may *sometimes* bound
upwards; pierce the clouds; & look over the doors of bliss, & behold
there 'each blissful deity, How he beneath the thundrous throne doth
lie': and I write to one who will know the difference between lofty
hope & complacent self-assurance. But hence! this auto-babblery.

Could you not bring over a bit or two from Donatello? If he
have left only a few such things as I know his St. George must be,
even from the outline I have seen of it, & which I suppose must

be scatter'd among the churches in various Italian cities; if there
be any more such things, so purely intellect, I would rather see
really fine copies of *them* on white or grey paper, than highly finish'd
pictures from most of Raffaelle's Frescos, beautiful as they must be:
for I can only admire works of art in the proportion of the abstract
mentality or power of thought which they display. Of this eternal
style, immutable by all the fashions of manners of opinion, from the
tower of Babel to the London University, Michelangiolo was a divine
master; and tho' I should like to see every work that his hand
touched, yet I think if I were in Italy I would not copy for engraving
such of his works as have been done by the old men, tho' their engravings are not perfect, but perhaps I should find out some trans-
cendent statue or picture of which we have no cast or plate. But
from one or two mere outlines I have seen from Donatello I would
particularly look after him; as we know but little of his inventions;
and if he compass'd many *St. George's*, have reason to desire to know
so much. I think if you were to do about a dozen highly studied
but bold drawings with the sense hanging a good deal on the turn of
their outlines, from works yet unknown in England, which, on grey
paper you might soon accomplish; it would not take long to make
expressive engravings of them, with broad lights; & with a slight
page of large letterpress to each, a fine book it would be: and tho'
I really doubt whether a dozen people in all England in the present
barbarous condition of the arts would buy it for the merit of the
designs; yet would fifty grave judges for the *names* of the designers;
a hundred travell'd gentlemen to shew it to their friends, & vaunt
that they had seen the originals in Italy, whether they remember'd
them or not; and two hundred more for the neat letterpress & clean
wide margin.—If it were etchings of a grinning monkey shaving
himself in the gloss of a boot, or sugarplums from a sirreverence ;
or of a fiddler, or a methodist preacher, or Mr. O'Connell, or a mounte-
bank, we might write the hundreds *thousands at least*! There will
be some choice as to the way of proceeding Romewards: I should
go thro' as many great & ancient cities as I could, & visit as many
Cathedrals & convents, for, by continually asking at every church
& monastery after pictures, you may light on one or two, shrined
up in the recessed twilight of some oratory, or cloister, worth the
whole journey. I would ask for pictures everywhere, & see every
collection I could get at, however small: sometimes one painting is
worth ten galleries. I have seen saloons of noblemen with five or
six nominal Raphaels or even Da Vincis, not altogether worth half
so much as some single effort of an obscurer name, & in a collection
on the whole perhaps much inferior. I would ransack the convents

& churches, & get to see some of the Clergy, who, when they know your object will direct you to what you want, & be, much more likely, polite and attentive than most servants or doorkeepers. You may find some exquisite Da Vincis! Then I would wheel back again by a different route; still hunting the pictures with the keen scent of a hound. The great object of an artist in a brief tour is to see pictures, statues, & buildings:—perhaps his second, the beauties of external creation:—afterward, places memorable in history;—universities;—manners, & customs, characteristic of the genius of the nation.—Were two ways indifferent as to the first aim, you would chuse the more beautiful, which, as far as I have tried, is always that running on, or close by a hilly ridge. I find also, that high roads cheat one out of the best scenery though they run thro' the heart of it. You may see glorious things among the Alps & Apennines! If I think on these things I shall catch the fury of wandering, which, however, is useless as I want the means: and I will not infringe a penny on the money God has sent me, beyond the interest, but live & study in patience & hope. By God's help I will not sell away His gift of art for money; no, not for fame neither, which is far better. Mr. Linnell tells me that by making studies of the Shoreham scenery I could get a thousand a year directly. Tho' I am making studies for Mr. Linnell, I will, God help me, never be a naturalist by profession. He has been twice to the valley, & is coming again in a day or two. Where-ever he is, nothing can be dull or stagnant. He is delighted with the scenery—Rook's Hill-Brasted Chart—Pig & Whistle Valley etc. and says he has seen higher hills but never finer scenes, in Wales or anywhere; & he makes it doubly delightful by his incessant flow of exuberant liveliness ingenuity & wit; interspers'd with hints and reflections of keenest sagacity, & reaching thoughts of the widest span, & highest arc of spiritual wisdom. Our conversation is an entertaining medley not unmix'd with Theology. On art, it is gentle sly hinting, between the *Kemsing Pig Style*, and the *Rustic Shepherd Style*—attacks & defences of cottages; tho' not so fierce and bloody as those of the Belle Alliance or Hougemont. I have not yet opened the campaign against the smooth antiques, but we remain in dreadful silence, not even breathing ourselves in flying skirmishes. Politics we dabble in: Mr. L. though of no party magnifies the peasants; I, also, as you know, of no party, as I love our fine British peasantry, think best of the old high tories, because I find they gave most liberty to the poor, & were not morose, sullen & bloodthirsty like the whigs, liberty jacks & dissenters; whose cruelty when they reign'd, was as bad as that of the worst times of the worst papists; only more sly & smoothlier varnish'd over with a thin shew of reason. On Theology, and church government, we keep up a perpetual running fight: I am for high church & the less of state expediency and money mix'd up with it the better:—my opponents, (for beside Mr. Linnell and my Father, here have been staying some of my anabaptist cousins) parting off severally, to the *One Man System*: the Three Man System, viz: one poor sectarian parson wedged between two rich *deacons*:—the *Many Man System*, or the brethren exhorting; and lastly, what I fear is the true end, & inverted climax of free-thinking and dissent, the NO MAN SYSTEM. Also in doctrine we have the Sandemanian or *Believe the Report System*: the modern hyper-calvinistic (forgive the jargon) or *Frame and Feeling System*, & *Sweet Hymn System*, an extreme, assimilating in this to its opposite, Wesleyism; & the Quiescent, Converted-contented, Placid or *Cast Iron System*, so christened by Mr. Linnell. One of our party, on being asked his faith, replies—'Sir, I am a Strict, Calvinistic, Republican Anabaptist'! Another, of a very mild disposition naturally, I ask'd, if he did not think Shoreham Church pretty from where we were looking:—after a pause he replied gloomily—'*Humph—I wish there was not one standing.*' He says 'the Church is Hellish'; he wishes he 'could dig as many holes as there are churches, & bury them in a moment'! Another of the family is more liberal in his notions, & they call him almost a papist.

I have been sketching a head from life, and life size on gray board, in colours, and heightened with Mrs. Blake's white, which is brighter, and sticks faster than chalk; & it seems such a quick way of getting a showy, but really good effect, that I was thinking you might do five or six at Calais, for people who would not sit for a miniature or picture, & so come to touch a few extra hundreds of francs; (as it is life size, & fit to frame & hang up;) which would help carry you to Italy; whither I really hope you may go without ceremony, (tho' I shall almost envy you;) for it is not always designs plann'd leisurely at home & long premeditated that realize best to us; but those things whose causes are not atal (*sic*) in our own power, and lie without the largest angle of our foresight, do come up suddenly from behind us, & hold out to our grasp such advantages as suspend, sometimes, the fortunes of our lives. Go, Sir, to Italy by all means, if you can only stay a fortnight; it will practise you for a longer visit if such wait for you; & it would be a pity to lose what may, for aught you know, so brief and busy is our existence, be your only time. You (may) marry; & you know what the bachelor rhym'd: 'Like a dog with a bottle tied close to his tail; Like a tory in a bog, or a thief in a jail'! which same, some

waggish friend chanted under his window on the poet's wedding
night by way of Epithalmium. The very clash of a sudden
impulse against obstacles ofttimes kindles up (a) directing light
even thro' darkness & danger. As to Paris, unless your profession
call you, or you pass thro' it to Rome, I do not see what good
you can be(hold) in that metropolis of Apes. If you go to Rome,
you will see many places renown'd in history, immortalized in
song, dignified by wisdom, & heroic virtue, & consecrated by
piety. It is a small thing to be snatch'd by a kind enchanter into
the 'Land of Faery'—*You* are going to tread a holy ground, where
St. Peter, & St. Paul have walked before you:—to traverse the site
of groves, & gardens which once were seen illuminated with rich
holocausts of Christian Heroes, & were music'd with their dying
triumphant alleluias!—to walk about the moulder'd desolation of
those vast amphitheatres where the flower & fashion of polite Rome
hunted the old martyrs with wild beasts, and shed that testamental
blood which cemented indissolubly the mightier fabrick of the eternal
Church. A visit, indeed, to Rome should reimpress upon us with
the force of local retrospection the spirit & genius of Christianity;
how it worked its peaceful irresistible progress thro' the scorn, the
hatred, the persecution, of the learned, the wise, the powerful; with
a reputed felon for its founder; tent makers & fishermen of a
tributary colony for its champions; the despised poor for its prose-
lytes; poverty for its true riches; simplicity its logic; its rhetorick
the tears of affliction, and the patience of the oppress'd; its eloquence
the groans of torture & the agonies of dissolution; its confidence &
ornament, its boast & glory, the detested & accursed death of traitors
& malefactors; the ignominy of the Cross! As a river, noiseless in
its fountain, & subterranean in its progress, it burst forth and over-
whelm'd the nations: as a seed of chance, trampled by the hind, or
by the cattle into an uncongenial & flinty soil, it spread and over-
topp'd the forest: it was a little spark; an ember which every gust
and damp threatened to extinguish; but the gust that should have
quench'd, fann'd it, & the wind spread it, & the heap that crush'd
it, became the fuel of its blaze: the weak things of God did confound
the mighty & His foolishness the wise; & those things which are
despised did God choose, yea, & things which are not, to bring to
naught those things that are esteemed all in all;—the kingdoms of
this world became the kingdoms of our Lord & of His Christ; and
He shall reign for ever & ever.

You will not fail to bring us home in a waistcoat pocket book,
outline sketches of some of the famous cities? You will enjoy the
music in the abbeys & churches, especially if it be like, on the whole,

some of the chants; simple majestical composition, and not flourish'd about, and tortur'd like the modern operas; it is easy to run up & down, & backward, & forward, & round & round, like a squirrel in his cage; but this is the art of music, to invent a sweet, pathetick or majestic melody; & to enrich it to the utmost, but not crush it even if it be a chorus, with full harmony & symphonies, & ever to be waiting as an obedient handmaid on the sense and prosody of the poet. Hence, I have thought that great poets should be their own musicians, that so, the high thought, the nervous march & rhythm of the words & tune might be found consenting together in one impression on the soul, 'Wed their divine sounds & mix'd power employ, Dead things with inbreath'd sense able to pierce.'

I hope you will not infer, because I talk so much of convents & pictures, that I am insensible to those other noble objects of travel so worthy the attention of an accomplish'd mind—but I speak of a hasty journey & brief stay—else, could I be insensible of the other noble opportunities of information which the most devoted artist would not pass over of the manner e:g: of treating the poor and prisoners, if he might ever indirectly serve them, there, or in his own country. We know that all ignorance is evil in a mind that is to live forever, hopes to company with angels; and, O! bliss inconceivable to see the face of his Creator & Redeemer!; but we know not that any useful knowledge, how remote soever from our calling can never at any time, or in any degree, contribute to individual happiness, or universal good; which, indeed, may be named the sum & aggregate of individual virtue. We know that all ignorance is bad:—we know not that any knowledge will be useless. This is wisdom; not, while we are seeking one knowledge, wilfully to shut us up & hide our eyes from any other presenting itself, either of less moment, or, as we may fancy superflous or antipathetic; but to know what we should learn first, above all things; which is the knowledge of God in Jesus Christ—what second; this is our business or profession—& what things to be content to happen upon and view passing; as a traveller by the straightest road turns upon some brows and corners whence delicious prospects greet his spirits; not retarding, but lifting him some miles upon his way—that we should know when to taste & when to spare such innoxious delicacies of cordial & spicy stimulus as quicken the arduous digestion of those high knowledges which are the pabula of the soul:—such as are the phosphor of her immortal lamp; the nourishment of her pure & fiery essence: tho' it be now as a wasted brand; as ashes cast away, as in a poor lanthorn of clay; but by and by it shall oxygenate, blaze up, fulgurate & dazzle in a more vital air: not in these charnel damps. You would like also, to ascertain in your travels the various modes of education, from infancy to accomplishment. You would not think it trouble to go a score or two miles about, to visit any shrine of piety & holiness; any field of patriotism or seat of ancient learning, or humbler walls that casketed any one of those pure diamonds of genius which help off the sorry complexion of our world, and make angels endure to look upon it. And it is a glorious use of our outward senses, turning them against their own fleshliness, to drink in thro' their grosser pores wisdom & virtue to the soul: to become wiser and better as we look upon & handle the very urn which holds the dead ashes of some noble heart that once was more capacious than the universe; & passing by the sculptured cemetries of proud conquerors, usurpers & oppressors; of all whose glories, whether thousands of bereav'd families; deposed monarchs; rivers of orphan's tears ; plunder'd cities; naked exiles; murder'd patriots; empty horror & blacken'd desolation; none are so innocent & beautiful as the solemn marble that records at once the triumph of their successes & the vanity of their hope—passing by these, to melt & glow at once, with penitence & devotion as you print the more neglected clay of martyrs & confessors; who, having lost all that they might win their Saviour, and enjoy Him at the last, possess'd nothing that death could take away, nor wish'd anything beside those beatitudes which his stroke would release their spirits to enjoy: who took the prey out of the lion & the bear; who woo'd the obstinate, reclaim'd the wandering & redeem'd the lost: labouring in sighs & tears, pleading with men, who oftentimes did rejoice those holy angels that joy over one sinner that repenteth—and who having come out of great tribulation, & washed their robes, and made them white in the blood of the Lamb, walk henceforth evermore in white robes with palms in their hands & wise in winning souls & having turned many unto righteousness, are now shining like the sun, and as the stars forever & ever.

The wise traveller would endeavour to find the causes, in religion, in government, national habits, popular virtues or vices, education, arts, literature, philosophy & sciences, which brought about the misery of happiness, the glory or degradation of the countries he passes thro' : nor would he fail where ever he went, to inquire with lively interest the real condition of the Church of God which He hath purchased with His own blood: its purity or corruption; its increase, or lukewarmness & decay. In the shortest tour, at home or abroad,—in a five minutes' walk, the lover of his brother's soul will know how to say a word of instruction *to him that is weary*. Who, that loveth not his brother will dare pretend to love his God?

Who *can* love his brother & refuse to follow the inward motion of the Spirit, which always urges in right season, to allure, or snatch his poor, blind fellow-sinner from the cliff-edge of damnation & despair? But I thank God you know these things & feel them, &, as I believe, are not an unfruitful hearer but a doer of the word; for which God be praised! Who knows but you may say a simple word to some poor fisherman on Calais beach, or to some rich towns-man or gentleman (tho' more hopeless) that shall be so sent home by the Convincing Spirit, as to be, under God, the mean of his eternal salvation, & through him, of whole families?—Yea, perhaps God intends that you are to do the like *This Moment*, sitting at home, or in your *Next Walk*! I am not for breaking open doors & windows, & howling out *Hell Fire & Damnation* at every innocent dance & merry meeting: the 'Word *in Season*' is often invited by opportunity, and sanction'd by discretion—tho' if it seem otherwise, we must obey the impulse—and, at the moment God is moving your lips to speak, He is opening an ear to hear and converting a heart to understand. Oh! if we lov'd one anothers' souls as we ought to love, methinks our eyes would so run down with rivers of water that we could scarce any more enjoy the shining of the sun: the changing splendour of the seasons would be as an universal blank; the song of the vineyards swell unheard; all the harvests disappear suddenly, as swoop'd into the horrible yawning of the bottomless pit: the whole scope of vision be smear'd with a dreadful confusion of horror; or blacken'd beyond a starless midnight with doleful obsequies of unpardon'd souls. With respect to the objects of travel, tho' you will move too quickly to notice many of them, yet go, Sir, to Italy if you can: perhaps it may be, in a tour; as you know we have found it in a day's excursion; generally more pleasant when done almost at a moment's suggestion. I am sorry, dear Sir, that you labour under such a load of depression. Trust in the Lord, and seek to Him for comfort upon your knees. Let your 'hope surely there be fix'd where true joys are to be found' for 'vain is the help of man.' I have suffer'd O! how bitterly! from a gloomy medium of perception which blacken'd every object and occurrence, & changed the meridian noon to darkness; & I found no help but prayer. Perhaps you may find afterward, that some of your best works were done in entire, humble chasten'd dependence on God, & renunciation of self. 'Heaviness may endure for a night, but joy cometh in the morning.' I have, for several months, been mercifully reliev'd from that overshadowing Horror which was wont to spread its numbing wings over me. It's a long grove indeed which has no light at the end of it. I am sorry I shall not see your large

fresco head.   I have pleas'd myself with trying to imagine it.   I
suppose you know that Mr. Sherman is, or has been with Dr. Monro [39]
at Bushy.   He likes an artist to live with him, and work for him
from the cottages &c thereabout.   He has had some of the first-
rate housepainters and sky sloppers and bush blotters there.   I fear
Welby won't do for him not having much of the requisite facility.
I know not how our London friends are, save Mr. Linnell, and Mr.
Walter who came with him to Shoreham.   I am rejoic'd to hear
Mr. Tatham is much better.   Pray write me a more minute account
than the last of what you do 'from morn to dewy eve.'   If you want
high amusement get Sir T. Browne's 'Religio Medici'; & I need
not say read it attentively through:—Sir Thomas has taken care of
that.   The price here is about 1s. 6d. or 2s. 0d.   Mr. Linnell has
borrow'd the excellent 'Cat o' nine tails,' [40] & says with me he should
like to be acquainted with the author.   *We were talking of going to
Exeter together to see him!!*   Mr. Linnell has given my Father
impressions of those Inferno plates dear Mr. Blake lived to execute:
nothing can be finer: they are Art in its sublime nakedness (not as
being unfinish'd) and in its eternal abstraction from cloggy corporeal substance.   They are not of this World.   When you write,
please to tell me if I can get the sketch of my Cousin which is in
your study: I can do without it if it be not quite handy.   Be pleased
to present my best respects to Mr. Waters. William [41] draws daily
out of doors: he has made some very pretty studies from Nature,
that great goddess Diana of nightmen, atheists, & bad artists—or,
as a dissenting preacher once named her, with a holy unconsciousness
of sex 'That great *God* Diana of the Ephesians!'   Some grey paper
with slight tinting & heightening would bring home some of those
marine effects capitally.   For this long epistle, dribbl'd, with scarce
adding or altering, at a spare minute or two, as I could snatch time;
partly in the act of walking to Lullingstone, partly in the park,
paddock, or Mr. Groombridge's Garden, & after supper, if it were
not for your double requisition of a long letter (tho' this has grown
undesignedly) you will perhaps say I should have ask'd rather your
forgiveness than your attention.   OCTOBER.   I have just returned
from London—these are the news—the bitter before the sweet to
make the sweet the sweeter.   Mr. Sherman went recommended by
Mr. Varley to Dr. Monro: he got there at night.   Next morning he
make a sketch of the Dr.'s house before breakfast.   After breakfast
two steeds were caparison'd, on one of which mounted the Dr. &
on the other Discipulus, & set forward to depict from Nature.   The
Doctor led the way to that selected scene which he intended to
commend first of all to his visitor's attention.   It did not consist

wholly of nature nor wholly of art. Had *we* had the happiness of beholding it, how must it have rais'd our esteem and admiration of *his* taste who first discover'd & explored it! Rara Avis! It consisted, I say, not of mere sylvan simplicity or unadorned grandeur, but presented that most rare, fortunate concurrence & due admixture of nature and of art in which great critics assert perfection to consist. Here was landscape in its flattest and most inoffensive simplicity; & uncorrupted architecture in its purest elements & *most primitive order*! At last the picturesque tourists arrived at the Arcadia of their destination:—and Behold!—It was a BRICK FIELD!!!!! The Doctor's outline was soon done & he went home to tint it; Mr. S. remained several hours, & made three sketches; one of which, when he came home in the evening, the Doctor (who by this time had quite finish'd his own) kept; & politely inform'd Mr. Sherman that his carriage was going to town the next morning and that he might if he pleas'd avail himself of that convenience; which he accordingly did. He is more miserable than ever. Mr. Varley has been very kind: teaching him something of that process in water & oil which is likely to please. He has also spoken to M. Lowry,[42] who is willing to try him with some engraving work. Mr. Tatham also has two or three days' work for him. He was, and perhaps *is* looking out for some place in a shop; he cares not what, and is thinking of going to sea. Pray write him a word of encouragement. I think he has been working hard. Mr. Varley told him he remember'd spending three days upon a drawing; walking all over London to get rid of it, & being rejoiced at last to sell it for a shilling! Now for good news. Mr. Linnell still mends. Mr. Tatham seems well, and is working most energetically. Mr. Calvert I found as I prognosticated in a former letter, risen from temptation, & finishing with surprising rapidity, the effect of prayer, a beautiful & luxuriant design of the cider pressing: a wood engraving. It did my heart good to see his poor dear little Willy after all his suffering quite well & looking if anything even more chubby than Johnny. Mr. Calvert has got another school. Farewell! and do for me what I have this moment done for you—intreat God to have mercy on me for Christ's sake; that He would be pleas'd to sprinkle this vile heart with that infinitely precious blood which is the only hope and last refuge

of Dear Sir

Your guilty but affectionate friend

Samuel Palmer.

P.S. Donatello's St. George is in the oratory of St. Michael at Florence.[43]

F

Many things in this monster of a letter, the talk of the schooling
and purifying of the soul, of the mind lifted up "to those altitudes of
her own unbounded hemisphere, whence she may serenely muse
and contemplate, beyond the waters of the extremest ocean, and
last cape and promontory of this transitory world," the "base, deject,
dirty and shameful barter for the treasures of the soul," the high
knowledges which are the "phosphor of her immortal lamp; the
nourishment of her pure and fiery essence," the "auto-babblery" of
piercing the clouds and looking over the doors of bliss, of the changes
by way of prayer from black gloom to exultation, the mention of
Blake's Dante illustrations which are " not of this world"—all these
things show that the heat of Palmer's self-dedication was still warm-
ing towards its height. He had no use for "landscape in its flattest
and most inoffensive simplicity"; [44] no use, in spite of Linnell, for
getting a thousand a year "by making studies of the Shoreham
scenery." His art is "God's gift of art," which he will not sell for
money or fame.

"Tho' I am making studies for Mr. Linnell, I will, God help me,
never be a naturalist by profession." Earlier on, Linnell had doubted
the value of his move to Shoreham; and before he had fixed himself
there, he had been "startled" (and wrote and told Linnell so) "by
this sentence in a letter just received from my father 'Mr. Linnell
. . . foretells that your voluntary secession from artists will end in
the withering of art in your mind. He has known it to be so.'" [45]
Linnell spoke then perhaps more truly than he ever came to realize,
even if the withering was to be caused less by secession than by the
dangers of winding too far up the pinnacle of an exclusive "enthusiasm"; but Palmer had enough conviction about himself and his
purpose to withstand Linnell then as well as now. And Richmond,
replying from Calais in November, wrote: "I was delighted to
hear of your inflexibility about (studying) the Figure, for though it
is certain *you will not* any more than *Mr. Blake* get a thousand a
year by it, yet you will have what he had, a contentment in your
own mind such as gold cannot purchase—or flimsy praise procure.
Mr. Linnell is an extraordinary man, but he is not a Mr. Blake." [46]

The minor points of the letter—that Palmer's father seems to
have left him, that his brother William had inclinations towards
being an artist, and that Palmer had only lately, as the wording of
his address indicates, moved into Waterhouse, near Shoreham
bridge—are to be noted; because with Richmond abroad, and his
other friends in London, Palmer does seem to be becoming rather
lonelier and more driven in on himself. And so Linnell's commission for studies from nature, in more than one way, may have come

just when it was needed most. It may have been a shrewd psychological judgment.

The next two pieces we have of his correspondence are again to John Linnell. If the first may in some ways be a slight sop to his mentor, it also raises up Palmer's own ecstasy to a new point:

"Shoreham, Kent, December 21st, 1828.

My Dear Sir,

I have begun to take off a pretty view of part of the village, and have no doubt but the drawing of choice portions and aspects of external objects is one of the varieties of study requisite to build up an artist, who should be a magnet to all kinds of knowledge; though, at the same time, I can't help seeing that the general characteristics of Nature's beauty not only differ from, but are, in some respects, opposed to those of Imaginative Art; and *that*, even in those scenes and appearances where she is loveliest, and most universally pleasing.

Nature, with mild reposing breadths of lawn and hill, shadowy glades and meadows, is sprinkled and showered with a thousand pretty eyes, and buds, and spires, and blossoms gemm'd with dew, and is clad in living green. Nor must be forgotten the motley clouding; the fine meshes, the aerial tissues, that dapple the skies of spring; nor the rolling volumes and piled mountains of light; nor the purple sunset blazon'd with gold and the translucent amber. Universal nature wears a lovely gentleness of mild attraction; but the leafy lightness, the thousand repetitions of little forms, which are part of its own genuine perfection (and who would wish them but what they are?), seem hard to be reconciled with the unwinning severity, the awfulness, the ponderous globosity of Art.

Milton, by one epithet, draws an oak of the largest girth I ever saw, 'Pine and *monumental* oak': I have just been trying to draw a large one in Lullingstone; but the poet's tree is huger than any in the park: there, the moss, and rifts, and barky furrows, and the mouldering grey (tho' that adds majesty to the lord of forests) mostly catch the eye, before the grasp and grapple of the roots, the muscular belly and shoulders, the twisted sinews.

Many of the fine pictures of the 13th, 14th, and two following centuries, which our modern addlepates grin at for Gothic and barbarous, do seem to me, I confess, much deteriorated by the faces, though exquisitely drawn, looking like portraits, which many of them are; and from the naked form, thwarted with fringes, and belts, and trappings, being generally neglected or ill expressed through a habit of disproportioned attention to secondary things, as the stuff and texture of draperies &c.; which ended at last in the Dutch school; with this damning difference; that in the fine old works the heads are always most elaborated—on the Flemish canvas, the least finished of any part; and yielding to the perfected polish of pots and stew-pans; a preference most religiously observed by the cleverest disciples of that style at present. An instance of this appeared in the last exhibition, where was a painting in which, against the sky and distance, beautiful, intense, and above the Dutch perception, there came a woman's head; hard to tell whether quite neglected, or laboriously muzzled—the least perfect object in the piece, with a careful avoidance of all shape, roundness, and outline. But nature is not like this. I saw a lovely little rustic child this evening, which took my fancy so much that I long, with tomorrow's light (God sparing me), to make a humble attempt to catch some of its graces. If I can at all succeed it will be nothing Dutch or boorish.

Temporal Creation, whose beauties are in their kind perfect, and made and adapted by the benevolent Author to please all eyes and gladden all hearts, seems to differ from images of the mind, as that beautiful old picture in the last British Gallery (I forget the name; it is that I miscalled Garofalo) differs from the conceptions of the Sistine Chapel, or the tomb of the Medici: were both called suddenly into breath, the simple shepherds would, I think, as they ought, modestly withdraw themselves from the stupendous majesty of Buonarroti's *Night*.

So, among our poets, Milton is abstracted and eternal. That arch-alchemist, let him but touch a history, yea a dogma of the schools, or a technicality of science, and it becomes poetic gold. Has an old chronicle told, perhaps marred an action? Six words from the blind old man reinvigorate it beyond the living fact; so that we may say the spectators themselves saw only the wrong side of the tapestry. If superior spirits could be fancied to enact a masque of one of the greatest of those events which have transpired on earth, it would resemble the historical hints and allusions of our bard. I must be called mad to say it but I do believe his stanzas will be read in Heaven: and to be yet more mad—to foam at the mouth, I will declare my conviction that the *St. George* of Donatello, the *Night* of Michelangelo, and *The Last Supper* of Da Vinci are as casts and copies, of which, when their artists had obtained of God to conceive the Idea, an eternal mould was placed above the tenth sphere, beyond changes and decay.

Terrestrial spring showers blossoms and odours in profusion, which, at some moments, 'Breathe on earth the air of Paradise': indeed sometimes, when the spirits are in Heav'n, earth itself, as in

emulation, blooms again into Eden; rivalling those golden fruits
which the poet of Eden sheds upon his landscape, having stolen
(them) from that country where they grow without peril of frost,
or drought, or blight—'But not in this soil.'

Still, the perfection of nature is not the perfection of severest art:
they are two things. The former we may liken to an easy, charming
colloquy of intellectual friends; the latter is 'Imperial Tragedy.'
That is graceful humanity; *this* is Plato's Vision; who, somewhere
in untracked regions, primigenous Unity, above all things holds his
head and bears his forehead among the stars, tremendous to the gods!

If the *Night* could get up and walk, and were to take a swim to the
white cliffs, and after the fashion of Shakespeare's tragicomic mix-
tures, were amusing herself with a huge bit of broken tobacco-pipe,
I think about half a dozen whiffs would blow down the strongest
beech and oak at Windsor, and the pipe-ashes chance to make a
big bonfire of the forest!

General nature is wisely and beneficently adapted to refresh the
senses and soothe the spirits of general *observers*. We find hundreds
in raptures when they get into the fields, who have not the least
relish for grand art. General nature is simple and lovely; but,
compared with the loftier vision, it is the shrill music of the 'Little
herd grooms, Keeping their beasts in the budded brooms; And
crowing in pipes made of green corn,' to the sound of the chant and
great organ, pealing through dusky aisles and reverberating in the
dome; or the trombone, and drums, and cymbals of the banner'd
march. Everywhere curious, articulate, perfect and inimitable of
structure, like her own entomology, Nature does yet leave a space
for the soul to climb above her steepest summits. As, in her own
dominion, she swells from the herring to leviathan, from the hod-
mandod to the elephant, so, divine Art piles mountains on her hills,
and continents upon those mountains.

However, creation sometimes pours into the spiritual eye the
radiance of Heaven: the green mountains that glimmer in a summer
gloaming from the dusky yet bloomy east; the moon opening her
golden eye, or walking in brightness among innumerable islands of
light, not only thrill the optic nerve, but shed a mild, a grateful, an
unearthly lustre into the inmost spirits, and seem the interchanging
twilight of that peaceful country, where there is no sorrow and no night.

After all, I doubt not but there must be the study of this creation,
as well as art and vision; tho' I cannot think it other than the veil
of Heaven, through which her divine features are dimly smiling;
the setting of the table before the feast; the symphony before the
tune; the prologue of the drama; a dream, and antepast, and

proscenium of eternity. I doubt not, if I had the wisdom to use it
rightly (and who can so well instruct me as yourself?), it would
prove a helpful handmaid and co-mate of art, tho' dissimilar; as
mercury sympathizes with gold, learning with genius, and poetry
(with reverence to speak it), with religion. Those glorious round
clouds which you paint, I do think inimitably, are alone an example
how the elements of nature may be transmuted into the pure gold
of art. I would give something to get their style of form into the
torso of a figure. And I must do my taste, if I have taste, the justice
to observe that I consider and have always considered your miniature of Anny, Lizzy, and Johnny, a perfect, pure piece of imaginative
art; [47] and I have a pleasing hope that its beautiful living models
will some day themselves be poets or intellectual artists. I care not
how, or from what a thing is done, but what it is. Pamegiano's
auto-portrait in the last British Gallery, I can't help thinking not
only superior to his other works that I have seen, which have been
rather composite, but the finest picture of any sort I ever saw: [48]
we have only the copy of Leonardo's, tho' I don't know what can
go much beyond that.

I beg to be understood as not so much positively asserting anything in this half-studied scribble on a very difficult subject which
is beyond me, as, for the increase of my knowledge, putting forth a
thesis by way of query, that where it is rotten it may be batter'd,
thus avoiding to choke the throat of every sentence with '*I humbly
conceive—I submit with deference*,' which had made these lines, if
possible, more tedious than you will find them. I will not correct
them, lest I overspend that time in talking which should find me
doing . . .

Mr. Richmond, in a letter from Calais, asks me very anxiously
about your health. He heard from his father that you were worse.
He says from enquiry, two might go to Rome and stay six months,
for ninety pounds between them. Is this credible? I should like
to hunt out some gems like the *St. George*, if I could go, and bring
them home on grey paper, especially such works as we have no good
engravings of. If, at any time, you feel the *cacoëthes scribendi* come
upon you, I wish you would favour me with your opinion how,
should I go Romewards, my time might be most profitably spent
there. I have no prospect of travelling yet; but some time or other,
God willing, most certainly shall, and wish to get together all kinds
of information on the subject . . .

With love to the little 'Ancients,' I remain, dear Sir,
Your oblig'd affectionate Servant,
SAMUEL PALMER.

P.S. I have just finished another attempt at a portrait on grey board in colours. I took pains, and it is a likeness, but whether tolerably executed or not, I cannot tell. I am desperately resolved to try what can be got by drawing from nature. I think the pictures at our exhibitions seem almost as unlike nature as they are unlike fine art. I am going also to try a little child's head: if anything would please me in the copying it is children's heads." [49]

There are many echoes in that letter, which is the noblest piece we have of Palmer's rhetoric—echoes of Blake's strictures on the Vegetable Earth as compared to Eternity, and on the Optic Vegetative Nerve,[50] echoes of Isaac Barrow and of Archibald Alison's "general nature." [51] His quotation about the "budded brooms" is out of Spenser's *Shepherd's Calendar* (and it is, incidentally, a curious example of inheritance—Spenser borrowing it from Chaucer's *House of Fame*, and Fletcher repeating it in *The Faithful Shepherdess*) ; but for the moment, it is Palmer's postscript which continues where the earlier letter left off: "I am desperately resolved to try what can be got by drawing from nature. I think the pictures at our exhibitions seem almost as unlike nature as they are unlike fine art"—desperately, I take it, because, even if Palmer was determined to be true to his visions, even if he had his small competence coming in, and the roof of the by no means uncomfortable Waterhouse over him, he was selling little or nothing, and realizing that "looking for a wife," or marrying one, demanded the making of something by sales. Linnell, who recognized the dangers of lonely enthusiasm, was also a shrewd enough business man, and to him the asses' bridge of superstition was also—as he must have pointed out—the bridge into penury.

The last of the extant letters to Linnell shows that his new drawing from nature did not overjump even the first obstacle to sales. He sent in his eight to the summer show of the Academy. Two of them, "The Deluge: A Sketch" (No. 70), and "Ruth Returned from the Gleaning" (No. 69, Plate 29), drawings in his more "outrageous" manner, were hung, to his surprise, and the others rejected:

"Shoreham, Kent, Saturday May (17), 1829.

My dear Sir,

Pray accept my thanks for the trouble you have taken in getting me the colours: they arrived quite safely. I have not been to town since you saw me; but in a few days, when I have finished a bothering little job of a likeness, shall come and have a look at the exhibition, and I hope, have the pleasure of your company back to Shore-

ham. Nothing but such pleasure has been wanting to perfect my
delight at the glory of the season. Tho' living in the country, I
really did not think there were those splendours in visible creation
which I have lately seen.

The ways of the Royal Academy are to me unaccountable—not
that it is unaccountable they should reject six of my drawings; but
that they should hang those two which I thought far least likely.
I expected they would reject the '*Whole kettle and boiling*,' as
they have for these two years, and intended, with the patience
of an ox, to prepare eight colour'd pictures for their rejection
next season; and if *they* were refused, a like dose on the year
succeeding. As they condescended to receive any, I wonder they
did not prefer the nature sketches, and perhaps the two little
moonshines, in which, I think, there was more look of light
than I got before; and less of my wonted outrageousness than
in the *Ruth* or *Deluge*.

I will immediately enquire about horses and asses. There are
plenty of *brutes* in Shoreham, but no asses that I know of, except
myself, and *I* don't answer the description, for I cannot say that I
am yet *able* to *draw*, tho' certainly most willing.

The artists have at last an opportunity of wearing the beard
unmolested; I understand from the papers that it is become the
height of the fashion! I hope they will avail of this. . . .

With best respects to Mrs. Linnell, and love to the children,
I remain, dear Sir, Your obliged and affectionate Servant,

Samuel Palmer." [52]

Palmer had had nothing in the Academy since 1826, and was
to have nothing again till 1832; and if he sent to the British Institution, he had been equally unlucky there, not succeeding between the
years 1822 and 1834. "A bothering little job of a likeness" makes
it clear that he did some portrait-making, against the grain; and
another point in this letter which should not be missed is the reference to beards. Like James Ward (who is reputed to have written
a pamphlet on them) [53] he approved of beards; and round about
now he grew one himself. There is a drawing of him by George
Richmond, done in February 1830, which shows him moustached
and bearded, with long hair curling down to his shoulders. It is
curious placed alongside his drawing of himself in 1828 (No. 58,
Plate 24); [54] and it shows how far he was at heart from any con-
forming. His style of hair is very much that of Dürer in his self-
portrait, and it is an outward expression of his inward convictions
of the primitive and the patriarchal.

V

There are some seventeen drawings which belong to this time of 1828 and 1829, to Palmer's analysing of nature. Five of them were among the studies done for Linnell, and till lately belonged to one of Linnell's grandsons. There is a peculiar authenticity about these drawings. Whereas in the series of 1825, nature was jacketed into a precision and stiffness of form, fitted into a Van Leydenish or Dürer-like quality of landscape, with however strong and glowing an apprehension, here in these drawings it is nature and Palmer, a presence of Palmer *into* a tree, into the dark velvetiness of a shadowed hill, into the fury of a tangle of branches, into all the eyes and buds of nature. Produced by a mind partly fed and fattened by literature, they belong in no sense to a literary, anecdotal art. They are of a family which includes Van Gogh and the blots of Alexander Cozens, Gerard Hopkins and John Clare, and the fulfilled apprehension, the insight of the prints of Herkules Seghers. They have none of the aridity of Dürer, whose forms Fuseli called "the thwarted growth of starveling labour and dry sterility." [55] A peculiar richness surrounds Shoreham—the river through watermeadows, the full curve of the hills, the intersecting of lines of growth and ripeness, the heavy and ancient timber of Lullingstone Park (beneath which is a small church, by the river, filled with an exceptional antique richness and suggestiveness of the past). The Lullingstone tree drawings are exactly described in that long letter to John Linnell:

"Milton, by one epithet, draws an oak of the largest girth I ever saw, 'Pine and *monumental* oak': I have just been trying to draw a large one in Lullingstone; but the poet's tree is huger than any in the park: there, the moss, and rifts, and barky furrows, and the mouldering grey (tho' that adds majesty to the lord of forests) mostly catch the eye, before the grasp and grapple of the roots, the muscular belly and shoulders, the twisted sinews."

Palmer, as you may see in "Oak Tree and Beech, Lullingtsone Park" (No. 60, Plate 25), contrives both the muscularity and the moss and lichen, and rifts, and barky furrows. Just as he had tried for the granulation of statues in the British Museum, for the "niggling," so he sticks to it in these drawings, only keeping it within bounds. In this particular drawing, he combines a quick growth of pen strokes with watercolour and a gouache, a paste of lichen and moss. Fine examples of his tufted gemming and jewelling are the celebrated "Shoreham Garden" (No. 78, Plate 34) (which I should say is later than the Lullingstone tree drawings) and "The Primitive Cottage" (No. 75, Plate 31), and the two extraordinary thatched roofs (Nos. 71, 72, Plates 30 and 1)—nature "sprinkled and showered with a thousand pretty eyes, and buds, and spires, and blossoms gemm'd with dew," and "clad in living green." The intricacy and solidity of the mossy roofs are extraordinary, dark green, light green, pale yellow, deeper gold, brown and pink and pale red and white in the "Barn" (No. 71, Plate 30); and in just this way he uses sheep as solid tufts on green fields, corn stooks on golden stubble, clouds on the sky. Living green, living solidity, as we have seen, are common enough to the language of mystical vision, as in St. Teresa's trees beginning "to button, and budd out towards flowring"; but this apprehension of living detail was not peculiar at this time to this one artist. It can be seen, for example, in drawings of holly trees and plants by James Ward, in the richest early work of Linnell's friend Hunt (the matrix of his later birds' nests and primroses); there is a rich gemming in miniatures by Samuel Shelley, and Linnell himself. Palmer, we know,[56] read on top of everything else, James Hervey's eighteenth century *Meditations and Contemplations* (also admired by Blake), in which there is a curling dance and emergence of leaves and tendrils reminiscent of such drawings as "The Shoreham Garden" and "The Pear Tree in a Walled Garden" (No. 77, Plate 33)—"why does the parsley, with her frizzled locks, shag the border; or why the celery, with her whitening arms, perforate the mould?" In John Clare's poems—particularly in many of the unpublished ones—is not only a quivering freshness of unity with nature, but the same taste for living detail—leaves and flowers which burn with light, the solidity of dew, the red of a cuckoo's open mouth, the purple light inside a Canterbury bell; and in this poet, twelve years older than Palmer, and like him a devotee of Blake—("Blake," he wrote, "is as great a warrior as Nelson, the one was honoured with titles, the other not")—there are oak tree descriptions which nearly parallel these Lullingstone drawings:

> Where old embowering oaks lift overhead
> An arch of powdered grains.

or

> The huge oaks splintered trunks appear
> When spring is in her pride
> As they were whitewashed every year
> Upon their northern side
> And where I climb the paddock's nest
> The side that faced the south
> The dust that rubbed off gen my breast
> Came bitter in my mouth.[57]

Moss and lichens had impinged, less violently, on the eyes of Crabbe (one of the poets whom Palmer enjoyed), and the Wordsworths, and Southey. And before much of this living physique of nature came into poetry and painting, naturalists had begun to peer into natural detail. James Sowerby, in the seventeen-nineties, had painted golden lichens for his *English Botany*, and Gilpin, the archbishop of the picturesque, had written in 1791, in his *Remarks on Forest Scenery*, a commendation of lichens (he includes lichen in the term 'moss') to the artist's attention: "In coloured landscape, it is surely a very beautiful object of imitation." He has an excellent passage on "the green velvet moss" on an oak; the "little rich knots and fringes." And, he says, in words that almost translate the detail of a Palmer drawing, "we may observe also touches of red; and sometimes, but rarely, a bright yellow, which is like a gleam of sunshine; and in many trees you will see one species growing upon another; the knotted brimstone-coloured fringe clinging to a lighter species; or the black softening into red." Again: "When they are blended harmoniously, as is generally the case, the rough and furrowed trunk of an old oak, adorned with these pleasing appendages, is an object which will long detain the picturesque eye"; and he adds that "the rooting of trees is a circumstance on which their beauty greatly depends." The hop, too, which Palmer so loved and so often drew, Gilpin commended to the painter: "In its rude natural state, twisting carelessly round the branches of trees, I know not whether it is not as beautiful as the vine"—although in cultivation he found hops "disagreeable."

Palmer sees such things, enters into them, and renders them with his own rare individuality and passion, his religious excess. So much of the analysis of nature in Ruskin, and in the Pre-Raphaelites, comes, not out of their originality but from this same process of the times, at work before them in Palmer; but in the Pre-Raphaelites the detail is colder and more literal, minus the religious "inscape," minus the coupling of tenderness, unity, and a passion of growth visible in such drawings as "Barn in a Valley" (No. 65, Plate 27), "The Bridge at Shoreham" (No. 68, Plate 28), or "An Ancient Barn" (No. 76, Plate 32). Pre-Raphaelite pictures are an assembly of detail, not condensations of nature.

VI

As this desperate attempt to see what could be done with drawings from nature proceeded, and the old outrageous manner receded, there occurred what, with Palmer, was inevitable—the drawings from nature became the foundation of a new outrageousness, a new excessiveness, equally unacceptable to the exhibitions of the day. The mystical accent, or temperature, rises in 1828 and 1829 through such drawings as the "Pear Tree" (No. 77, Plate 33) and "The Shoreham Garden" (No. 78, Plate 34), which I have mentioned, towards the moonlight drawings of raving-mad splendour, and the amazing climax of "The Magic Apple Tree" (No. 92, Plate 45) and the "Yellow Twilight" (No. 89, Plate 42).

There is little to document these months, although there are hints of a crisis full of meaning. Palmer's "looking for a wife" had boiled up. He was in love, and he failed. That is about all there is to say, but he did not take it easily; any more than he took a death without being totally possessed and bowed by it. It is tempting to hazard that he had fallen in love with one of Frederick Tatham's "sweet sisters"—a match which their snobbish father would certainly have opposed just as he opposed his daughter Julia's engagement, two years later, to George Richmond, so much so that Richmond had to elope. Palmer talks of it afterwards in a letter to Richmond of 1834, mentioning the very many ties which bound them together: "Besides the kindness and sympathy of yourself and Mrs. Richmond when crossed in love I was a nuisance to others & to myself—that alone would be sufficient to fix you both in my heart which would want a very rough jerk to tumble you out of it." [58] In whatever way George Richmond and Julia Tatham may have helped, there is a gap for this particular year, 1829, in the letters from Palmer to Richmond, although Richmond was back in England before the end of May.[59] A. H. Palmer talks of the matter as "another time of great sorrow in 1829" (the sentence before concerned Blake's death), and then quotes from a letter in which Palmer, referring to his trouble, declared: "The allurements of this world promise much and reward little, but the studies and exercises of wisdom, virtue, and holiness, seeming at first crabbed and dull, hold in their hard shell endless and unsating variety of true pleasures." [60]

And obviously into those studies and exercises he drove anew. His father and his brother William were no longer at Shoreham, but his nurse Mary Ward still kept house for him and gave him affection that he needed. She stayed with him, through all his Shoreham years, eventually returning with him to London.[61] In 1829 she gave him Tonson's two-volume edition of the *Poems of Milton*, which he inscribed, "Samuel Palmer, Shoreham, Kent. The gift of his beloved nurse, Mary Ward, 1829." [62] Inside the cover of the first volume he wrote down a list of all those lines

referring to the moon.   His "moonlight of moonlights" was always
the Fuseli-like one called up by the description of the hell-hounds at
Hell gates:

> Nor uglier follow the night-hag, when, call'd
> In secret, riding through the air she comes,
> Lured with the smell of infant blood, to dance
> With Lapland witches; while the labouring moon
> Eclipses at their charms . . . [63]

But his moons now were neither the eclipsed nor the "horned
moon . . . Amongst her spangled sisters bright"; but the full moon,
the "moon globose," the moon "stooping through a fleecy cloud,"
the moon "rising in clouded majesty"—

> . . . now reigns
> Full-orb'd the moon, and with more pleasing light
> Shadowy sets off the face of things . . .

These are the moons—the Beulah moons—of "A Kentish Idyl"
(No. 79, Plate 35); "Shepherds, under the Full Moon" (No. 87,
Plate 41); "Full Moon and Deer" (No. 81, Plate 37), and "A
Shepherd Leading His Flock under the Full Moon" (No. 80, Plate
36)—four closely related drawings; and of the painting "Coming
from Evening Church" (No. 83, Plate 38), which was finished at
Shoreham in 1830.   It has a Gothic arching of trees like the earlier
painting, "Hilly Scene," and it may be a reworking of an earlier
design in the new frenzies of the moment.   There is another moon
which may also belong to this year, the "moon globose" of Dr. and
Mrs. Gordon Bottomley's watercolour (No. 93, Plate 46)—which Dr.
Bottomley describes to me as being in "a range of filmy variations
on a dark rich umber."   This may be a drawing leading up to the
"Harvest Moon" exhibited at the Royal Academy in 1833, for
Palmer brooded plenty of images in his mind, and then worked
them out into pictures a year or two later.

    There are several cornfield and moonlight, cornfield and twi-
light, or sheep and twilight pastorals of this same time.   "Cornfield and Church by Moonlight" (No. 88), "Cornfield by Moonlight, with the Evening Star" (No. 86, Plate 40), and "Evening:
A Church Among Trees" (No. 85, Plate 39), are clearly much of
a date; and to these can be added "A Village Church Among Trees"
(No. 84), "A Church with a Bridge and a Boat" (No. 94), and "A
Country Road Leading Towards a Church" (No. 91, Plate 44).   In
all these drawings there is a passionate draughting, a passionate
vision, but the particularity has broadened.   The forms of things
are known so well, so much entered into, that they can be recorded
and assembled and simplified, so as to be there in the elements of

their existence with all their light and shade.   Quick lines dash
about the cornfields, quick masses blot in the tufted trees; and the
"look of light" and its distribution are easily satisfying.   In this
matter of shade and the "look of light" Palmer contributed much
to English art.   It is not only Palmer's forms which are so fascinating, and so display his union with nature.   Perhaps even more
this union is shown in his mastery of light.   Talking of an art-
critic's statement that he and Monet had "no conception of light"
before they came to England in 1870, Camille Pisarro made a remark
which is relevant to Palmer's light and shade.   "The fact is,"
Pisarro wrote, "we have studies which prove the contrary.   He omits
the influence which Claude Lorrain, Corot, the whole eighteenth
century and Chardin especially exerted on us.   But what he has no
conception of is that Turner and Constable, while they taught us
something, showed us in their works that they had no understanding of the *analysis* of *shadow*, which in Turner's painting is
simply used as an effect, a mere absence of light." [64]   Palmer's
shadow is never a mere absence of light.   He too had gone to
Claude, and to Bonasone, and to nature.   Bonasone, as we have seen,
he called later his "great coppermaster of shadows," who "never
commits the grievous fault of making shadow, as such, rich and of
a positive texture."   He gives a lesson of "texture in its proper
function, and shadow in its poetic sleep."   Palmer's shadow, especially in these moonlight drawings, is a darkness sleeping upon
substance, a darker light in relation to the light which flows, or
hovers among his trees, or spreads behind his hills.

Perhaps Alexander Cozens, as well as Claude and Bonasone,
helped him to this.   He investigated light and shadow more thor-
oughly and tenderly, I believe, than Cozens, but there are black-
and-white drawings, calmer a little and more precise, by Alexander
Cozens, which gave something of the same vision of nature, half a
century before—the same leaves, for example, black against the
light; and Palmer drawings still ahead—"The Weald of Kent"
with its Cozens-like trick of looking through dark into light, and
the Bright Cloud drawings—have already been paralleled in Cozens's
closer eighteenth-century idiom.   "I will studdy beauty of Form,"
Cozens wrote in his Roman Sketch Book (which Mr. Oppé ascribes
to 1746), "& injoy elegant Ideas set the Image of a charming face
fore my Mind feed on its lovely Innocence & by it flatter my longing Soul with Visions of happyness tho' but in Picture, for I will
immure myself in solitude & paint the Graces act Truth and
contemplate Virtue." [65]

But the results of Palmer's solitude and contemplation flamed into the "Yellow Twilight" (No. 89, Plate 42) and "The Magic Apple Tree (No. 92, Plate 45). Reproduction without colour can give no notion whatever of these two exceedingly, supremely exquisite works of vision. We know something of the genesis of "The Magic Apple Tree" (magic is, by the way, a poor word to apply to it: in Palmer's eyes magic it certainly was not: "divine" comes nearer), because there are two drawings for it. One is the sepia of "A Country Road Leading Towards a Church" (No. 91, Plate 44), which I have just mentioned, and which gives, roughly, the framework of the "Apple Tree"—the spire cut across by the fruit branches, the yew tree across the church, the arching trees, the lane leading downward between high banks, and the sheep. The other is the "Study of a Bough loaded with Apples" (No. 90, Plate 43), which is dated 1830, and round which Palmer has written some analysing notes:

"Principle of size
"Medium or large Apples universal bright
"Exceptions {some still a little larger & some very much smaller—often in gradated clusters
"Gen. Effect in bright sun the whole tree apples & leaves very golden in the same tree will be some boughs of darker apples dim in relief but exquisite in finish
"boughs next in size to smallest twigs—are I think of a crusty texture and a pale dead gold

"Apple boughs fall in long shapes like the branches—or the same foreshorten'd which is fine, the boughs are pull'd down by the weight. N.B. some trail along on the green ground."

The finished watercolour hits the eyes with what A. H. Palmer has called "a conflagration of colour"; and its colour is indeed so essential an element in the design that reproduction without it presents only a quiet, almost mean travesty. What you immediately take in are the dark leaden sky and the conflagration immediately below of the corn and stubble covered hill-slope, in tones from orange to the clearest, most luminous yellow. The sheep in the foreground have their backs lit up with yellow and white, the shadows around the piping brown-faced shepherd boy reflect more weakly the leaden mauve of the sky. Every fragment has its colour carefully adding to the total, and here and there a scurry of quick pen lines runs up a tree trunk or along a sheep's back. I repeat, the name given to it, I believe by A. H. Palmer, is not fortunate: not only are the apples not magic: bright red, and touched some of them with white and yellow, they have no overweight in the picture, and are not, as A. H. Palmer describes them, "a tremendous and utterly abnormal crop"; what is tremendous, what is abnormal, is the lemon-yellow light of the hill; and some such name as "Yellow Harvest" would have come closer.

"Orange Twilight," or "Twilight, Orange Sky," the name A. H. Palmer gave to the watercolour I have rechristened, and called "Yellow Twilight," is again a misnomer; and the watercolour again cannot easily be reproduced. In the lemon-yellow sky hangs a very pale crescent moon, and above the moon stretches out a band of pale blue. To the left, there are bands of orange above a sunset patch of red on yellow. This red is reflected on the tufted tree-tops on the right. The hillside below the moon is in deep purple shadow; the trees, some outlined again with quick pen strokes, are rendered in various warm tints of brown.

In a half-lit room the drawing seems luminescent; both startling and tender. Yet it is an accurate "effect," and I have seen it almost exactly paralleled, with a crescent moon over the dark wooded hill of a bay in North Devon. There are Turner sunsets in which the exaggeration of a splendour, the forcing of effects, appears to be little else than forcing and exaggeration, little else than a splendid frippery. What Palmer has contrived is different: it is a tender, imaginative truth, a sunset sky which is, precisely, a visible image of an invisible, hardly attainable blessedness. In few things painted by an English artist is vision held so securely and with such simplicity and such delicate, grave concentration. He wrote—and it applies to these watercolours—in 1830, presumably in a letter: "Let not the painter say 'I have done many pictures, and therefore should be able to do this less carefully'; for each time invention is a new species, though of the same genus. . . . If the painter performed each new work with that thirsting of mind and humility of purpose with which he did his first, how intense would be the result." [66] And how intense it was.

VII

If there is little evidence of Palmer's life in 1829 and 1830, the next year is still more barren of letters, or memoranda, or of any drawings which can certainly be dated. Belonging to 1830 there is one letter to George Richmond, which shows a continued liking for Fuseli, that Palmer was working to send (without success) to the Academy, that the monthly meetings continued,[67] that Palmer still hoped his brother William would become an artist, that Henry Walter was with him at Shoreham, and that he was still on good terms with the Tatham sisters at their home in St. John's Wood, Alpha Cottage:

Dear Sir   "Shoreham, Kent, March 15, 1830. sent 16.

I trouble you with particulars about the flat for the frame you so kindly offer'd to lend me. The flat must be $15\frac{3}{4}$ inches by $12\frac{1}{2}$ inches, *Sight*, and 7/8ths of an inch thick as the panel is 6/8ths. Mr. Steggle lives at No. 1 Green Street Leicester Fields. He can show you a little Fuseli I believe. Please to insist on his making the flat of an equal breadth all round that it may be afterwards useful for a drawing; unless so doing would injure your frame by demanding too much rabbet to be cut away—but I think it will not, as frame and picture are very nearly of the same proportion. I do not know the size of the frame so perhaps you would measure it and give Mr. Steggle the breadth of the flat. If you will house it, pray tell him to send it to you as soon as possible. Next time you are very near Mr. Linnell's senr., will you ask him if he have receiv'd my letter about frames:—& if he objects to making the flats of the same breadth all round please to insist upon it most positively & on my having them in time to work at least two days on the pictures in them before the sending them to R. Acad.ʸ I should like to be quite certain whether he can do what I want by Exhibition time—if he cannot, or if the 28 shilling frame which I have order'd be sold, would you drop me a line. Should you see William,[68] please to exhort him to do his best for the next monthly at Mr. Calvert's, and to begin directly. Mr. Walter desires me to say he will feel much obliged if, should you be near his brother's you would ask him whether he has any frames of his & if you will let him know the sizes, as time hastes. If I knew that my frames and flats were all in progress without hideous blunders and delay I should work most comfortably.

I hope your picture goes on well & that your man's head will glow like fine gold. Do get the upper half of the figures to a finish & all will be safe.

> I am Dr Sir
> > Yours very affec.ʸ
> > > Samuel Palmer.

P:S: I had a singular accident which would amuse the ladies at Alpha. Going across the kitchen in a hurry part of the floor broke under me with a great crack, and in a moment down went one of my drumsticks a good way into the cellar. I was filled with

G

the most unaffected surprise on finding that I had only one available leg to rise with: however having discover'd that the other was not quite lost but only below stairs; I slowly releas'd it; made a quiet effort to bend it, in which I succeeded & concluding thereby that it was sound & whole, dragged it after me to dinner.

How much smaller a thing has plunged some into eternity! Our life should be one holocaust of gratitude, for we live by a perpetual miracle—if Providence take His eyes off us we die.

Mr. Steggle must name the price before he has the order—of both which be pleased to make a Memorandum that if he makes it a wrong size it may not be imputable to us. Please at the bottom of my order to write your description ask him to name the lowest price as I am very straitened for money.

> "To Mr. Steggle.
>
> Sir
>
> Please to make a flat for me according to the description Mr. Richmond will have the goodness to give you & at the price agreed on by him, *if it can be done quickly*, and to send it to Mr. Richmonds address. I shall be in town soon & in three weeks will pay you for it.
>
> Samuel Palmer." [69]

But that letter reveals little enough. And it helps little to know that Richmond had done a miniature portrait of Samuel Palmer, which he exhibited in 1830,[70] or that Palmer's name, with two addresses, Waterhouse, and 2 Temple St., Fleet St., was given in the *Literary Blue Book, or Kalendar of Literature, Science and Art,* for 1830, with his speciality as "Design." [71]

Still, after the excessive height of that year, it is reasonable to expect a period of calmer, less extreme drawing. One certain fact is that in this year, in January, George Richmond and Julia Tatham having determined to run away to Gretna Green, Samuel Palmer lent Richmond the £40 which he needed. £12 was also borrowed from Henry Walter. And when they came back from Scotland, he gave them a home for the time being in Shoreham.[72] Richmond was a careful creature. On Palmer's loan he paid interest at $3\frac{1}{2}$ per cent., and had returned the whole £40 by the end of the year, having made "for 73 Portraits & teaching in Gower St." a total for 1831 of £207, 19s.—"and from that time forth by God's blessing my income rapidly increased." [73]

Palmer's income did not increase. It is true that his run of bad luck with the Academy was broken in 1832, when seven out of his eight submissions were hung. These were, "The Sheep Fold," "Scene near Shoreham, Kent," "A Pastoral Scene, Twilight," "A Pastoral Landscape," "A Harvest Scene," "Landscape Twilight," and "Late Twilight." There is no means of identifying any one of these for certain, though it is likely from the letter he wrote to Richmond in September [74] that all or most of them were indian ink drawings. In the letter he says: "If there is a desire to see some things of mine my Father will be so kind as to get my blacks which were in the Exhibition conveyed to Miss Sawkins." [75] Fifty years later, George Richmond pencilled across the top of this letter, "Exhibited woodcuts to be restored to owner," so it looks (though "woodcuts" must be a mistake?) as if the blacks, or some of them, had been sold. "The Flock and the Star" (No. 98, Plate 48), an ink drawing from George Richmond's collection, may have been one of them; "A Cornfield, Shoreham" (No. 99, Plate 49), also once the property of Richmond, may have been the "Harvest Scene"; and "The Sheep Fold" [76] is probably identical with "The Folded Flock" (No. 100, Plate 50), another ink drawing (which A. H. Palmer lent to the Palmer Exhibition in 1926 as "The Sheep Fold"). "A Church with a Boat and Sheep" (No. 95), a sepia now in an American collection, also fits in (to judge from a photograph) with these drawings in style.

All are more cool and calm than the work of 1830, and I take it they were done between the summer of 1831 and the spring of 1832. The four of them are twilights, and the "Cornfield," "The Folded Flock" and "The Flock and the Star" each have in them a house with a lighted window. The sheep have gathered solidity, the stooks of corn stand still, the trees do not grow so furiously; and to my mind the "Cornfield" (though I can judge only from the autotype reproduction in the *Memoir of Samuel Palmer*) is one of those drawings in which Palmer draws on all that he has discovered by furious analysis and derives from it a serenity altogether satisfying. The watercolour of an "Old House on the Bank of the Darenth" (No. 97, Plate 47) should also be given to this time. A letter from Henry Walter to George Richmond, written on March 24, 1831, shows that Walter was still at Shoreham, and that Palmer was on one of his visits to London, and that Palmer's father was back at Shoreham. Richmond is to tell his newly married wife that "although I value gravity etc. very much, I would willingly sell her two or three pennyworth at half price—I think she wants some. I can get more on the hills by late twilight." Between now and 1833 Palmer bought two cottages at Shoreham, and the letter shows that he had already begun to negotiate for them.

Not long after the 1831-32 drawings, to judge from similarities
of manner, and either in 1832 or 1833, Palmer must have made
the series of studies which led up to his pictures of "The White
Cloud" and "The Bright Cloud"; but since the chronology of his
work from now to the end of his residence at Shoreham must
become fuller of "may" and "probably" than ever, it will be as
well to round off this time of serenity with the one letter of 1832,
which displays a calmer mind, less rhetoric, but opinions no less
firmly held.

It pictures him with one room at Waterhouse fitted up as a
private chapel, where portraits are to be hung of the now sanctified
Fisher and More (he named his first child, several years later, More
Palmer, much as Coleridge christened his children after Hartley
and Berkeley); [77] and he talks of the Richmonds' first of many
children who had been born the month before:

"Friday   September 21st. 1832.

Please to excuse great haste & a wafer instead of a seal

My dear Sir

Pray do not fail if you see Mr. Knyvett to tell him how sincerely
and exceedingly I am obliged to him for his kind remembrance of
me.   I will be in town on Monday or Tuesday at farthest, and in the
mean time if there is a desire to see some things of mine my Father
will be so kind as to get my blacks which were in the exhibition
conveyed to Miss Sawkins.   I have been working very hard at art
which I now love more than ever, and recreating myself with good
books: Sir T. Browne's Christian Morals & the life of holy Bishop
Fisher, of which the first is the little casket of wisdom & the second
a most comfortable cordial in this cold heartless & Godless age—I
mean to get a print of the venerable Fisher & one of his friend &
fellow martyr Sr T. More & hang them cheek by jowl in my little
chapel, that they may frown vice, levity & infidelity out of my
house and out of my heart.   I have greatly desired to see your little
daughter & indeed have already loved her though unseen, and
while so many children, innocent & beautiful at first, lose daily as
they grow up the similitude of their divine parentage, and become
weeds & thistles instead of olive-branches in the church, what if by
the hearty prayers of her parents and friends your child should be
like St. John the Baptist filled with the Holy Ghost even from her
mother's womb, & like Samuel the prophet minister while yet very
young in the temple of the Lord?   Yet such glorious things can
earnest prayer accomplish!   Nothing is beyond its power.

How is the situation of a Christian changed in becoming a parent! an immortal soul placed under his controul & guidance for eternity—and that at his immediate responsibility! all sanctimonious whining and canting apart, it really is a most awful thing—and so indeed is everything influencing the salvation of damnation of a soul. It has now I know become quite unfashionable & unbearable to talk of Hell even in the pulpit, but none will fully enjoy the comfort & peace who do not know also the terrors of the Lord, the plague of their own heart & the deadly evil of sin. If people knew how deeply the whole world lieth in wickedness, and how totally it is estranged & set in opposition against God; they would I cannot help thinking, no longer wonder why all kinds of sects & schisms may not equally be term'd the churches of Christ—& think the robe of the true Church too mean & narrow without tacking upon it the abominable vestments of Quakerism Socinianism—yea the church of Mahomet, to swell it to the dimensions of modern Charity but would gladly press into the sanctuary of the Apostolic Church for refuge from the wrath of God & lay fast hold of the horns of her altars. Once I was full of this lightness & folly—yea even to the present time my old Adam can see no reason why the sleek & sober Quaker or the meek and moral Unitarian should be beholden to the Church, claiming the power of the keys of the kingdom of Heaven— But blessed be God I am changed even since you saw me—I am a free thinker in art in literature in music in poetry—but as I read of but one way to Heaven & that a narrow one, it is not for me to chuse which way I will be saved & make it a pretty speculation or matter of taste, & run to seek my Saviour in holes & corner, but go at once where He is ever to be found, at the Apostolick altar of the Melchisedekian priesthood. Elsewhere; whatever the *uncovenanted mercies* of God may be, we have no ratified charter, no sealed covenant of salvation—at that glorious altar, that Holy of Holies within the rent veil, may our friend Mr. Arthur Tatham (whose promotion in the Church I much rejoice to hear of) long live to minister oblations of acceptable praise to God, and good gifts to men, and in the fiery trial which is coming to prove & purify the Church, may he be never daunted or dismayed, but live through it & come forth as gold, or die in it & obtain a glorious & eternal crown of martyrdom.

I remain in great haste Dr Sir

Yours most affectionately

S. Palmer." [78]

Palmer's isolation was now becoming more extreme. His father was only at Shoreham on and off and his brother was gone; Arthur

Tatham was already ordained, and Richmond, hitherto closest to him in sympathy of all his artist friends, was now married, busy, and with a family. His contacts with Francis Finch and Calvert continued at the monthly meetings. His cousin John Giles (who, as a stockbroker, looked after his business affairs) was never out of his heart, but Welby Sherman and Walter were the only artists of the circle who were free to stay long and frequently at Shoreham. And new troubles, which Palmer hints at in the close of his letter, were beginning to start up. These were the times of Reform; and Reform, I take it, is "the fiery trial which is coming to prove & purify the Church," no less than it was coming on the country; and Palmer's thoughts of Arthur Tatham living through it and coming forth as gold or else dying and obtaining " a glorious & eternal crown of martyrdom " were neither extravagant nor exceptional among those who shuddered at the portents.

CHAPTER VI

THE LAST SHOREHAM YEARS

I

ALL the same, Palmer's letter of September 1832 is in some ways deceptive. The year had been one of perpetual excitement, and a fever heat of politics, a climax of several such years. The Reform Bill had kept coming and going, there had been riots, threats of suppression, cholera, rick-burnings, especially in Kent, to break in upon the ideal of Palmer's earthly paradise, and in June 1832 the Reform Bill had finally been passed by the House of Lords.

One should remember the background of excitement behind Palmer's life from 1829 and 1830, the years of his intensest visionary work. Palmer looked back with concern on the Acts of 1828 and 1829 which had given relief to the dissenters and the Catholics. The Church most in tune with his visionary realities was, to him, the Anglican Church of his fathers, the church of spires under the steep slopes of his Kentish hills; and the political party, as we have seen,[1] from his letter of 1828 to George Richmond, the High Tory: "I, also, as you know, of no party, as I love our fine British peasantry, think best of the old high tories, because I find they gave most liberty to the poor, and were not morose, sullen and bloodthirsty like the Whigs, liberty jacks and dissenters." 1831, Palmer's year of relative calm, after his visions of 1830, was the year of Edward Irving's prophecies, and the gift of tongues among his followers,[2] and with one thing and another, a man did not need to be what Palmer called himself later, a "quaint crinkle-crankle Goth," to be uneasy and apprehensive. More ordinary hard-headed individuals than Palmer, better disposed towards reform, felt the riots and mutterings of change, the earthquakes, eruptions, disasters, and universal uncertainty, just as much. Harriet Martineau, in her *History of the Peace*, quotes Arnold of Rugby, who thought in the autumn of 1831 that, whether Irving's activities were a real sign or no, the day of the Lord was coming, "i.e. the termination of one of the great $ai\hat{\omega}\nu\epsilon\varsigma$ of the human race. . . . The termination of the Jewish $ai\hat{\omega}\nu$ in the first century, and of the Roman $ai\hat{\omega}\nu$ in the fifth and sixth, were each marked by the same concurrence of calamities, wars, tumults, pestilences, earthquakes, etc., all marking the time of one of God's peculiar seasons of visitation." And Arnold ended

103

this letter, "We talk as much as we dare talk of anything two months distant, of going to the Lakes in the winter." [3]

As the years moved on to the final passage of the Reform Bill, Palmer must have felt the walls of his paradise increasingly threatened; and he broke out in peculiar fashion for a countercharge of his own. His whole art, all he had done, all the moons, and leaves against the evening light, all his rich fruit trees and oaks, and thatched roofs, and round hills and spires and pastoral sheep and brown-faced shepherds, his reading of the Christian fathers, the English divines, and the poets, his feeling for the pure and primitive, his love for Sir Thomas More and Bishop Fisher, his whole being and all his visionary years at Shoreham, fought, ineffectually, on his side against the Reform Bill. And if it was passed, it would be the beginning of the new $\alpha i \hat{\omega} \nu$, the enthronement of a new art for rich manufacturers, and the end of an epoch in Palmer's own life.

The moons and the twilights had charmed away neither fire nor reform. The ricks had burned around Shoreham, within sight of Waterhouse, and the Kentish papers of the year were full of savage evidence of distress, transportation for life for stealing a gold watch and chain, for stealing seven fowls, for stealing a shilling, "a jacket and other articles of clothing." Palmer wrote years afterwards of a visit he paid about this time, when he "dined with Mr. Daniel Whibley, farmer at Edenbridge and saw the old manners— the farm labourers clumping in in their many-sounding hobnails, and dining cheerily at the side-tables,—instead of meditating rick-burning while they eked out a quarter meal of baker's bread bealumed and rancid bacon under a hedge." [4] As an anti-Reformer I suppose he still saw some hope in the General Election which followed the Reform Act after the dissolution of Parliament in December. And while purple banners were being stitched for Sir William Geary, the Tory candidate in West Kent, with the arms of the county, with St. George and the Dragon, and "King and Constitution," he made his counter attack, and left painting for a moment to gesticulate in print against change and the future. He wrote a violent anonymous pamphlet, printed at Sevenoaks. I have not managed to trace a copy of the pamphlet, but Palmer sent it for review to the Kentish papers: the *Kentish Observer*, the Tory paper, which promised to notice it, and never did—"*The Address to the Electors of West Kent* forwarded to us from Sevenoaks, shall be attended to in the way that is suggested"—and to the Reform paper, the *Maidstone Gazette*, which luckily gave it a column of quotation and abuse.[5] The pamphlet was "by an Elector," and Palmer had now qualified himself as an elector by his purchase of the two cottages at Shoreham.[6] "The ravings of this maniac," the *Gazette* called it, believing it to have been written by a Kentish clergyman, no doubt one of the clergymen who believed with *Blackwood's*, that "it is notorious that in all other countries, the overthrow of religion has speedily followed the triumph of the democratic party." But the ravings are authentic Palmer, in his rich, archaic, Sturm-und-Drang, pseudo-Miltonic periods. Here are the extracts given in the column review:

"It is true we vastly, and beyond comparison outnumber the enemy: but then we are men of peace; and they are beasts of prey. We are strongest by day: they ravine in the night; for their optics are adapted to darkness. And it is now a very dark night for Europe. The Radicals are elated; for it is a dark and foggy night when thieves are always on the alert. They are housebreakers: we are quiet householders, who have drawn the curtains, and retired to rest!"

"Some have strangely refused to support SIR WILLIAM GEARY on account of their being, from early associations, attached to the Whigs. Alas! it is but an ill compliment to the Whigs of sixteen hundred and eighty eight, to mistake for their successors a rabble of incendiaries and jacobins. The policies promulgated by our adversaries are not those of MARLBOROUGH or CHATHAM, but of THISTLEWOOD and BRANDRETH!" [7]

(Then, "in allusion to the tardiness of the Tories in proposing reform"):

"But let it be so no longer! Put on, once more, the invincible armour of old English, of old Kentish Royalty. Strangle the snake corruption wherever you shall find it; and everywhere promote, in God's name, effectual reform: but leave not your hearths and altars a prey to the most heartless, the most bloody, most obscene, profane, and atrocious faction which ever defied God and insulted humanity."

"You will NOT suffer those temples where you received the Christian name to fall an easy prey to sacrilegious plunderers! You will NOT let that dust which covers the ashes of your parents, be made the filthy track of Jacobinical hyenas!"

"Our mistakes lie in not clearly understanding *what it is* that we rent of our landlord. We may, perhaps, imagine that we pay him for the whole of the crops which we produce; and that the tithe cart takes away a tenth of that produce, for the whole of which we have made our landlord a consideration: but it is no such thing: we never paid for that tenth: it was not charged in our rent. In short, we pay our landlord for the land; and if the other tenth were not removed by the titheman the landowner would take care to demand it in rent. It is irksome to be put to the proof of anything so self evident, where every argument is like a truism."

"The best informed authors will inform us that the ancient landowners who built most of our parish churches, left to their children only nine tenths of the profits of the estates which descended to them: the remaining tenth they bequeathed in the shape of the present tithe, to their respective churches for ever: and that bequest was and is ratified by the laws of our country. Therefore the landowner who is possessed of a thousand acres, receives only the profit of nine hundred: tomorrow, were the tithe law repealed, he would have ten hundred, bona fide disposable to his own use and benefit."

"As to the very ancient triple distribution of the tithe, which has been spoken of in certain quarters; one part to the poor; another to the parochial clergy; and a third towards the repairs of the Cathedral; a moment's reflection will convince us of its impracticability at present; when by the blessing of God our parish churches are so vastly multiplied; and I am happy to add multiplying. The solicitude of our enemies for the beauty of our cathedrals is a little out of character: we may believe it to equal their sympathy for the poor: with respect to whom, be it remembered, that the clergyman pays his full share of poor rate upon his income; to say nothing of the innumerable private charities, and neighbourly benefits conferred on their parishioners, by the great majority of that amiable and venerable, though most shamefully calumniated order."

"Brother Electors: we have been requested to return to Parliament two Gentlemen, who have, unhappily, ranked themselves under the standard of the so-called Radical Reformers. I would remind you that the Radicals have ever been found adverse to the agricultural interest: that, whatever they may pretend, they will, if possible, sweep away your protecting duties.

Farmers! They were the wretched leaders of this wretched faction, who, during the late dreadful fires, strenuously encouraged the incendiaries! Some of the most abandoned of them published cheap tracts for distribution among the poor, stimulating them to fire their masters' property. But now, if there be a Radical Parliament, the starvation produced by free trade, and the consequent reckless desperation of the peasantry, will supersede the necessity

of all other stimulants. If, then, you patronize Radicalism, in any
shape, you will have yourselves to thank for the consequences.

Already the fires have begun. Do you wish them to blaze
once more over the kingdom? If you do, send Radicals into Parliament; make Radicals of the poor; and as those principles effectually
relieve all classes from every religious and moral restraint, neither
property nor life will be for a moment secure. Conflagration has
already ravaged your harvests.

Landholders, who have estates confiscated or land in ashes:
Farmers who have free trade, and annihilation impending over
you: Manufacturers who must be beggared in the bankruptcy of
your country: Fundholders, who desire not the *wet sponge*: Britons,
who have liberty to lose: Christians who have a religion to be
blasphemed: now is the time for your last struggle! The ensuing
Election is not a question of party politics: much less, a paltry
squabble of family interest: but Exhistence, or Annihilation to good
old England!''

"False statements," cried the *Maidstone Gazette*, "weak arguments, accusations, and charges, as groundless, as they are base—
gross invectives, and foul vituperations, all of them striving for the
mastery, and all of them couched in Billingsgate phraseology, or
copied from the more elegant vocabulary of St. Giles's." The discussion of tithes no doubt led the paper to declare that it proceeded
"from the pen of a Reverend Divine . . . although he attempts to
hide his cassock under a veil of mystery, and misrepresentation, for
the cloven hoof will show itself, the 'galled jade will wince';" and
that therefore "we are led to treat all its wild declamations and
frothy nothings, as a certain other gentleman in 'black' did the shearing of swine 'great cry but little wool.'" Sir William Geary "must
feel himself heartily sick of so parasitical a Quack. It is almost too
lenient, however, to treat thus the ravings of this maniac." And
Sir William Geary was at the bottom of the poll, the Jacobinical
hyenas were in.[8]

II

In spite of this passionate squib, in spite of all the fever of the
year, Palmer did much painting in 1832. In fact, 1832 and the next
two years ripened his experience into a good harvest, even if now
began the gradual change and decline of Palmer's art. Stepped up
too high, it was soon to fall too low in the new England of the
nineteenth century. By exhibition time in 1833 he had his quota

ready for the Academy: five were accepted. Six were accepted in
1834; two in 1835. He had five things in the British Institution
in 1834, and four in 1835.

Of all this only a fragment is visible, several watercolours, a few
drawings, and eight pictures, but they show the character of the
work of his last Shoreham years. By 1832, long before the General
Election and the pamphlet, Palmer had begun his retreat from
Shoreham. He had been left another bequest and with this he must
have bought the Shoreham two cottages.[9] But he also bought
himself a small house in London, in St. John's Wood—No. 4 Grove
Street, Lisson Grove [10]—a street now swept away by railway yards.
The Richmonds were not far off; Calvert and Linnell lived near,
and so did the Tathams in Alpha Cottage. But he did not move
altogether from Shoreham, and was certainly there on and off until
the autumn of 1834. He gave No. 4 Grove Street as his address
on the back of his Academy pictures; and seems to have spent
some of his time there, and some in Shoreham, starting to work up
a teaching connection.[11] In a sense he was giving out, rather than
receiving: he was no longer in the full creative grip of Shoreham
twilights and the Valley of Vision; and this seems reflected in the
pictures. It is not easy to date them, and titles of more than one
of them no doubt differ from the original exhibition titles. My own
belief is that they are pictures worked up in the main from Shoreham sketches made before 1832. "The Bright Cloud" (No. 136,
Plate 62) and "The White Cloud" (No. 135, Plate 61), for instance.
I believe that the firm and exquisite drawings on which these are
based were done when his eyes and mind imaged such drawings as
"The Flock and the Star," "A Cornfield, Shoreham," and "The
Folded Flock." Set, for instance, against "The Flock and the
Star" (No. 98, Plate 48), the drawing now in the Ashmolean (which
Randall Davies picked up on a stall for a few shillings) on which
"The White Cloud " is based: here are the same fullness of weight,
the same vision of foliage, the same mottling of light and shade.
The Tate Gallery drawing for "The Bright Cloud" (No. 118,
Plate 55) is a touch coarser in detail and in its forms, but this too
must certainly be much earlier than the painting. The same is true
of the drawing (No. 109, Plate 52) for the "Scene at Underriver."
The mysterious "Sleeping Shepherd" (No. 140, Plate 64) summar-
izes many earlier recordings of the vision of twilight glowing behind
a dark mass of wooded hill, and the figure, as I have mentioned,[12]
is taken from Palmer's early love in the British Museum, the Graeco-
Roman figure of "Endymion the Shepherd Boy Asleep on Mt.
Latmos." And it recalls the 1831-32 drawings of twilight with a

2. Scene at Underriver (131). *c.* 1833-4. *Oil and tempera.* 7 × 10
[*Opposite page 108*]

lighted window. So does "Landscape: Twilight" (No. 141), which bears an Academy label on the back of the panel and is no doubt one of the two of the same name in the Academy of 1833, and the Academy of 1834.

One can get some idea of the way Palmer kept an image or a drawing in his mind from the relation of "The Skylark" (No. 110, Plate 53) to the much later picture,[13] and the etching. "The Skylark," with its Miltonic text, with its full felt sky, its curling interwoven cloud, its delicacy of early light, comes from a time of pervading emotion, and power to order it and record it. But many years later, when his power of fulfilling such an image had gone, he used this early drawing first as the basis for a picture, and then, in 1850, for his etching. "Evening," the mezzotint of 1834 (No. 142), is also likely to be a translation of early vision; it was a job given to help and keep up the respect of Welby Sherman, the weakest member of the group.

All of this—and dates, except in relation to the meaning, depth, and development of an individual art, have no point—is not as much as to say that the pictures are devoid of Palmer's moving and remarkable power. Looked at in one way, they are the pause before his power weakened and tailed away into a sensitive distinction. They are full, serene, and balanced,—words true, above all, of "Scene at Underriver" (No. 131, Plate 2), with its procession of figures moving the eye into a rich and mysterious centre, into a heart of fruitfulness. It is not mannerism, it is not anecdote. It is the form and language of nature, heightened and compressed, condensed into a completeness. And how deep and how far Palmer had mined in eight or nine years is evident when "Scene at Underriver" is compared with an early picture such as "The Repose of the Holy Family" (No. 30, Plate 9), with its palm trees out of Dürer. Less fulfilled, the two Cloud paintings—"The Bright Cloud" especially—are rare and exquisite things, and the drawing for "The White Cloud" (No. 120, Plate 57) is superlative.

For the study of Palmer's aids and nourishment "The White Cloud" sets a problem. A careful comparison of the way it is composed with Breughel's "Corn Harvest" shows resemblances too striking to be due to a kinship of vision. In both, birds flying over the corn to the left; in both, figures walking from left to right between walls of corn; in both, a tree trunk sloping out of the picture to the right, a tree firmly placed to the right of the centre, and to the right of that tree a spired church; in both (though, in Palmer, enlarged and brought forward), a high gabled barn. I have pointed to earlier affinities between Palmer and engravings after

Breughel; [14]   but in those there is no difficulty. "The Corn Harvest" was acquired by the Metropolitan Museum in 1921, and had been purchased from the Doucet sale in Paris in 1912. "Its pedigree is unknown beyond this point." [15] It is assumed to be the missing picture of the five seasons which were in the Gallery of the Archduke Leopold William, and afterwards in the Belvidere, of which two at least were carried off to Paris by the French in 1809. I have been unable to trace any engraving after "The Corn Harvest." Whether Palmer can have seen the picture or a version of it in England, or whether Richmond can have seen it and copied it for him in France in 1828 or 1829, are unanswerable questions; but the resemblance remains.

For all these cloud drawings, it is worth mentioning, there is a warrant in Milton (in *Paradise Lost*) which Palmer must have been familiar with, though I do not know that he ever quotes it:

> Why in the east
> Darkness ere day's mid-course, and morning-light
> More orient in yon western cloud, that draws
> O'er the blue firmament a radiant white,
> And slow descends, with something heavenly fraught?

"The Bright Cloud" was called by Palmer "A Rustic Scene," and it is either No. 356 of the Academy of 1833 or No. 517 of the 1834 exhibition. "The Harvest Moon" in the National Gallery (No. 130, Plate 59) can hardly, as the catalogue suggests, be "The Harvest Moon" of the 1833 Academy—a smaller picture, $8\frac{1}{2}$ by $10\frac{1}{2}$ inches, minutely described by Palmer's son.[16] The picture and the description do not tally, and the National Gallery picture is perhaps "The Gleaning Field" (R.A. 1833).

If Palmer was less receptive in these years, and drew rather from his accumulation of images, his eye was still active. The "Study of a Kentish Hop-bin" (No. 147) is dated July 7, 1834, and was certainly done at Shoreham. It is not a very compulsive drawing; but the longer note [17] analysing the colour of hop leaves, the bin clothes, the ground—"The ground much of it fine crumbly mould. There are a great many grey withered leaves about the ground & pieces of bine about the poles are quite dark" etc.—show again, like the notes around the bough of apples, how Palmer had the habit of grasping directly at natural appearances. The character of this drawing suggests that 1834 is the date of "The Shearers" (No. 139, Plate 63), painted on a heavy oaken panel. There are two undated studies (Nos. 137 and 138) for the group of instruments leaning up against the entrance to the barn, and it may bear upon the date that Henry Walter, from Shoreham, exhibited a "Boy Shearing" at the British Institution in 1834. Though rather hot and sharp in colour, this panel is still one of the most vigorous and condensed of all Palmer's Shoreham work.

I have still left out of account "A Pastoral Scene" and its attendant drawings, which we shall come to presently; and three watercolours of great loveliness. These are "The Weald of Kent" (No. 132, Plate 60), and "The Timber Waggon" (No. 133), and "The Golden Valley" (No. 134), both of which are reproduced in colour in Binyon's *Followers of William Blake*. "The Timber Waggon" and "The Weald of Kent" go obviously together. All three spring of Palmer's love of the ridge view, and all have obvious links with such pictures as "The White Cloud" and "The Bright Cloud" with their solemn pastoral processions. I should date them 1831 to 1832. The Weald, with its dark tree trunk specked with red, shows the study of lichen-jewelled trees absorbed and "naturalized"— the underlying truth replacing the particular. As in some drawings by Alexander Cozens, the spectator (more than can be realized from a reproduction) looks out through a dark frame of ground and tree trunk and foliage lapped with heavy blue into the easy light and depth of the wide landscape down below. The colours are cool and harmonious and unexpected, the effect is rich and strong, the recession into the far distance immediately arresting. It ranks high, in its visionary sense of a double image. In "The Timber Waggon," note the resemblance—I think a reminiscence—of Palmer's waggon and oxen to the timber waggon and horses of Turner's "Poole" in the *Southern Coast of England*.

III

We know that in these years, from 1832 to 1834, Palmer was ill at ease and unhappy. He was uncertain about his finances, his powers, and his future. Buying the cottages and the small house in St. John's Wood was no doubt a cautious investment, a cautious way of using the bequest that came to him, at a time when the pillars of the world seemed very shaky. Otherwise, he had only whatever few sales he might make, whatever little sums he earned by teaching, and the small income from the money left him by his grandfather. His son, who had his accounts to go by, says, "My father, towards the end of his stay at Shoreham, had discovered that 'the expenses of one person living as an epic poet should live' could be cut down to 5s. 2d. a week," and he adds that his father, to be within this limit, cut himself to a nightly allowance of one candle, which "grievously curtailed the nocturnal talks and readings." [18] He was even reduced to cleaning a portrait by Opie.[19] And whatever his views on being "an epic poet," he must have looked a bit askance at the way in which George Richmond was earning and keeping a wife, and already a child.   Richmond's sitters between 1832 and 1834 included Wilberforce, Lord Teignmouth, the Bishop of Chester, Lord Sidmouth.[20]   "Grant O Lord that I may not waste," Richmond wrote in his account book.[21]

Palmer also put down a memorandum of his shortcomings :

"Some of my faults.   *Feebleness* of first conception through bodily weakness, and consequent timidity of execution.   No first-conceived and *shapely* effect.   No rich, flat body of local colours as a ground. No first-conceived foreground, or figures.

| Whites too raw | Greens crude |
| Greys cold | Shadows purple |

RIDGES OF MOUNTAIN ALONG OPEN COUNTRY

"(1) Base the subject on a neutral-tint effect like Varley's little drawing so that at the beginning the great shapes of the lights shall be forcibly announced.   (2A) Invent at once the great masses of Local Colour, and aim at once at a splendid arrangement.   (B) Blocks of local colour before the small varieties.   (3) Carry on the drawing till real illumination be obtained.   Investigate on some simple object what are the properties of illumination and shade.   (4) If possible, complete at whatever struggle the foreground and figures at the time.   (5) Let everything be colour, and not sullied with blackness. Think of some of Titian's things, as *The Entombement*.   (6) CLEANNESS OF TINT.   Try to get something beautiful in the first design." And along with this were "records of many and elaborate experiments in oil vehicles" and "long tables relating to colours."[22]

The view from a ridge which made landscape into "the symbol of prospects brightening in futurity"[23] is something Palmer was thinking about back in 1828 (p. 74); but his concern now for colour points forward to his whole change of conviction, his apostasy to old principles, which was to follow his study of Venetian pictures when he went to Italy.   He had followed Blake in disliking the "most outrageous demon Rubens" (though there seems a Rubens-like quality of colour, in spite of himself, in some of these pictures of the early thirties), and he used to tell the story of how Samuel Rogers thrust colour at him: "'Colour is the attraction,' as the Poet Rogers bade me observe, when he was shewing me his Rubens"— colour as the "sugared spoon which will make us swallow the ideal or severe" that "as a People" we dislike.[24]   Certainly there is a crudeness of colour, a rawness of green, and a purple of shadows, in some of these late Shoreham pictures, a certain mannerism and combination of eclectic elements, an afterthought adding of figures; but his doubts went deeper than worries about cash or style. He asked himself questions about his whole view of life, his whole pursuit of the Ideal of heavenly beauty, his old desire to "bound upwards; pierce the clouds; & look over the doors of bliss." [25] It was not simply that he had decided to come back to London, that the Ideal had been rudely assaulted, and that the Jacobinical hyenas were howling in triumph among the ruins. Palmer must have met in his time many of the warnings against Enthusiasm, may well have read the popular Zimmermann on *Solitude, or The Effects of Occasional Retirement*. "Certain it is, that we owe to the spirit of enthusiasm whatever is great in art, sublime in science, or noble in the human character. . . . Who would not willingly pierce the pensive gloom, or dwell among the brighter glories of the golden age, or acquire, by a warm and glowing, but correct and chaste, contemplation of the beautiful and sublime works of nature, these ravishing sensations, and gain the noble fervour of the imagination? A proper study of the works of nature, amidst the romantic scenery of sylvan solitude, is certainly the most likely means of inspiring the mind with true enthusiasm, and leading genius to her most exalted heights; but"—and this is the *but* that Palmer had been able to disregard—"the attempt is dangerous." Zimmerman was hard on fanaticism, mysticism, and the saints. "Excluded from those social communications which nature enjoins, with no means of gratifying the understanding, amusing the senses, or interesting the affections, fancy roves at large into unknown spheres, and endeavours to find in ideal forms entertainment and delight. Angelic visions, infernal phantoms, amazing prodigies, the delusions of alchemy, the frenzies of philosophy, and the madness of metaphysics, fill the disordered brain. . . . From the prolific womb of solitude sprung all the mysterious ravings and senseless doctrines of the new Platonists." [26]

There were many other voices of prudence, many other warnings which make the bridge from romanticism to the Victorian painter's horses and carriage and butler. And one of these warnings Palmer certainly did absorb. In place of the works of "Sanctity and Ideal beauty"—he read Foster's *Essays*. "Once," he wrote as an old man looking back to his creative youth, and thinking over "the battle of life," "once I thought that I had hit it and that one should try to be a Christian bulldog. The Christian element would make it harmless, and the bulldog would come even upon the best things with the advantage of 'holding them fast.' . . . I would fain hope

H

that everyone is always 'beginning again,' and never trusting to another what he should do himself. I think I found benefit from reading Foster's essay on Decision." 27

John Foster was a Baptist. He had been a romantic himself, an early admirer of Coleridge, and before that "a nervous, gloomy, sensitive child" who shut himself up in a barn with Young's *Night Thoughts*; and his *Essays in a Series of Letters to a Friend* went into a great many editions through the century, putting down paving stones for prudence and Victorian virtue. "Yet though it is improbable that a very irresolute man can ever become an habitually decisive one, it should be observed, that as there are many degrees of determined character, and some very defective ones, it might be possible to apply a discipline which should advance a man from the first degree to the second, and from that to the third, and how much further I cannot tell; he may try." 28

Linnell was sniffing about the asses' bridge of superstition. Tatham was off with the Irvingites. Richmond was prying open the world. Calvert was veering to paganism. Finch was a Swedenborgian; Blake was dead; and Palmer had no spiritual director to support him in his nature and pass him through the next stages of vision and pilot him over the dry rocks. The new age was closing in on him. And next to the *Essay on Decision of Character* comes a thundery chapter *On the Application of the Epithet "Romantic"* which must have disturbed Palmer as he read it:

"Imagination may be indulged in till it usurp an entire ascendancy over the mind, and then every subject presented to that mind will excite imagination, instead of understanding, to work; imagination will throw its colours where the intellectual faculty ought to draw its lines; imagination will accumulate metaphors where reason ought to deduce arguments; images will take the place of thoughts, and scenes of disquisitions. The whole mind may become at length something like a hemisphere of cloud-scenery, filled with an ever-moving train of changing, melting forms, of every colour, mingled with rainbows, meteors; and an occasional gleam of pure sunlight, all vanishing away, the mental like this natural imagery, when its hour is up, without leaving anything behind it but the wish to recover the vision."

Imagination was necessary "in early life, to cause a generous expansion of the passions by giving the most lively aspect to the objects by which they ought to be interested." Imagination may even "be allowed the ascendancy in early youth," but "the case should always be reversed in mature life; and if it is not, a man should consider his mind as either unfortunately constructed, or unwisely disciplined."

Two curious and characteristic letters, written in the autumn of 1834 (Palmer was now twenty-nine), show his doubt, his isolation, and the cooling of the iron to red and milder glow. Both come from Shoreham, where (Henry Walter having gone back to London) he had no company but that of his nurse and Welby Sherman:

"The other sheet also is scribbled over. There is something about cyder which you must read directly—

OBSERVE! As this letter ran I don't know how into the subject of costiveness which is touched on in plain terms do not give it to any one to read to you if you are engaged when you get it.

My dear Sir   Shoreham Kent   Oct.ʳ 14th.   1834

As you are now become a great man I will address you on a sheet of my best writing paper, not gilt edged and delicate like yours but rather too extravant (*sic*) for me who may perhaps be composing a set of King's Bench Bucolics in the winter months.

I have to speak also upon subjects that, in the opinion of this world are two of the most important which can "disturb the passions or perplex the intellects of man"—a gentleman and a groom. Mr. Baily knows a young man son of Hoare who has been a long time in the service of Mr. Wilmott—of whom he gives the highest character for honesty civility & sobriety—who is an excellent groom & has had some experience in Farriery & would make himself generally useful in a house if required—he recommended him so strongly that I thought I would write to you as you might know somebody who wanted such a man—I should think he would be just the thing for Mr. Knyvett if he keeps a man servant—it is a melancholy thing for a very willing young man to be out of employ—*I know it by experience*, and have no club nor artists' Trade Union to fall upon—and should therefore be much obliged if as you kindly promised you would let the little mezzotint flock hang up somewhere where it can be seen as it might be of some service to Sherman or myself who are both at present pinched by a most unpoetical & unpastoral kind of poverty—I seldom taste animal food and know when I do that I am exceeding my year's supply so that tho' sweet in the mouth it turns sour on the conscience—& therefore I prefer bread and butter & apples washed down with a draught of my only luxury weak green tea which is about as cheap as bad table beer— And this brings me round to the main drift of my letter of which as it was written in tender compassion for your own & Mrs. Rich-

mond's insides I shall let you pay the postage. Know then that
you may now have from Mr. Waring's the rich farmer at Chels-
field as much of the best possible cyder undiluted and unadulterated
as you please at one shilling per gallon. Baily can buy a strong cask
cheap and if you have so little as a barrel 36 gallons, it will not
stand you in more than about fourpence pr. quart carriage & tub
included—the larger the quantity the less in proportion the price of
the tub & I suppose of the carriage. Baily says that mixed in the
glass as you drink it with an equal quantity of water it will be better
than the water cyder which Mr. Walter & I found such a delicious
& wholesome beverage at Mr. Willis's & as you have contracted by
herding with the pork-vision German students a sovereign scorn of
Hyson & Gunpowder I suppose you may want something to supply
their place. Bailey says that cyder causes a most powerful appetite
for solid food and I knew your digestive organs had not been in fine
order for a long time, I really thought it might be the very best
thing you could take. I hope you have some contrivance by this
time for getting wholesome bread—Consider what a responsibility
you incur by aluming up your childrens' entrails every day to a
wrought iron rigidity. Even occasional costiveness by hardening the
fæces which should have passed first—prevents the timely passage
of such as are in a wholesome state & renders the whole system an
alembic of excrement! But I know what people would say—Ah!
he's got some queer notions, hasn't he?—but I would rather have
queer notions than queer *motions*. While the poor soul flaps about
in the cage of the body the more open that cage is kept the better.
When one ought to have a motion and can't I always think the cage
feels sensibly more narrow—My Grandfather died at eighty-two
having a most excellent natural constitution—and the doctors said
he would have seen a hundred if he had minded his bowels. As to
taking physic it is the Crown of the art of Health: a little is quite
necessary & we should always have it by us—but diet—diet is the
thing—diet & gymnastics—Look at pregnant women sitting all day
on sofas and cushions thimbling away at babies' caps & lace trumpery
instead of bustling about the house & going to market—jammed up
in their tight stays—why doctors are obliged to physic them forever
—they are so costive & withal they can only pass slimy motions
which do them no good while the hardened & still increasing fæces
which ought to be got rid of, are as tense as a bronze cast in the
mould of their peristaltics. You may laugh at this as you like or
say it's filthy talk but it's too serious & too true.

Why there's Mrs. Baily she's so big that she looks as if she had
got the dome of St. Peter's under her apron—there she is bustling

about all day like a girl—well she'll just drop her kitten into the
basket without any caudle or parade & in a day or two be just as well
as ever again.   They used to be golden days for me when my poor
Mother was confined!   Boy-like I knew the closet where all the
diet-bread & cakes & cold boil'd chickens were kept and I took care
to be as much confined to that spot as my Mother was to her room
except when the nurse pushed me out.   Don't think I'm writing
when I ought to be painting—I'm just come from work after dark—
& have cleaned my palette etc., with scrupulosity & just scribble a
little while the tea is drawing—I am in solitude & poverty but very
fat & well & if I could but get a twenty guinea commission even if
it were to take a view of Mr. Stratton's conventicle or to draw the
anatomy of a pair of stays should be as happy as the day is long—and
feel a kind of presentiment—I hope not a false one—that Providence
will not suffer me to come into embarrasment.   I have a slowly but
steadily increasing conviction that the religion of Jesus Christ is
perfectly divine but it certainly was not only intended to be en-
throned in the understanding but enshrined in the heart for the
personal love of Christ is its beginning & end & while deeply abased
because it so slowly winds into my affections & though most unworthy
even to speak of it—yet I cannot help daily anxiety for a dear friend
of yours & mine [29] who though the most amiable & conscientious
of men—if he knew what was right & true—we have beheld now
for years remaining in deliberate hostility to the gospel of Christ—
do let us pray for him & at all seasonable opportunities not contend
with but 'perswade' him 'knowing the terrors' as well as the unspeakable mercies of our Lord—for if translated out of natural
darkness into the marvellous light of the gospel I think he would
be an ornament to the Christian profession—but alas! it seems he
cannot believe because the darkness hath blinded his heart & his
children however good they become in other respects will remain
hoodwinked in that darkness if 'Salvation' do not 'come to his
house' 'through the faith that is in Jesus Christ.'   I feel for parents
but I feel still more for poor little children who whether from the
darkness, or most cruel neglect of their natural guardians who do
believe—are kept from the nurture & admonition of the Lord, and
are brought into the world to gratify a momentary pleasure that
they may perish body & soul forever.   How fearful is the responsibility of parents: how urgent their call to set their children from the
tenderest years an example of almost sinless perfection & that not
negatively but by a positive & visible devotion of the whole household to God—by openly delighting in Him—by the seriousness of
penitance & prayer, by the merriment of Hymns & spiritual songs

with which they should be waked & lulled to sleep—and we have the blessed assurance & promise that a child brought in in the way he should go will not depart from it when old—but I am afraid that *Way* is nothing short of the devotional & openly holy life exhibited to their children by Apostles & Patriarchs & in later times by a few such devoted & affectionate parents as Sir Thomas More, whose house was as much a Church, as an academy of sublime wisdom & heroic virtue. I feel more energetic & ambitious for excellence in art than ever, but yet I hope with a more innocent & less selfish enthusiasm—our purest & best motives are sadly debased with every kind of alloy—but really a handsome income & personal influence do enable a man while sitting in his study at his daily duties to be at that very moment spreading the light of the gospel into the most distant lands. I do not think (tho' I am very likely quite wrong) that Christianity is meant to damp the spirit of enterprise or the desire of success—but certainly entirely—utterly to change its ultimate object from vile all-absorbing self to the Poor, to the Church, to the welfare, the eternal welfare, of all around us—to the promotion of the Kingdom of God, to the glory of the Lord Jesus Christ. And though the selfishness of ambition, that 'last infirmity of noble mind,' may linger for a good while after nobler things have entered the heart yet it will soon, I should hope, be absorbed like the damps of morning into the beams of the rising sun. But it is a very trying situation in which I am at present placed—wishing as soon as possible to struggle up into repute—I have not the money nor influence to do good with & I am in danger of having all my thoughts & affections absorbed into the means—but I shall endeavour to use rational means & I do not think I shall if I live send any pictures to the next exhibition smaller than kit-cats and three quarters—I hope I have already the materials for one kitcat & two—perhaps 3 three quarters and if I can but get time before the rain sets in, hope to have 2 more kitcats—where the frames are to come from I know not—I must try to hire them for the exhibition. I have heard there is in one of the late Quarterlies a very interesting article on Coleridge—it was, I think, before his death. For conclusion of Cyder subject see the other letter." [30]

The other letter was written two days later:

"Shoreham Kent Thursday 16th. Oct. 1834.

There is a long rigmarole on the other sheet *which read first.* There is something about cyder which you must read directly.

My dear Sir,

I received your kind and welcome letter the next morning after I had scribbled the foregoing, and though I believe our old friendship can subsist very long without fresh nourishment, yet you afforded it a very pleasant & nutritive meal and I took it the kinder as you sent it me from the abodes of the great, among so many alluring and attractive objects where the simple & the poor are very apt to be forgotten or despised, but be assured that there were no other ties—and there are very many that bind me to you—beside the kindness and sympathy of yourself & Mrs Richmond when crossed in love I was a nuisance to others & to myself [31]—that alone would be sufficient to fix you both in my heart which would want a very rough jerk to tumble you out of it. With respect to the studious lamp it is just what I wish and hoping to be much more beforehand than usual with my exhibition subjects shall be able to clean up the palette by dark & devote, if I live, the winter evenings to the figure —I should like to tackle two or three very fine hands and feet & to dissect an arm—first finishing the old bust if ever we can manage to get it quite in the right height & position again. I thirst vehemently for your legend of the Rhine & hope to hear it elaborately wiredrawn over six large bowls of Hyson which I am glad to hear you have not learned to despise as I feared. Mr. Calvert told me something about the skies there, which has set me all agape. If you were only to put down in your memorandum book the names of places at which you arrived each day before you forget them, it might help you to keep in mind some of the minutiæ which may perhaps slip the memory and I should like to hear an eight hours' description at least. I would not have been without the Devonshire reminiscences on any account—I hardly ever try to invent landscape without thinking of them. You may go for five shillings now by the steamboat to Plymouth, close to the cluster of little rivers, that fall from Dartmoor, and see the wonderful Titian etc.—not as a deck passenger as I heard before—but lie on a sofa in the cabin & vomit quite genteelly! I long to see some first rate distances—& hope you have brought a line or two of some of the quaint rocky or wooded summits of the Rhine. I believe in my very heart (but the heart's a great liar tho' it's the truest part about us) that all the very finest original pictures & the topping things in nature have a certain quaintness by which they partly affect us—not the quaintness of bungling—the queer doing of a common thought—but a curiousness in their beauty—a salt on their tails by which the imagination catches hold on them while the sublime eagles & big birds of the French academy fly up far beyond the sphere of our affections—One of the very deepest sayings I have met with in Ld. Bacon seems to me to be 'There is no excellent beauty without some strangeness in the proportion' The sleeping Mercury in the B. Museum has this hard-to-be-defined but most delicious quality to perfection so have the best Antique jems & bas reliefs & statues—so have *not* the Elgin Marbles graceful as they are, but it is continually flashing out in nature & in nothing more than in the beamings of beautiful countenances. But I begin now to be quite humbled & to speak of all things as modestly as an impudent man can speak. Every day convinces me with wise & good Dr. Johnson that this life is a state in which 'much is to be done & little to be known'—and what is known is apprehended by doing—and whatever *is* done is wrung out of idle fallen wretched man by necessity immediate or foreseen—& what is done at leisure is done wrong & whatever is done best, is done when there is hardly time given to do it in—talk of putting thistles under donkeys' tails to make them go! why *man*, imperial Man, unless he sits upon thorns will sit still forever. Dr. Johnson would scarce have written anything if he had not been hard driven by want—and as to Milton he had plenty of other business which he was obliged to attend to, and most likely came to poetry etc. as a relaxation—and as to artists who paint to please themselves—perhaps they would get thro' ten times as much work & improve thirtyfold—if they were forced to sit half a day behind a desk in the custom house. Happy the artist who has half his time bespoke in commissions, & half to paint what he loves—I intend if I live to keep the lower Port Royal cell [32] neat all the winter & work upstairs, and perhaps knock down the partition—& carefully exclude every inch of prospect from the window as I purpose never again to see London by daylight when I can help it—though I would gladly visit the great national dust hole once more if it were only to enjoy the grand Rhenish tea festival: and at that celestial assembly Mrs. Richmond our fair Hebe will want every particle of her present health & spirits to bear the task of dealing about bowl after bowl of the Oriental Nectar to the Gothic Mythology which will surround her. I am very glad to hear of poor Bolls' improvement,[33] & of the Chevalier New-come whose melodies when agitated by the poetic fury are I daresay become by this time remarkably sonorous. You shall see my body as soon as I come to town—but as to my poor mind I have been vegetating so long in solitude that I hardly know whether I've any left.

Mr. Baily was told this evening that Mr. Warings stock of apples for cyder are this year remarkably fine indeed. R. B. says it is good to drink directly and he likes it best quite new—though I suppose it cannot be so spirituous as afterwards—I have written to my Father & to Mr. Linnell & Mr. Calvert about it & I hope they will not lose the opportunity—if you all want some, one message will do sent to Bailey at the White Hart Inn, Boro', before ten o'clock next Thursday morn^g, stating the respective quantities and with the accurate directions where each is to be sent, inclosing for R. Bailey the price of the several quantities & about ten shillings extra upon each for cask & carriage—N.B. all the money for cyder—tub etc.—should be inclosed & sealed directed to *me* who will pay Bailey when I hear of its safe arrival—there must be an *order very accurate* given to R. B. to make him responsible—but there should also be a duplicate inclosed for me in the money parcel—there can be none had without sending cash as I have none. Please to be very particular to give my love to Mr. Walter & inform him of every particular relative to the cyder—as I think it very likely he may wish to have some—and had he not the opportunity of knowing about it by this letter I should have taken great care to let him know of it separately—Give my kindest remembrances to Mrs. Richmond & love to Bols—the Chevalier is too young to remember me—Monday 20th. OBSERVE! OBSERVE! Please not to go to sleep over the fag end of this letter for the best comes last I have just heard (it came from Mr. Waring himself) that the expense of the cyder will be NINE PENCE instead of one shilling per Gallon—apples & pressing— So that the whole price when tub & carriage are paid for will be about Three pence & *not* Four pence pr. Quart—& if you like to lay in a good stock for family consumption & have in several smaller barrels, ONE PIPE of it, it will only take three men one day's work to press it at half-a-crown each—wages—The apples at one shilling & sixpence pr bushel—one bushel makes about three gallons of cyder—and you may have as many bushels as you like at that price brought with the cyder if you please, to make pies & puddings of—Being threshed & not gather'd by hand they will not keep very long but they will keep a month I believe— and I should advise you to give your poor bowels a month's opening with roasted apples—instead of all those pills and filthy trash which you now twist them about with. One of the Shoreham Farmers is going to have a very large quantity of this cyder from Mr. Waring's to give his labourers while at work instead of table beer, it is so cheap—if you want any cyder or apples & cannot send by Thursday morning to the Boro' you may send a parcel containing the instructions & money to the George Inn, Boro' on Saturday Morn^g before ten o'clock & have it book'd & directed for me by R. Foreman Carrier & if possible have it put into Robert Foreman's hands but without telling him anything about the cyder

I remain   My dear Sir

Yours most aff<u>ty</u>

Samuel Palmer." [34]

The change in Palmer had so far been gradual and cumulative; —"a more innocent & less selfish enthusiasm" marks what was happening. There was a lessening of his visionary power, but Palmer was clearly uneasy about the other demands of prudence and the world. He had drawn out—probably at this time in this process of arguing with himself—"a diagram showing in the form of a tree the respective claims of the Poetic, the Rational, the Scientific, and the Prudential aspects of life." [35]   But his painting of 1834 and 1835 was still in the Shoreham mould. His mention in the second of these two letters to Richmond of the Devonshire reminiscences is a bit puzzling. Richmond and his wife had taken their first holiday together, in company with Henry Walter, in Devonshire, two years before, in 1832; [36] and Palmer must mean the descriptions which Richmond and Walter had given him of Devon; yet between this time and the week before the sending-in day for the 1833 Academy, Palmer himself must have made his own first journey to North Devon. The Academy took two pictures, "The Cornfield" and "Scene from Lee, North Devon," and one or other of these is likely to have been identical with the "Pastoral Scene" (No. 156, Plate 66), now in the Ashmolean. It is Shoreham-like, but to a Shoreham cornfield, and a pastoral Shoreham foreground, and a moonlit Shoreham twilight, he had added North Devon rocks, a North Devon coomb with the deep purple shadows of those coombs below Exmoor, and a vista of blue sea. It agrees very much with the nature of the high and heaped-up and wooded coast around Lee Abbey, west of Lynmouth; and there exist Palmer drawings, perhaps made on the same journey, of the tower on the cliff-top at Lee Abbey. It is the only traceable work (besides the small companion drawings, Nos. 154 and 155) which can with some certainty be given to this final moment of his Shoreham life. In the British Institution (where he had had five exhibits in 1834) he showed in 1835, "A Scene from Shoreham, Kent," "At Filston Farm, Kent," "The Lane Side," and "The Cottage Window," and at the Society of British Artists in 1836 an oil, which he named "The Hop Pickers."

CHAPTER VII

AFTER SHOREHAM

I

SHOREHAM, in effect, was now over; and this study of Palmer's early years covers only his development up to the age of thirty, his climb to a point of intuition and power as an artist which he never reached again in the forty-six years that he had to live. But the dwindling and close of his effective, realized idealism needs to be clarified by showing what in fact he did become. Up to 1835, as I have said, the change was gradual. Then, after his Devonshire journey, after his determination to "struggle up into repute," the change in his style was quick and obvious, although the clinching step did not take place until after his marriage in 1837 and his hard-working honeymoon visit to Italy. After the beginning of 1835, he still disliked the necessity, as he now saw it, of settling in London; but he made two more departures from the rich pastoral scenery of his Kentish vision. It was as if his Shoreham lode had been worked out, as if, in his words, he wanted new "materials of imagination." And by steamer from London, in the summer of 1835, he went off to North Wales, with Henry Walter.[1] On the way back, he enjoyed the Gothic luxury of stopping at Tintern Abbey, and drawing it. He and Walter were stranded there without enough money to get back to London. So he wrote off to Richmond:

"Tintern   Very deep Twilight   Wednesday August 19th, 1835.

The address for letter is to us at Mr. William Hiscock's—Black Lion, Tintern Abbey, Monmouthshire.

My dear Sir,
Our Ossian Sublimities are ended—and with a little more of McPherson's mist & vapour we should have had much more successful sketching—but unfortunately when we were near Snowdon we had white light days on which we could count the stubbs & stones ome miles off—we had just a glimpse or two one day through the hasms of stormy cloud which was sublime—however we have this vening got into a nook for which I would give all the Welch mountains grand as they are & if you & Mrs. Richmond could but spare

a *week* you might see Tintern & be back again. The Bristol Stages start daily, the fare I believe is low & there is a steam boat daily thence (only three hours' passage) to Chepstow within 6 miles I think of the Abbey—& such an Abbey! the lightest Gothic—trellised with ivy & rising from a wilderness of orchards—& set like a gem amongst the folding of woody hills—hard by I saw a man this evening literally 'sitting under his own fig tree' whose broad leaves mixed with holyoaks & other rustic garden flowers embower'd his porch. Do pray come—we have a lodging with very nice people under the walls & three centuries ago might have been lulled with Gregorian Vespers & waked by the Complin to sleep again more sweetly—but the murderer of More & Fisher has reduced it to the silence of a Friends' meeting house. Mr. Walter was shown the inside & says it is superb. After my pastoral has had a month's stretching into epic I feel here a most grateful relaxation & am become once more a pure quaint crinkle-crankle Goth—If you are a Goth come hither, if you're a pure Greek take a cab & make a sketch of St. Paul's Covent Garden before Breakfast. Addison speaks of the Cathedral of Sienna (one of the richest in the world) as the work of barbarians—clever savages almost—what a 'Spectator' —he could not bear too *lofty* & *pointed* a style—pity he died before the œra of Doric watchhouses, Ionic turnpike gates & Corinthian ginshops!—his taste outran his age—ours hobbles after—

Thursday Even^g Poetic vapours have subsided and the sad realities of life blot the field of vision—the burthen of the theme is a heavy one. I have not cash enough to carry me to London—O miserable poverty! how it wipes off the bloom from everything around me. Had I conceived how much it would cost I would as soon have started for the United States as Wales—but I have worked hard—seen grand novelties & enlarged the materials of imagination—if I could but sell a picture or clean another Opie or two or— but I am all in the dumps 'shut up & cannot come forth' & feel as if I alone of all mankind were fated to get no bread by the sweat of my brow—to 'toil in the fire for very vanity'—If you've a mangy cat to drown, christen it 'Palmer'——If you could oblige me by the farther loan of three pounds my Father will repay you I dare say if you can call at Grove St.—but I shall very soon be in town myself only—I want enough both to bring me home & enable me to stay a little longer in case I should find subjects which it would be short-sighted policy not to secure—but I hope not to spend so much—If the Movement Party want a professor of drawing in the Marylebone Charity Schools pray canvas for me. Things are come to a crisis now & I must begin to earn money immediately or get embarrassed

—horrid prospect—the anxieties of debt on the back of the perturbations of aspiring studies. The refuge I know is in Faith & Prayer—but is daily bread promised to those who over-spend their income—which I am afraid is now my case—however I was deceived by the strange mistatements about cheap living in Wales—otherwise my muse should have donkeyfied upon thistles from Husky Hampstead this summer—with a log at her leg. Well! I must come to London sell my pianoforte & all my nice old books—& paint the sun moon and seven stars upon a signboard I suppose——would I could get it to do! I find I am writing strange stuff & boring you with my own selfish troubles so I'll have done. If you can favour me with the three pounds would you have the farther kindness to send it as soon as possible and with a very full & legible direction on the letter—what if it should miscarry! I must stay at Tintern & go to plough——could you send by return of post? The candle is going out as did the light of my mind some hours ago so I must wish you miserably good night.

Mr. Walter desires me to give his love & say that he wishes to return directly but not having the means would be obliged if you would make it up a Five Pound Note—I will pay the postage of this when I see you—

With kindest love to Mrs. Richmond and such old friends as you may happen to see I remain
My dear Sir
Your affectionate friend
Samuel Palmer." [2]

And to this, reading it over in his old age, George Richmond has added, "How sad to think that at 30 my dearest friend should be struggling to earn a few pounds in the year unsuccessfully." It has been suggested that Henry Walter's drawing of Samuel Palmer sitting on a chair in hat and coat and muffler [3] was made during this journey. He still has longish hair, but a clipped, close beard and a slight moustache. But the face has aged, and changed much from the Dürer-like visionary of George Richmond's miniature, six years before.

In 1836 Palmer went off again to North Wales; and by this time there is little doubt that he had finally uprooted himself from Shoreham and settled with Mary Ward, his nurse, now an old woman, in the house in Grove Street. On this second journey he went with Edward Calvert; and as usual wrote to the Richmonds. It is a less miserable letter, referring as usual to Sir Thomas More, whose life had now for several years been one of the stays and springs of his existence. The handwriting is firmer and more assured:

> "At Mrs. John Davies's   Coach & Horses   Conway   North Wales.
>   Tuesday   June 5th.   1836.

MY dear Mr. & Mrs. Richmond

It is the 'witching' & the soothing time of night, when the traveller's remembrance turns to those he loves. All is solitude & utter stillness, except the fall of a mountain stream, & the ticking of a clock: and to such an accompaniment the heart may utter its full music. Mine, however, you will call a cracked fiddle, not have (*sic*) heard from me yet; but a real Cremona it still is, I assure you, in matters of love & friendship—though my artistical part, my poor mind, in the process of excentricity—cleaning Nature should serve as the housemaid did her master's violin one morning—scrub off the tone of a century, & so fetch a pot lid out of the shield of Scriblerus. My sufferings are like those of the 'Friends'—'considerable.' I am walked & scorched to death, & have then to make living pictures of dead nature. I regale on heating eggs & horny ham; the stove within me rages, having fuel from within & without; consuming all vain partiality for socks or shirts, of which last I convince the good people that I have one to my back by leaving it in my bedroom. To get the means however of obtaining some new ones should I take to wearing these out I must be up betimes in the morning, & so wish you both good night.

Even^g 2nd.—I have just received a letter which has put me in good spirits. O what gracious people you married ones ought to be! —Youthful passions at rest—mutual good example & most sage counsel—participation of prosperity—sympathy in adversity, & sugar'd sweet tempers. And then, the 'dear pledges'—'Good night dear Papa!' 'Good night dear Mamma!'—just before they cuff & scratch the nursery maid all the way up stairs, and kick over the basin as she washes them. 'Speak! ye whom the sudden tear surprises oft.' As Mr. Calvert & I walked through a romantic dell we saw a very young Welsh Girl of more than ordinary beauty, & loveliness of expression—her features were softened with that delicate shade of pensiveness &c. &c.—She timidly approached, & offered, I think for sale, a large winged beetle not yet impaled on a pin, but girt with packthread: it was taken away from her & let fly to her astonishment. O for a safe passage to that World where undivorced beauty shall ever be the form & index of goodness—O for a heart with none of the girl & beetle in it though perhaps she knew no harm—& the best men will only glance at the evil—except of their

wn hearts—but study and contemplate what is good. Yet we are
f a bad stock after all—we went astray from the cradle, speaking
ies—killed flies at church, & came home telling where the text
vas. See therefore the worst of your children as they grow up,
e yourselves not the censors but the caterers of their pleasures.
Vhile it is their pleasure to romp, romp with them, & whip them
or vice & disobedience. I am glad when I think of your children
—dear friends of mine I hope some day—to know that you both
ave the good sense to despise the super Bible, super Solomon,
tupid, twaddling sentimentality—the French Revolution philan-
hropy which would disuse the Rod. I agree with you that con-
inued beating is barbarous & ought to be bestowed on the parents
hemselves who have managed clumsily enough to find it needful:—
ut depend upon it, fear, of one kind or other, as well as hope is
ecessary to move either adults or babes to effective wisdom &
oodness. With sunshine before, & a thunder cloud behind, we
ake way. I believe the dread of ultimate bodily correction is the
nly real bugbear to children—while on the other hand are the
leasures & holidays which may be made for them; nay, by great
kill, even their learning may be given them in sugar—The right
and may shower indulgence if the left hand hold the rod—but the
arents who will not correct their children always become their
aves or their dupes. And now that I am hortatory I hope you,
ir, take care to cater for yourself after your professional labours a
oothing evening, something to look forward to through the day—
nd you, Madam, take a basket & go to market & buy a skipping
ope & be jocund & don't think of the 'thirty one.' It is a good
hile since I tried my hand at a bit of twilight poetry;—but here
oes—

Evening

'Then evening comes at last, serene & mild'—THOMSON.

Dedicated to George Richmond Esqre.

When each has been working all day like a horse,
And Master looks crusty and Mistress looks cross;
He combing his mind, & she knitting her stockings;
The door beat with craftsmen & carpenter's knockings,
And the maids in & out, & the candles want snuffing,
And Babbington's come from his errands all puffing:—
Then vow you'll not stand it; but get out your Handel;
And a kind friend will call in & give you some scandal:
When gone, get your Jebb & your Knoxy [4] so deep,
And quiet at last,—you will fall fast asleep.

Then Mistress will pinch you, & say 'At least when
'Mister Palmer's not here, you might chain up at ten:
'And *I* know some persons who'd beg him to go
'At half after nine, let him like it or no!'
You rise, with a yawn that would swallow an ox;
And leisurely lengthen the latches & locks:
When Hark!—A low tapping at which your heart fails
'You're the first friend I've called on since come from North Wales'
Then some Art, & some gossip, & free will & fate
Will sweetly refresh you for 'sitters at eight.'

Even.g 3d   I hope you have secured the proposed Saturday for
favorite studies: I think it would improve your health and spirits
beside the intellectual solace & profit.   How many blessings does the
future promise!   How do the present & the past belie it.   How
beautifully & usefully may the hours of the day be parcelled out
even in a moderate & sober plan of life: but an allowance must be
made for accidents & ugly etceteras.   However, if the leading
points of a good scheme be generally secured, it will be more than
one in a thousand is able to accomplish; so few have any plan ata
(*sic*); or see the two or three leading advantages which are worth
securing at almost any cost.   How does all animate & inanimate
creation, all the range of high arts & exquisite sciences proclaim
the immortality of the soul, by exciting—as they were intended to
excite—large longings after wisdom & blessedness which three score
or three hundred years would be too short to realize.   We are the
chrysalis dreaming of its wings!   The simplest division of our time
seems to me to be into a portion first for Religion, & its fruit active
benevolence: next for business: thirdly for bodily exercise;   &
lastly for soothing intellectual recreation.   It would be well if Christians in easy circumstances divided the poor of the neighbourhood
among them, & had each a little circle of sick & indigent to visit by
turns; say one every day.   This with other walking might be done
in an hour, & would secure the arrangement for bodily exercise.
There are visiting societies, I believe, belonging to some of our
churches, which enter the lowest haunts of wretchedness:—but
there is many a fine modern Christian who would have stopped his
nose at poor Lazarus.   Combination will do very much at the expense
of very little individual labour.   I am inclined to think that the
happiest hours of many people are those in which they work at
their calling: and if recreation itself were something both useful &
necessary, & not a mere hulling about, & kicking of one's shins, it
would be much more effectual relaxation than it usually is.

I should think the amusements of Sir Thomas More & his family
were, beside bodily exercise, little other than changes from the sever-

o the elegant studies, or still more lovely charities. O! blessed biography which hast embalmed a few of the graces of so many great
& good people! Perhaps to those who are in earnest for improvement no literature is so useful. Principles & precepts are the
grammar of morality—example is its eloquence. Though I have
often talked of the importance of quiet intellectual evenings to those
who are fagged in the day, & though I think them a delicious &
never-cloying luxury, yet I do not mean that we should make
pleasure of any sort the aim of life: on the contrary, as things are
so constituted that every little self denial & agonizing brings after
it "a sacred & home-felt delight," so on the large scale our whole
earthly existence ought to be a short agony to secure eternal blessedness. But as in a long sultry walk we choose our shade places now
& then, to sit down in, so I think none will agonize so effectually as
those who take the mental bath & balsam of a little daily leisure.
Blessed thoughts & visions haunt the stillness & twilight of the soul;
& one of the great arts of life is the manufacturing of this stillness.
The middle station of life, where more is demanded to be done than
there are hands enough quietly to do, almost forbids it; & the rooms
of our houses are so crowded together that we less enjoy life than
listen to the noise of its machinery. It is like living in a great Mill
where no one can hear himself speak. So I think the fewer wheels
the better——but what matters how I think—who am mad on this
subject?—Mad I mean to be till I get more light, & wherever I find
it will turn to it like the sunflower. For obstinate though I may have
been in trifles—much to my shame—I am not stubborn about
greater matters, but like a little babe crying out for food—for which
I expect kicks & buffets. However I am prepared; and with a
body & mind pretty well adapted, so far as that is concerned, to get
through life with—oil outside, & adamant within: but I hope less
& less oil of vitriol every day of my life.

I have not seen a paper, but suppose things are going on as
they have been for some time: occasional reform of real abuses,
accompanied, as good & evil always tangle together in this world,
with a gradual demolition of institutions which Englishmen ought
to hold sacred. Jews, Turks, Infidels & Heretics have broken down
the walls of bigotry, & I suppose will soon be throwing the stones at
each other. In the mean time, as long as the still small voice of
friendship can be heard—with kind love to Mr. Walter believe
me Dear Mr. & Mrs. Richmond

Ever your affectionate friend, Samuel Palmer.

Though I should delight to hear from you I know your time

I

is so occupied that I ought scarcely to expect it but if an opportunity offers a letter put into the post not later than two days after
you get this will find me

at Mr. John Davies's
Coach & Horses
Conway
North Wales.

I have been hindered altogether about three weeks by rain but
hope the weather is now more settled." [5]

But that letter is not the only evidence of Palmer's activities in
Wales. He was still in Wales in August and fell in with two other
tourists, Crabb Robinson and his friend Masquerier the portrait-
painter. Here is Crabb Robinson's description of the meeting from
the note-book in which he recorded his Welsh journey:

"Aug. 4 1836.

"This was one of the best days of my journey and reminded
me of my travelling in early times—I arose and was on my way at
$\frac{1}{2}$ p 7 and at 9 had reached the small house at Dol y Melynllyn where
is one of the three famous cataracts of this vicinity—Telling the
landlord that I had heard of this house from a painter whose person
I described, he said—he is now in the house, would you like to
breakfast with him—I at once acceded and this led to one of the
most agreeable incidents or rather the most agreeable incident of
the journey—M[asquerier] had fallen in with this pedestrian tourist,
making sketches and had conceived a low opinion of him as an
artist—I was pleased with his appearance on our return from Llan-
berris, and had alighted from the car, to give M: an opportunity of
inviting him to ride the last two miles—For this good nature on my
part I have been rewarded—After our breakfast the yet unknown
artist, whose eye of deep feeling and very capacious forehead had
inspired me to predilections for him, prepared to set out to one of
the waterfalls I had come to see, I Proposed to accompany him and
so an acquaintance was formed. He incidentally spoke of Blake as
the greatest genius in art of modern times tho' little known—This
made me more interested in him—I spoke at length of Blake and
my acquaintance with him, and soon satisfied him, that in calling
B *insane* I was not repeating the commonplace declamation against
him. He at length yielded to my statement—Tho' he at first tried
to maintain that in asserting the actuality of spirits he was but giving
personality to ideas as Plato had done before. On my mentioning
my name he said he had heard of me both from Blake and his

wife—I found too that he had been to see Mr. Aders pictures [6] and had heard of Gotzenberger.[7]

I enquired whether *Linnel* is not a man of worldly wisdom—He understood the insinuation and said, only *defensively* and he represented Linnels conduct as having been very generous towards Blake. This is contrary to my impression concerning L: [8] Palmer, for so he named himself, is also acquainted with *Daniell* who he says did him a service in showing some of his sketches to Mr. Boddington who bought them—I was so much pleased with Mr. P: that I mean to buy of him a sketch of Pistl y Cayne to which we went by the road on the left bank of the Maw which we crossed by the white footbridge I crossed the day before. It was a new way even to P: and we therefore entangled ourselves in a forest, but the mountain torrent afforded us great pleasure. In less than two hours we came to the waterfall Rhaiadyr y Mawddach which is a double and very fine one especially on the South side on which we were—Above the fall is a bridge—We crossed it and after looking at the fall on this side we came to the spout of the Cayne, a single lofty and most elegant fall which I left Mr. P: to take a sketch of, which I mean hereafter to buy. He has promised to call on me. I left him at one." [9]

Palmer did indeed call on Crabb Robinson in November 1836, and Robinson bought for ten guineas "A waterfall with a distant view of Snowden" noting in his journal that Daniell "seems to have a very high opinion of P: and I am very desirous of rendering him a service." Daniell was the distinguished amateur artist, the Rev. E. T. Daniell, at this time curate of St. Mark's, North Audley Street. He was a year younger than Palmer, who had probably known him, through Linnell, since early days at Shoreham. When Daniell was still at Oxford, Linnell had infected him with Blake. He had fallen, so he wrote to Linnell in 1826, "into a violent fit" about Blake's Job engravings, and had persuaded Parker, the Oxford bookseller, to order a set (which Parker could find no one to buy); and later he took lessons from Linnell, who painted him, and whose pictures he bought.[10] Palmer saw much of Crabb Robinson. They spent an evening together in December of the same year, "looking over the Churchyard of Pisa fresco engravings," and Robinson noted, "He pleases me as much as ever tho' he is merely a man of amiable feeling and probably genius for the arts"—continuing a bit more severely, "He is so much behind on moral subjects as to disapprove of the repeal of the Corporation & Test Act! He believes in witchcraft." [11]

Of Palmer's waterfall drawings I have seen one only—a sketch, a slight note in watercolour and black chalk, on buff paper, of Pistil Mawddach, done on his first journey into Wales in 1835,[12] and one of the studies for the "Pistil Mawddach, near Pistil-y-Cain, North Wales," a watercolour in the Academy of 1836, and also, it seems, at the Society of British Artists in the same year; where it accompanied his "Hop Pickers" and a watercolour of "Trefriew Mill, on the Road from Bettws y Coed to Conway, North Wales," drawn on the spot." In 1836, too, he exhibited a "Rhyd Dhu, or the Black Waterfall nr. Dolgelle, N. Wales" at the British Institution; and in 1837 a "Pistil-y-Cain, North Wales" both at the Academy and at the British Institution, together with two other Welsh subjects at the Academy. Another waterfall subject was Rhaiadyr-y-Wenol. But enough of his Welsh work is visible to enable its character and Palmer's change of style to be understood; and the change can be seen in the two drawings reproduced. One of these he made at Tintern in 1835, of a fig tree and cottage (see p. 124); a gentle, delicate watercolour with a gentle charm of sub-dued colour, now in the Ashmolean (Plate 68). The other, the "Mount Siabod" (Plate 67) has more dash, and a harmony of gentle greens and browns, and the distant blue peak. Another, "Llyn Gwinedd & part of Llyn-y-ddinas between Capel Curig & Beddgelert, N. Wales," is a strong, sweeping, cool watercolour of a great mountain valley, blue mountains, and brown mountains touched with green, stormy dark clouds overhead, and a blue river winding in the foreground. It is a panorama finely conceived as at one blow, cool and sombrely harmonious.[13] The tufted solidity, the double vision have both vanished. Instead, a *personal* landscape, struck out in a quick, masterly way, but embodying, as Constable's pictures so often do, a human, individual mood, a sense of uneasiness and disturbance. The colours, in these Welsh drawings, have quietened; and the excellence of the work is more in keeping with the norm of nineteenth-century watercolour: it must not be judged by the criterion of the Shoreham idealities. These watercolours show a direct, untainted grasp of nature, but they are nature without paradise, and they are what Palmer was in a later habit of calling "a batch of imitation," material to be worked up. A number of his Italian drawings—in fact, a good many of his later "batches of imitation" up to the fifties—were in the same key; and had Palmer been content with this direct interpretation, had he not wanted always to rise beyond this honesty to an idealism which he could no longer fulfil, we might have been spared all these hot watercolours, those elaborations in a Copley Fielding and Birket Foster idiom, which seem to us so false.

II

Palmer at least had some encouragement in 1836 and 1837. Daniell was a friend of influence and wealth, a member of the Athenaeum, with a wide acquaintance. Crabb Robinson, liking Palmer, also found his waterfall subject "a beautiful drawing independently of the inducement to buy from personal consideration;" [14] and helped him by interesting other people in his work. "As I believe you take a very kind interest in my welfare," Palmer wrote to a friend in 1837, "I will tell you what has been my manner of life since we met, at the risk of egoism. I have foresworn other loves and devoted myself exclusively to my Art—have made two long tours in Wales which have been the means of making me some useful connections, and what I value much more, of laying the foundation, I hope, of solid attainments. Meanwhile the cranium becomes stuffed with gallipots and varnishes; the blessed winter-evening talks are curtailed; and with the exception now and then, of a whole play of Shakespeare at a gulp and now and then your favourite *Christabel*, matters go on much more prosily and orderly.

"It is very much easier to give vent to the romantic by speech than to get it all the way down from the brain to the fingers' ends, and then squeeze it out upon canvas. However, I should be sadly grieved to forswear all the nice, long, old-fashioned talks . . . and know of no one with whom I should more enjoy a revival of them than with yourself. The little knot of friends remain united as you left them, only, if possible, more closely cemented than ever. We talk, now and then, of old times and wish you were with us; which desire, no one feels more sincerely than, my dear Sir, Yours faithfully and affectionately, SAMUEL PALMER." [15]

But 1837 was Palmer's fatal year. His nurse and foster mother, who had been with him since he was a baby, died: "Jany–18–1837 at about ¼ past 4 I asked Mary Ward to bid God bless me—& to kiss me (as I kissed her) she said 'May the Lord bless you forever & ever' & kissed me quickly several times on the cheek though so exhausted—my Brother William asked her to bless him & kiss him —& she said 'May the Lord God Almighty & Jesus Christ'—here her voice failed—& she kissed him on the cheek—

"My dear Nurse & most faithful servant & friend Mary Ward died at 5 minutes to five o'clock 18th Jany 1837 the same day of the same month on which my Mother died confined to bed 11 days." [16]

Mary Ward's death no doubt helped him to a decision. In

February he had been thinking of another waterfall tour. He had gone round to see Crabb Robinson: "Feb. 20 1837. I had calls— *Palmer* the painter to enquire about Westmoreland waterfalls." But now he thought about two things—marriage and Italy. His brother William had been a liability and a failure without talent or determination, but he was safely dealt with by July, when he was made an attendant on the Greek and Roman side of the Department of Antiquities at the British Museum.[17] On September 30, 1838, Palmer married Linnell's eldest child Hannah, in the registry office in Marylebone, with Calvert and Richmond as witnesses.[18] The civil marriage was insisted upon by John Linnell, and a fortnight later Palmer and his wife and the Richmonds were in France on their way to Paris and Italy.

III

Both Italy and marriage were fatal. Wiser artists resisted that Italian bait. Delacroix never went to Italy, wishing to keep the purity of his own style. Constable, no doubt deliberately, did not go to see the great Italians. Turner went, but, after a bad moment or two, continued to be Turner. Brought up on the lessons of Blake and Fuseli and Flaxman and the Ideal, full of the Italian visions of Claude, expectant of all the grandeur of the Sistine Chapel, and anxious to continue his climb into repute, Palmer set off from England ready to accept, worship, copy, and slave. He was amazed by the brilliance of Italy, and possessed by his new experience of the Venetian landscape painters.

It is not so easy for us to understand how fatal such trips could be into sharp light and Old Masterland. Our painting since Seurat has been one, on the whole, of shape and surface, not of degrees of atmosphere. A "composition" can be as well devised in a Euston Road fog as in a French olive orchard. The lighting of a dream or an episode in the womb does not owe much to local peculiarities of sunlight; and what Sickert once called "the roofy school of Collioure and Fitzroy Street" has dealt more in the generalized (and rather dull) ordering of tiles and walls than with aerial subtlety. But Palmer's light, moonlight, or twilight, or the flush on the summit, or the wet light of Welsh valleys, the light of Constable or Cotman, or the light of Caspar David Friedrich, was the northern light to which they were habituated and through which they knew how to express their vision.[19] Italian light and colour, however justified by too much veneration for holy ground and by the nineteenth-century yearning to be scientific and "accurate," were alien

to Palmer; and in 1839 he wrote to Richmond from Florence: "I
have been lately wholly absorbed in Meditation or study of the
ancient art of Landscape as practised by Titian, Giorgione etc., &
am scarcely able to think of anything else—it has worked or is
working a complete renovation of my tastes & habits of thought—&
appears to me so uncongenial with the most talented efforts of
English art—clever as they are, that I am really afraid to come
within the seducing atmosphere of living talent—knowing by
experience its exciting & intoxicating influence." [20]

He came back after the Richmonds, having suffered from being
snubbed and neglected, while the Richmonds had mixed with Gladstone and Manning, as well as everyone of an older generation of
importance in Florence and in Rome; and then began that long
series of pastoral subjects in a mixed manner of Italian light,
Venetian colour, and English-cum-Italian scenery with which Palmer
tried the tumbler's job of being true to himself, to his past, to Italy,
and to the market.

And he suffered also from being Linnell's son-in-law, personally,
and probably also professionally. The Linnell with whom Blake
chose to be friendly and the Linnell whose daughter Palmer married
must have changed. Linnell was determined, able, and invincibly
quarrelsome. Detested by other artists, he was hated by few more
than by Constable, who never concealed his loathing for him in his
unexpurgated letters to Leslie. He was never elected to the Royal
Academy, simply because of his hard and prickly eccentricity, a
certain malignancy in his character mixed with greed and religious
fanaticism. He ruled his family like Jehovah, and determined also
to rule his son-in-law, and surrender no control over his daughter
or over his daughter's mind. He gave Palmer shrewd and encouraging advice by letter when Palmer felt himself cold-shouldered in
Rome; [21] but what Palmer's son calls his "parade of dreadful
religion" soon enough began to weigh on Palmer after his return
to London. He pried into Palmer's affairs. "My dear Sir," John
Giles had to write to him on one occasion, "You have no right to
ask me any questions about Mr. Palmer's affairs, and if I had done
as I ought I should not have answered you, but I was induced to
answer you, from your saying 'Secrecy will be the worse for Mr.
Palmer.'" [22] Disagreement merged into what A. H. Palmer called
"implacable hostility," years in which Palmer was "reviled and
insulted," and called derisively and malignantly "the Jesuit" or
"the Puseyite," because of his modest leanings now, in a mild way,
towards High Church.

"After the Shoreham and Italian periods, the whole of my

father's life became a dreadful tragedy," A. H. Palmer wrote; [23] and in another letter: "Linnell's life was more like that of a mental pugilist, he cared not who he attacked, feared no enemy and bore very little spite. Peace he never attained to; either spiritual or otherwise. I knew the whole family intimately . . . and I can vouch for the fact that the incessant warfare between its members has been underestimated." [24] "On my maternal grandfather, sickness, nigh unto death, of children, and bereavement, made no impression whatever. His journal shows that he hardly ever lost an hour's work on such occasions—He derided those who did show feeling. He was in the room when my father was taken by the doctor from his dead son's side—taken at once far away. Linnell did his utmost to persuade my mother to leave the lad to be buried by strangers— to leave the arrangements to chance. . . . He quoted his favourite words 'Let the dead bury their dead.'" [25]

There is little doubt that A. H. Palmer was not exaggerating— there are, as I have said, too many other independent, if guarded, expressions of distaste for Linnell—not exaggerating when he compared Linnell's household to the household of the Brontës and Linnell himself to the asylum doctor in Charles Reade's *Hard Cash*, whose "turn of mind cooperating with his interests, led him to put down any man a lunatic, whose intellect was manifestly superior to his own." And there is a sentence in *Hard Cash* which fits Palmer's marriage into the family: "The tenacity of a private lunatic asylum is unique. A little push behind your back and you slide into one: but to get out again is to scale a precipice with crumbling sides."

Palmer never retaliated, never climbed out, never enjoyed understanding for the real nature of his work from his puritanical wife, who "was not really in sympathy and touch with him" [26] any more than her father was—a wife to whom her father wrote letters "chiefly intended to subvert her allegiance to her husband and her husband's and her own faith." [27] Of Linnell's children A. H. Palmer wrote, that "the whole of that family was in thought and other ways under Linnell's dominance throughout life to a degree probably unknown in biography" [28]—a condition that led to more than one dark event. As far as Palmer and Linnell were concerned, there were no doubt faults on both sides; Palmer never once spoke an ill word in return, though often he showed neither tact, decision, or a sense of the world. Linnell's son, John Linnell junior, drew up a series of notes on Palmer's character which he supplied to Story for the *Life of Linnell*: they give the Linnell view, and well serve to round off this melancholy business of a worried and unhappy life:

"S. P. (Character)

mind too fanciful, and wild, extravagant, not controlled sufficiently by reality, and sober *truth*

indulged a sentimental extravagance and exaggeration of expression in his writing and talk till this became habitual

rather puerile sentiment indulged in, in some matters

Indulges in conventional and fanciful sentiment, with exaggerated expression,—as to words used (& in painting—of colour)

lived in atmosphere of sentimental imagination and feeling not always in touch with truth, or *real fact*

perceived as reading his written ideas   His feeling and desire was for something pungent

Gastronomy—art or science of good living (gastros, nomos)
he was a Gastronomist—(versed in gastronomy) 'judge of the art of cooking'

S. P. his sentimental state of mind (called by some poetical?–!!) leads him to descriptions, that are partly fictitious, mixed with humour, and charactertures. . . .

—and his recipe for health (*goose* monthly)

S. P. had a decidedly humourous side (has A. H. P. represented this?)   In the letter from Shoreham why is the part cut out where S. P. expresses his delight in 'roasted goose'?

. This was not a mere sentiment, but an actual *fact*, a permanent characteristic, and a life-long liking of the artist

S. P.'s character had a humourous side—a salient and pronounced feature.   If this is omitted, or taken out or suppressed, in any account of his life and character we have *not the true man*. . . ." [29]

IV

The wonder really is that, after Linnell, Palmer ever again had any moments of security and clear vision.   But neither Italy nor Linnell overcame him quite so much as it is now the fashion to think.   He did not become altogether so sharp and heated a painter as many of the things suggest, as they appear in sale-rooms and galleries.   Occasional cool watercolours, occasional drawings of sensitivity and lyrical handling occur again and again; and behind his hot Venetian pastorals, too far behind often, was a close and selective observation. In his once over-praised, and now under-praised etchings, too, tenderness and depth struggle with a soft, blunted pastoral formula, partly Shoreham, partly Italian, part English, part Virgilian. He went on—in spite of his practice, in spite of the Venetians—admiring and yearning for all he had admired at Shoreham, Blake, Bonasoni, Fuseli, Claude, Elsheimer, Dürer. He went on admiring excess and fanaticism as principles for the artist—in spite of Foster's *Essays*. But pastoral without passion becomes vacant and soft—a sheep is either a paradisaical creature or a woolly object; and by sticking to pastoral, Palmer missed the fullness of life, shut, or limited, it would be fairer to say, both his eyes and his mind, turned his old powerful bias into a weaker prejudice, and prejudice into dogma. He had been a considerable artist, an artist of altogether exceptional style and insight, because, for some fourteen years, he had harmonized in a passionate headlong expression the ideas he felt with the things he saw, the earthly things made in the image of Paradise. Without the Paradise, he was not (as in his cool Welsh "batches of imitation") with the things and with himself. He drifted, longing for Shoreham and his youth, when all was glowing and fresh, into that final state which Foster had described: "The whole mind may become at length something like a hemisphere of cloud scenery, filled with an ever-moving train of changing, melting forms, of every colour, mingled with rainbows, meteors, and an occasional gleam of pure sunlight, *all vanishing away, the mental like this natural imagery, when its hour is up, without leaving anything behind but the wish to recover the vision.*"

Did Palmer ever admit that his Shoreham years produced the deepest painting of his life? I do not think so. He still praised excess, but was diffident about his own excessive past, and was careful about those he allowed to look into his Shoreham portfolio, where the evidence of it was kept.[30] And in 1856, in some notes for a pupil, he wrote, "When (you) see anything *very* rich, put it into drawing at once—but only a little. Nature, never strong in extremes—fault of young artists to be struck with richness of nature." [31]

No doubt Palmer was buried under the changes of the 'thirties and also under the nineteenth century in the prim Surrey villa in which his wife made him live, but his spiritual and imaginative stamina, and his ill luck, and not history, were to blame. He had gone courageously outside his call as a painter, had tied his talent too close to religion and a view of the world, and his talent suffered

with the kick to that view and the inescapable cooling of his religious
flame. He could not develop, that is the trouble. Clare developed
in the madhouse:

> I loved, but woman fell away;
>   I hid me from her faded flame.
> I snatched the sun's eternal ray
>   And wrote till earth was but a name.
>
> In every language upon earth,
>   On every shore, o'er every sea,
> I gave my name immortal birth
>   And kept my spirit with the free—

But Palmer hutched his spirit with the maids and scones, guarded
by conifers and begonias. He did not yield to the century. No, but
he could not grasp it, use it and overcome it. He could not gain the
deep, necessary worldliness of a Delacroix, or continue on the
mystical road he had first taken. He commented pathetically, as an
old man, upon his visionary youth. In his late sixties he wrote
against the annotations he had made on Payne Knight: [32] "I knew
the positive and eccentric young man who wrote the notes in these
pages. He believed in art (however foolishly); he believed in men
(as he read of them in books). He spent years in hard study and
reading and wished to do good with his knowledge. He thought
also it might with unwavering industry help towards an honest
maintenance. He has now lived to find out his mistake. He is
living somewhere in the environs of London, old, and neglected,
isolated—laughing at the delusion under which he trimmed the
midnight lamp and cherished the romance of the good and beautiful;
except so far as that, for their *own sake*, he values them above choice
gold. He has learned however not to 'throw pearls to hogs'; and
appears, I believe, in company, only a poor good-natured fellow fond
of a harmless jest." [33]

   He had become peculiar and ineffectual, a disappointed, perse-
cuted eccentric. "Anyone can have talent when he is five and
twenty," said Degas, "the thing is to have talent when you are
fifty." Palmer's talent might have had better chances of that sur-
vival had he never married Linnell's daughter, had he belonged,
not to his own twilight generation, but to the slightly older, worldlier
generation of Keats, Delacroix, and Danby, or the slightly younger
generation of Tennyson, Madox Brown, and Gautier (how would he
have taken Gautier's preface to *Mademoiselle de Maupin* with its
fun against the new morality, the poetry of Catholicism, and the
painters of the Angelic School?).[34] But might have beens are all
barren—barren except as definitions of what was; and Palmer was

an absorbed but limited visionary—a splendid visionary: who stood
out for one moment in the glide of a free, full romanticism in firm
possession of ideas towards sentimental romanticism, approved by
morality and devoid of ideas; or towards that romanticism of defiant
sensation, which grew in the air like a fine orchid without roots.

Palmer believed in the mystery of God. Rossetti believed in
mystery. Sir William Blake Richmond, R.A., son of Palmer's
friend, son of the successful Victorian portrait-painter who had closed
Blake's eyes—he believed in smooth, elongated prettiness from
which all mystery had been squashed and squeezed.

The wheel had turned completely; for it was also Sir William
Blake Richmond who was outraged, upon inherited principle, when
an uncompromising truth and naturalism came back to England
with Whistler, with Degas, and with Sickert.

And in our time, the successors of Sickert and Gilman and his
friends have asked themselves whether naturalism cannot be en-
livened with some of the richness and roundness (though not the
aerial subtlety) of Palmer. But they may ask themselves, how much
did the richness and roundness, how much did Palmer's vision and
its discoveries depend upon his belief?

NOTES

CHAPTER I (pages 1-9)

1 *Baptist Magazine*, 1825, p. 434.
2 *Portfolio*, 1872, p. 163.
3 *Life and Letters*, p. 3.
4 The Subscribers' list to *A Collection of Poems on Divine & Moral Subjects, selected . . . by William Giles*, 1775, includes Uwin's father, who was a clerk in the Bank of England.
5 Somerset House : Wills. The privately printed *Aegidiana or Gleanings Among Gileses, by One of Them* (A. H. Giles), 1910, gives details of Palmer's Giles relations.
6 At St. Mary Newington, Oct. 25, 1803.
7 Sale Catalogue, British Museum. See p. 50.
8 *L. & L.*, pp. 87-88.
9 *Portfolio*, 1872, p. 163.
10 March 13, 1838: Linnell MSS.
11 *Life of William Blake :* Mona Wilson, pp. 34-35: J. H. is probably Joseph Hogarth, London print and bookseller, whose Blakes, etc., were sold at Southgate and Barrett's, June 7, 1854.
12 *L. & L.*, p. 59, where it is stated by Palmer that his birth was registered at Dr. Williams' Library. It cannot be traced now in the Library registers.
13 *L. & L.*, p. 5.
14 From Edward Young's *Paraphrase of Job.*
15 *Portfolio*, 1872, p. 163.
16 Story's *Life of John Linnell*, vol. i. p. 255, and Linnell MSS.
17 *L. & L.*, p. 5.
18 Records at Merchant Taylors' Hall. He was entered on May 26, 1817, in the Second Form. His name appears in the Probation Book (list of Forms) for October 1817, but not in the subsequent Probation Book for March 1818.
19 *L. & L.*, p. 5.
20 Victoria and Albert Museum: *Catalogue of an Exhibition of Drawings, Etchings and Woodcuts by Samuel Palmer & other Disciples of William Blake*, 1926, p. 25. For Palmer's statement of the sharp sword, see *L. & L.*, p. 6.
21 This Giles uncle of Palmer's married one of Palmer's aunts, and was a blind stockbroker with many children, one of whom, John Giles, was Palmer's intimate friend.
22 *i.e.* Wylye.
23 *Portfolio*, 1872, p. 163.
24 *L. & L.*, p. 34.
25 He desired in his will, proved Nov. 26, 1831, to be buried with his wife and child in St. Bartholomew's Church.
26 *L. & L.*, p. 6.
27 *L. & L.*, p. 7.
28 *V. & A.*, 1926, p. 21.
29 Letter to F. G. Stephens, May 4, 1872 : *L. & L.*, p. 325.
30 Letter to Sir W. B. Richmond: *The Richmond Papers*, by A. M. W. Stirling, 1926, p. 296.
31 *Life of William Blake*, by Alexander Gilchrist, 1863, vol. i. p. 301.
32 Letter to Mrs. Robinson (Julia Richmond), Dec. 9, 1872 : *L. & L.*, p. 343.
33 *L. & L.*, p. 7.
34 *L. & L.*, p. 8.
35 *L. & L.*, p. 8.
6 *A Memoir of Samuel Palmer*, by A. H. Palmer, 1882, p. 47.
7 From Flaxman's *Lectures on Sculpture*, 1829, Lecture VI on " Composition."
8 *L. & L.*, p. 8.
9 *L. & L.*, p. 14.

CHAPTER II (pages 10-17)

1 *England and The English*, by Edward Lytton Bulwer. 2nd ed., 1833, vol. ii. p. 239 *seq.* Cf. also the statement made to Count Raczynski by " one of the most distinguished painters in London," when he visited the Academy in 1838: " The first and chief object of the English school is, to delight the eye. If there is no glow of colour, all other merit is not cared for."—*Histoire de l'Art Moderne en Allemagne*, vol. iii. p. 496.

[2] MS. Autobiography.

[3] But see note on 8, p. 191. There seems usually to have been a good alloy of self-interest in Linnell's kindness.

[4] *L. & L.*, p. 8. For Bell Scott on Varley, see *Autobiographical Notes of The Life of William Bell Scott*, 1892, vol. i. p. 118.

[5] Letter from A. H. Palmer to Martin Hardie, Aug. 5, 1920.

[6] *A Memoir*, p. 7.

[7] " Of these oblong Whatman books, I had a number, and used them in the Life and Letters of S. P. Then alas I destroyed all but one, which Mr. Richmond left to me." (A. H. Palmer to Martin Hardie, Aug. 5, 1920.) A. H. Palmer wrote to F. L. Griggs, March 18, 1923, of a bonfire at Sennen before he left for British Columbia: " Sooner than that multitude of slight sketches, blots, designs, etc., which my father valued so much . . . shld be scattered to the winds, I burnt them, and so much more before we sailed, that the fire lasted for days."

[8] *Portfolio*, 1872, p. 163. Linnell also gave him some of his first lessons in oil, Wate having instructed him in watercolours only. Letter from A. H. Palmer to Martin Hardie, March 14, 1920.

[9] *Reminiscences of Solomon Alexander Hart, R.A.*, edited by Alexander Brodie, privately printed, 1882, p. 11.

[10] *Portfolio*, 1872, p. 163.

[11] Letter to P. G. Hamerton, February 1874 : *L. & L.*, p. 346.

[12] Letter to P. G. Hamerton, Nov. 19, 1872 : *L. & L.*, p. 336.

[13] *L. & L.*, p. 13.

[14] Oct. 16, 1834 : *L. & L.*, p. 183. Cf. on the Romantic modernity of Hellenistic art March Phillipps's *Form and Colour* (1915), pp. 152-5.

[15] Letter to L. R. Valpy, Sept. 1864 : *L. & L.*, p. 261.

[16] For the Aders Collection, see Passavant's *Tour of a German Artist in England*, 1836, vol. i. pp. 201-219. Gilchrist describes the Aders household.

[17] J. C. Young, in his *Memoir of Charles Mayne Young*, 1871, describes a visit to the Aders chateau at Godesberg, and meeting there Coleridge, Wordsworth, and A. Schlegel: vol. i. p. 170 *seq.*

[18] A. T. Story's *Life of John Linnell*, vol. i. p. 155. Lord Cowper owned two celebrated Raphaels of the Madonna and Child, one of them now in the National Gallery, Washington.

[19] *L. & L.*, p. 14.   [20] *L. & L.*, p. 14.

[21] *L. & L.*, p. 15.

[22] " Portrait of a Young Man," No. 258, *Dulwich Gallery Catalogue*, 1926, p. 153, now attributed to Piero di Cosimo.

[23] *L. & L.*, p. 15. George Barret the younger's pictures are very well described as " too light and superficial." They are sentimentalized reflections of Claude, of precisely that order of feebleness that Palmer was to fall into in his middle-age.

[24] *L. & L.*, p. 13.

[25] *L. & L.*, pp. 12, 13.

CHAPTER III (pages 18-34)

[1] *Portfolio*, 1872, p. 163.

[2] Even the *Catalogue* of the V. & A. Exhibition of Palmer and his circle talks of them a " disciples of William Blake."

[3] *Blake's Poetry & Prose*, 1932, p. 980.

[4] A. H. Palmer has maintained (*Samuel Palmer*, by Martin Hardie, 1928, p. 9) " that his father was wrong in this recollection," and that Blake must have been at work on the *Job*, not the *Dante* drawings, saying that the unpublished Linnell-Blake accounts show that " the Dante scheme had not been thought of in 1824." These accounts now in the Yale University Library, mention a payment of £5 to Blake in 1825 " for Sketches of Subjects from Dante," but Blake may well have been designing from Dante before the actual commission from Linnell, and Palmer is not likely to have been wrong in describing one of the big events of his life—especially as little time seems to have passed between the event and the record. Gilchrist, vol. i. p. 332 says the *Dante* drawings were begun in 1824, while he was still working on the *Job*.

[5] *L. & L.*, pp. 9 and 10.

[6] *L. & L.*, p. 9.

[7] Gilchrist, vol. i. p. 300.

[8] Gilchrist, vol. i. pp. 301-304.
[9] See p. 131. Constable writes of " such a thing as Linnell " in one of his letters to C. R. Leslie, R.A. He opposed Linnell's election to the Academy. When he was after votes, Linnell, Constable declared, " spoke long to Landseer in Regent Street with his hat off all the time—I should not have wanted any other reason not to vote for him."—*The Letters of John Constable, R.A., to C. R. Leslie, R.A.*, ed. Peter Leslie, 1931, pp. 59 and 95.
[10] *A Memoir of Edward Calvert*, by Samuel Calvert, 1893.
[11] Gilchrist, vol. i. p. 278.
[12] Letter to P. G. Hamerton, Oct. 13, 1879 : *L. & L.*, p. 380.
[13] *A Memoir of Edward Calvert*, p. 23.
[14] Letter to L. R. Valpy, Sept. 1864 : *L. & L.*, p. 260.
[15] *A Memoir of Edward Calvert*, p. 86.
[16] Gilchrist, vol. i. p. 303.
[17] Letter to Mrs. Gilchrist, July 2, 1862 : *L. & L.*, p. 245.
[18] Gilchrist, vol. i. p. 303.
[19] Letter to L. R. Valpy, Sept. 8, 1878 : *L. & L.*, p. 374.
[20] Gilchrist, vol. i. p. 301.
[21] Letter to Mrs. Gilchrist, July 2, 1862 : *L. & L.*, p. 244.
[22] Gilchrist, vol. 1. p. 321.
[23] Letter to Mrs. Gilchrist, July 2, 1862, *L. & L.*, p. 246.
[24] A. H. Palmer in *The Portfolio*, 1884, p. 146.
[25] Gilchrist, vol. i. p. 312 (certainly contributed by Palmer: see also Ruthven Todd's Everyman edition of *Gilchrist*, p. 392).
[26] Annotations to Wordsworth's poems : *Poetry and Prose*, p. 1024.
[27] *Portfolio*, 1884, p. 146.
[28] " My father valued the Calverts more highly than he did his Blakes. At one time three of Blake's finest panel pictures were stored away in the basement with a lot of rubbish ; and it was barely possible to see that they were pictures." (Letter from A. H. Palmer to Martin Hardie, April 29, 1920.) Besides these four pictures, of which the " Pitt " is now in the National Gallery, " The Bard " (Palmer had given this to Richmond) in the Tate Gallery, and the " Satan " in possession of Mr. Graham Robertson (the " Napoleon " cannot be traced), Palmer owned a good many more things by Blake. He owned a sheet of impressions of the Thornton's Virgil wood-engravings, printed and signed by Blake in his presence ; an impression of Blake's own engraving of " Death's Door "—one of the designs for Blair's *Grave* ; and at least four of his drawings, the " Prophet Isaiah foretelling the Crucifixion and Ascension in pencil " (British Museum) ; " Satan Calling Up His Legions " (in an American collection) ; a drawing in pencil and indian ink of James Barry, inside a copy—which belonged to Blake—of Barry's *An Account of a Series of Pictures in the Great Room of the Society of Arts*, 1783 (also in the U.S.A.) ; and a red crayon drawing of the central figure in " The Stoning of Achan " (Fogg Museum).

Besides the Barry, he owned several important books which had been Blake's : Blake's annotated copies of Lavater's *Aphorisms on Man*, Bishop Watson's *An Apology for the Bible*, and Bishop Berkeley's *Siris*. Other Blake books he acquired were Potter's translation of *The Tragedies of Aeschylus*, Chatterton's *Poems, Supposed to have been written at Bristol by Thomas Rowley*, three copies of Blake's own *Poetical Sketches*, and the MS. of *An Island in the Moon*. (See Keynes, *Bibliography of William Blake*, 1921.)

Palmer was also one of those who copied out for himself the annotations on Sir Joshua Reynold's *Discourses* (Gilchrist, vol. i. p. 97). His father took a copy of the *Job* engravings (*Job Account Book*: Yale University Library), and, after Blake's death, received impressions from Linnell of the *Dante* plates (see p. 80).

Palmer wrote his name and the year, 1833, inside the *Aeschylus* and the *Siris*. Presumably he acquired most of his Blake treasures through his friend, Frederick Tatham ; and since most of them came to him after Blake's death, they came after Blake's influence on his work had passed its maximum.
[ ] *L. & L.*, pp. 15, 16.
[ ] *L. & L.*, pp. 16, 17.
[ ] *V. & A.*, 1926, p. 3.
[ ] See Catalogue, No. 24 (4).
[ ] From a letter from A. H. Palmer to F. L. Griggs, Aug. 28, 1924.

34 See Catalogue, No. 24 (7).

35 From A. H. Palmer's letter to F. L. Griggs, Aug. 28, 1924.

36 *L. & L.*, p. 13.

37 C. H. Collins Baker, " The Sources of Blake's Pictorial Expression," in the *Huntingdon Library Quarterly*, iv., No. 3, April 1941. Blake's donkey is taken from a plate in Alexander Browne's *Ars Pictoria*, 1675.

38 Story's *Life of John Linnell*, vol. ii. p. 254.

39 *L. &. L.*, p. 17.

40 *L. & L.*, p. 17.

41 *L. & L.*, p. 17.

42 Quoted from *The European Magazine* in W. T. Whitley's *Art in England*, 1831-1837, pp. 90, 91.

43 *Paradise Lost*, iii. ll. 694-698.

44 *L. & L.*, p. 18.

45 *L. & L.*, p. 33.

46 *L. & L.*, p. 33.

47 *L. & L.*, p. 38.

48 *L. & L.*, p. 37.

49 Gilchrist, vol. i. p. 297.

50 See p. 27.

51 For Blake's " Beulah " see the second book of *Milton* (*Poetry & Prose*, pp. 524-528). " From Blake's description of it . . . it appears either as something a little lower than the perfection of Eternity, or, though less distinctly, as the proximate highest if not the highest mode of visionary communion possible to mortals."—(D. J. Sloss and J. P. R. Wallis, *The Prophetic Writings of William Blake*, 1927, vol. ii. p. 30.) The moon (cf. Palmer's moons) " is the symbol of Beulah, since the moon reflects the light of the sun, and makes it endurable to the eyes of those on this earth."—(S. Foster Damon, *William Blake : His Philosophy and Symbols*, 1924, p. 423.) Palmer echoes Blake's language in *Milton* in his letter to John Linnell (pp.83-86) ; and the guardians of the gate towards Beulah were " Fenelon, Guion, Teresa, Whitefield & Hervey. . . ."

> . . . " with all the gentle Souls
> Who guide the great Wine-Press of Love."
>
> (*Jerusalem*, iii. 72 ; *Poetry and Prose*, p. 696.)

Palmer certainly read St. Theresa and was familiar with Hervey's *Meditations* (see *L. & L.*, p. 263, and his letter to George Richmond, Nov. 14, 1827), p. 62. Beulah—Bunyan's, and Blake's Beulah imperfectly understood—is the territory of Palmer's moonlights in sepia and indian ink. " Blake at this time was full of Bunyan, and was busy with his illustrations to *Pilgrim's Progress*, which are now in the Frick Museum, New York."

52 *Pilgrim's Progress.*

53 " The whole tree together in flower is a glaring object, totally unharmonious and unpicturesque."—(*Remarks on Forest Scenery*, vol. i. p. 65 ; 2nd. ed., 1794.)

54 " A cedar and a chestnut are just the best trees you could be employed upon " : Palmer to his pupil, Louisa Twining, August 1856.—(*L. & L.*, p. 213.)

CHAPTER IV (pages 35-48)

1 *L. & L.*, p. 17.

2 " Now when about eighteen, I gave some little part of the sacred daylight to music but a friend, only a little older than myself, warned me, and I *instantly* left an amateur musical society, and thereafter sang or fiddled only in the evening."—(Letter t W. Williams, Dec. 26, 1879, *L. & L.*, p. 384.)

3 Perhaps the obscure artists, " Mr." Bird and J. Denham should be added to the circle They were on its fringe, at any rate. Bird had to do with Calvert's first visit t London. " Well I remember his first visit, prompted by Mr. Bird, a prosperou stalwart country gentleman when I met him at the 1826 exhibition."—(Letter t George Richmond, June 7, 1880, Richmond MSS.) He also bought a copy of Blake Job in 1826 (*Job Account Book*, Yale University Library). Denham was a sculptor. H bust of George Richmond is in the National Portrait Gallery, and he exhibited " colossal bust " of Frederick Tatham at the Society of British Artists in 1830. Wit Richmond and Tatham, both were at Mrs. Blake's funeral in 1831. To mark th

Tatham presented Bird with an inscribed copy of Blake's *For the Sexes, The Gates of Paradise*.—(Geoffrey Keynes, *Bibliography of William Blake*, p. 177.)

4 Purcell's *Life of Manning*, vol. i. p. 443.

5 A. H. Palmer to Martin Hardie, Dec. 6, 1927.

6 For his engravings and those after Calvert and Palmer, see *Edward Calvert's Engravings*, by A. J. Finberg (*Print Collector's Quarterly*, vol. xvii. p. 139), in which Richmond's drawing of Sherman is reproduced, and *The Engravings of George Richmond and Welby Sherman*, by Campbell Dodgson (*ibid.*, vol. xvii. p. 353). Mr. Dodgson's list is not quite complete. Late in life, to his account book entry of July 1827 that he had begun a miniature of Sherman, Richmond added a note that he "was a fellow student of ours, but did not turn out as he began, alas," and this is confirmed by A. H. Palmer's statement about theft and France, made in a letter to Martin Hardie, Sept. 9, 1930. For Sherman and Dr. Monro, see p. 80.

7 See *Memorials of Francis Oliver Finch*. Edited by his wife (Eliza Finch), 1865. Palmer's references to him will be found in a letter to Mrs. Gilchrist, January 1863 : *L. & L.*, p. 251. See also Gilchrist's *Blake*, vol. i. p. 299.

8 Linnell's Autobiography : Linnell MSS.

9 *The Letters of William Blake, together with a Life by Frederick Tatham*, ed. A. G. B. Russell, 1906. For Blake's earlier knowledge of C. H. Tatham, see Keynes, *Bibliography of William Blake*, p. 136. Tatham had a copy of *America* inscribed "From the author to C. H. Tatham Oct 7 1799."

10 Letter to Mrs. George Richmond, July 15, 1878 : Richmond MSS.

11 *Times Literary Supplement*, January 28, 1939.

12 *A Memoir of Edward Calvert, by His Third Son*, 1893, p. 59.

13 In a letter to Miss Mona Wilson, Nov. 16, 1925, A. H. Palmer talks of him as "a curiosity of weakness, ineptitude and foolishness," and mentions his "singular character and baleful activities," and "his connection with Frederick Tatham."

14 Samuel Palmer to Mrs. George Richmond, Feb. 25, 1874 : Richmond MSS.

15 Introduction by W. B. Yeats to W. T. Horton's *Book of Images*, 1897.

16 His son's *Memoir of Edward Calvert* is unfortunately a thin, verbose account with few facts or early details.

17 Samuel Palmer to George Richmond, June 7, 1880 : Richmond MSS.

18 George Richmond in *The Athenæum*, 1883, p. 251.

19 In a letter to his son : *Memoir*, p. 19.

20 See note 18.

21 See note 18.

22 For the engravings see *Edward Calvert's Engravings*, by A. J. Finberg, *Print Collector's Quarterly*, vol. xvii. p. 139.

23 *Memoir*, p. 97.

24 See p. 68.

25 *Memoir*, p. 39.

26 See p. 81.

27 See p. 117.

28 Story's *Life of John Linnell*, vol. i. p. 157. Blake and Taylor had friends in common, and Mona Wilson assumes that he derived his knowledge of Greek thought through Taylor and his writings.—*Life of William Blake*, pp. 31, 52, 87. Several of Taylor's translations were in the library of Palmer's intimate friend, John Giles.—*Christie's Sale Catalogue*, Feb. 2, 1881.

29 *A Memoir of Edward Calvert*, p. 25.

30 "Your kindnesses to me are among my few pleasures of memory. . . . You hated me for three days for singing you 'The British Grenadiers' and that was all!"—Palmer to Calvert, in his old age : *L. & L.*, p. 28.

31 *Coleridge on Giordano Bruno* : Alice D. Snyder, *Modern Language Notes*, xliii. 7.

32 Article 13 of "The Platonic Philosopher's Creed" in Taylor's *Miscellanies in Prose and Verse*, 2nd ed., 1820.

33 *Vaurien, or Sketches of the Times : Exhibiting views of the Philosophies, Religions, Politics, Literature and Manners of the Age* (1797) is a store of rather smartly ordered evidence for romanticism. The Platonist (*i.e.* Taylor) is mixed up with the Gothic and the primitive. He had "resided in a romantic part of Scotland," in a "picturesque landscape" ; in "a cottage retaining an antique aspect," which was "formed from the small remains of an abbey." There are comments on the building of the Pantheon in London as "novel extravagance of Platonism." The granddaughter of T. L.

K

Peacock, Taylor's friend, recounted the story of the sacrifices in the lodgings.—*Thomas Taylor, the Platonist*, by W. E. A. Axon, 1890. For the rumpsteak, see *E. W. Field : A Memorial Sketch*, by Thomas Sadler, 1872, p. 126.

[34] *The Richmond Papers*, ed. A. M. W. Stirling, p. 99.

[35] *A Memoir of Edward Calvert*, p. 151.

[36] *A Memoir of Edward Calvert*, p. 184.

[37] *The Richmond Papers*, ed. A. M. W. Stirling, p. 24.

[38] *My Life*, by T. S. Cooper, 1890, vol. i. p. 115.

[39] Sir William Blake Richmond in *The Richmond Papers*, p. 25.

[40] This is reproduced in *The Richmond Papers*.

[41] " In one of the letters written by Richmond to S. P. when they were both in Italy, is the direct admission that he considered the pursuit of sentiment at Shoreham a waste of time. On his part it was merely a pose."—A. H. Palmer to F. L. Griggs, Feb. 2, 1926.

[42] A note added to his early account book, which records his early sitters, the marriage loan made to him by Palmer, etc.

[43] Toynbee, *The Industrial Revolution*, 1908, p. 141.

[44] Harriet Martineau, *History of The Thirty Years' Peace*, vol. ii. p. 97 (1877 ed.).

[45] J. A. Froude, of his brother R. H. Froude, in *Good Words*, January 1881, quoted in John Stoughton's *Religion in England*, 1884, vol. ii. p. 36.

[46] E. S. Purcell's *Life and Letters of Ambrose Phillips de Lisle*, 1900.

[47] Palmer's intimate friend John Giles, as one might expect, had in his library a complete set of Kenelm Digby's works.—*Christie's Sale Catalogue*, Feb. 2, 1881.

[48] *The Richmond Papers*, ed. A. M. W. Stirling, p. 23.

[49] " The masterpiece of Lievens is, the Resurrection of Lazarus, a work which, in sublimity of conception, leaves all attempts of other masters on the same subject far behind."—Fuseli, in his edition of *Pilkington's Dictionary of Painters*, 1810. Palmer, who knew either the picture (now in the Brighton Art Gallery) or Lievens's etching, or both, often refers to this masterpiece. Passion for the spirit and drama of the subject led Lievens away from the Gospel account, in which Lazarus " came forth, bound hand and foot with grave clothes " ; but Lievens's liberty of the hands stretching up from the tomb was not likely to upset either Fuseli or Palmer : Lievens caught the sentiment.

CHAPTER V (pages 49-102)

[1] *V. & A.*, 1926, p. 5. They evidently fell out again. A letter, many years later, from Linnell to Palmer on his Italian honeymoon, talks of a reconciliation and of the allowance being restored.

[2] *Catalogue of a Miscellaneous Collection of Books including the Stock of Mr. Samuel Palmer, late of Broad Street, Bloomsbury, Retired from Business, which will be sold by auction by Mr. Southgate . . . No. 22 Fleet St., on Friday, March 2nd, 1827, and six days following.* The British Museum copy of this catalogue is priced, and makes it clear that the first three days of the sale were Palmer's stock.

[3] Richmond MSS.

[4] *Memoir*, p. 9.

[5] Letter to P. G. Hamerton, Aug. 4, 1879 : *L. & L.*, pp. 377, 378. The " learned traditions " of the vicarage refer to its tenure from 1728 to 1785 by Vincent Perronet, the Methodist and friend of John Wesley.

[6] MS. Letter to George Richmond, Sept. 1876.

[7] Richmond MSS.

[8] *L. & L.*, pp. 35-37.

[9] Palmer to George Richmond, Nov. 14, 1827. See p. 61.

[10] *L. & L.*, pp. 49-50.

[11] " Bonasoni is to me the great copper master of shadows : he never commits the grievous fault of making shadow, as such, rich and of a positive texture."—Letter to P. G. Hamerton, July 8, 1871 : *L. & L.*, p. 315. " Let any one who can draw, copy exactly in pen and ink some boldly-shadowed limb of Bonasoni's, and afterwards turn it into a tree trunk by vigorous line work expressing the textures of the bark, and he will then see texture in its proper function, and shadow in its poetic sleep."—Letter to P. G. Hamerton, Nov. 1872 : *L. & L.*, p. 333. Palmer was first shown the work of this fifteenth century engraver by John Linnell, who urged on him the study not

only of Dürer, but of Bonasone and Michelangelo (*L. & L.*, p. 11), and he praised him all through his life. Blake's friend, George Cumberland, had written *Some Anecdotes of the Life of Julio Bonasoni*, with a catalogue, published in 1793, and reprinted in 1827. Cumberland's Bonasone Collection is now in the British Museum. Cumberland spoke of him as a " great and original genius," with " a manner of his own purely ideal, founded on the principles of nature and the antique." He was commonly admired by all the young artists round Linnell and Blake—Wainwright, for example (who had had lessons from Linnell), eulogises Bonasone in his *Sentimentalities on the Fine Arts* (*London Magazine*, April 1820). Wainwright, Linnell, Palmer, etc., admired his engravings for Bocchius's *Emblems* (*Achillis Bocchii Bonon. Symbolicarum Quaestionum de Universo Genere quas serio ludebat* : 1555), which contain some of the designs which fed Palmer's vision—for example, the dark, rolling clouds or the sheep-shearing scene (*Symb.* xxxii.) with its shepherd under a tree, dog in the foreground, and sheep, profiled in the Blake manner, one against another. His Lullingstone Park tree drawings are in debt to the broad limbs of Bonasone. For Calvert on Bonasone, see *A Memorial of Edward Calvert*, p. 19.

12 Letter to P. G. Hamerton, Nov. 9, 1872 : *L. & L.*, p. 338. As a warranty for the Great Gorge, cf. Opie : " Next to the study of nature and the fine examples produced by the art itself, reading of various kinds, chiefly of history, natural history, voyages, travels, works of imagination, and, above all, of poetry in all its branches, may be considered as affording the most copious fund of materials, and imparting the most powerful stimulus to invention . . . we cannot wonder that drinking deep of the Pierian spring should have been forcibly recommended by all writers on the subject, as having the most direct tendency to exercise, warm, invigorate, and enrich the imagination, and excite noble and daring conceptions."—Lecture II, Feb. 23, 1807 : *Lectures on Painting by the late John Opie, Esq.*, 1809, pp. 60-61.

13 *L. & L.*, p. 18 (June 23, 1880).

14 Letter to W. Williams, August 1880 : *L. & L.*, p. 391.

15 *Memorials of the Late Francis Oliver Finch*, by Mrs. Finch, 1865, pp. 44-45.

16 *Lectures on Sculpture*, 1829, p. 339. All the same, Milton as a poet was one thing, and Palmer's High Anglicanism and High Toryism made it difficult for him to accept some of Milton's teachings in prose. See Linnell's comment, Chapter VI, Note 8.

17 Letter to his cousin Samuel Giles, Oct. 28, 1838 : *L. & L.*, p. 206.

18 *The Mystic Will, Based on a Study of the Philosophy of Jacob Boehme*, by H. H. Brinton, 1931, pp. 21, 28.

19 See p. 67.

20 *The Flaming Heart, or The Life of the Glorious S. Teresa*, translated by M. T., Antwerp, 1642, Chap. XIV, p. 173.

21 A good account of the mystical and allied influences at work in romanticism is given in *Observations Respecting the History of Physiognomy* by the natural philosopher Thomas Cooper, in the *Memoirs of the Literary and Philosophical Society of Manchester*, vol. iii., 1790. For the influence of Boehme on Coleridge, and Boehme's help in keeping " alive the heart in the head," see Chapter IX of *Biographia Literaria.*

22 Quoted by Dean Inge, *Christian Mysticism*, p. 296.

23 *God is Love the Most Pure, My Prayer and My Contemplation, freely translated from the Original of M. D'Eckarthausen by John Grant, M.A., Minister of Kentish Town Chapel*, 1817.

24 Letter to Rev. J. P. Wright, June 9, 1877 : *L. & L.*, p. 370.

25 Richmond MSS. Note in one of George Richmond's two early account books, added in 1889.

26 " I seemed doomed never to see again that first flush of summer splendour which entranced me at Shoreham."—S. P. to his wife, 1859 : *L. & L.*, p. 118.

27 " When I was first introduced to dear Blake, he expressed a hope that I worked ' with fear and trembling.' Could he see me over an etching, he would behold a fruition of his desire copious as the apple-blossoms of that village, where I lost, as some would say, seven years in musing over many strings."—Letter to J. J. Jenkins, July 28, 1879 : J. L. Roget's *History of the Old Watercolour Society*, vol. ii. p. 280.

28 *L. & L.*, p. 113.

29 *The Richmond Papers*, p. 15.

30 His letter to Richmond of Sept. 1828 (see p. 70) begins specially " Please to direct, Water House, Shoreham, near *Dartford*, Kent," as though the move had just been made.

[31] Richmond MSS. The " Mr. Waters " of this letter was a patron of George Richmond.

[32] See p. 53.

[33] The changes of Palmer's state from drought to fertility, darkness and terror to light and sweetness, his vision of exuberance is worth comparing with the fantastic *Vision of a Maniac Artist*, contributed to *Arnold's Magazine of the Fine Arts*, Jan., 1834, and purporting to be " by a young artist lately dead." It wants Palmer's Christian mysticism, but here are the alternations, the exuberance, " the tender bud," which " timidly peeped forth into the genial region, but with an almost instantaneous fertility leaped into a glowing existence," the influence of Fuseli, and so on. The introductory note writes of " The dry style of the early German schools and some modern imitations, the gorgeous and unbridled vigour of the Rubens school, the seductive style of the Paphian painters, the harrowing and immoral tone of overstrained imagination, and, ultimately, the pure imitation of Nature," which are all displayed.

[34] Richmond MSS. Endorsed later by George Richmond, " Feb. 22, 1828. *aet.* 18."

[35] Richmond MSS.

[36] Richmond MSS. This letter is sealed with the family crest.

[37] The MS. is now in the Victoria and Albert Museum. It is given in full in *V. & A.*, 1926, pp. 23, 24.

[38] Linnell MSS., from one of the letters written to Palmer in Italy.

[39] The celebrated Thomas Monro, the physician and amateur artist who had patronized Turner, Girtin, Linnell, etc. Now an old man of sixty-nine.

[40] *Cat-o'-Nine-Tails*, by the Rev. J. Dennis, B.C.L., Prebendary of the Royal Collegiate Church of the Castle of Exeter. Exeter, 1823. A violent, curious championing against changes, abuses, puritanism, radicalism, popery, and infidelity, written in a lively, exaggerated English. Like Palmer, he was against Catholic emancipation : " Know, then, that LIBERTY'S PALLADIUM is PROTESTANT ASCENDANCY ! Know too, that such Ascendancy at once will be destroyed, if Popery's demand of functions legislative, executive, judicial, be at length, through thy ingenious schemes, conceded."

[41] Samuel Palmer's brother.

[42] ? J. W. Lowry (1803-1879), engraver, and son of the engraver, Wilson Lowry.

[43] Richmond MSS.

[44] Cf. Fuseli : " . . . the last branch of uninteresting subjects, that kind of landscape which is entirely occupied with the tame delineation of a given spot."

[45] *L. & L.*, p. 39.

[46] *V. & A.*, 1926, p. 9.

[47] Still in possession of the Linnell family : it is a rich, rounded painting of three large-headed children, with their cat.

[48] Now in the Earl of Strafford's Collection at Wrotham Park, Barnet.

[49] *L. & L.*, pp. 173-177.

[50] Cf. Blake's *Milton*, i. 31 (*Poetry and Prose*, p. 522) ; and " This World of Imagination is Infinite & Eternal, whereas the world of Generation, or Vegetation, is Finite & Temporal. There Exist in that Eternal World the Permanent Realities of Every Thing which we see reflected in this Vegetable Glass of Nature " : *A Vision of the Last Judgment : Additions to Blake's Catalogue* (*Poetry and Prose*, p. 830), from the Rossetti MS. (which belonged to Palmer's brother).

Essays on the Nature and Principles of Taste, 1825 ed., p. 62.

[52] *L. & L.*, pp. 177 and 178.

[53] " Well below average height, he wore a long beard when everyone was shaved."—*Memories of Ninety Years*, Mrs. E. M. Ward, 1924, pp. 141 and 142. According to Mrs. Ward his pamphlet (not in the British Museum) gave thirty-one reasons for wearing a beard.

[54] See p. 64.

[55] " The forms of Albert Dürer are blasphemies on Nature, the thwarted growths of starveling labour and dry sterility—formed to inherit his hell of paradise."—*Aphorisms : Life and Writings*, ed. Knowles, vol. iii. Fuseli asks in his seventh lecture what can be more disgusting " to an eye accustomed to harmony of frame," than the starveling forms of Albert Dürer " unless it be the swampy excrescences of Rembrandt ? "

[56] See p. 62.

[57] Unpublished transcripts.

[58] See p. 119.
[59] Richmond MSS. : early note-book.
[60] L. & L., p. 45.
[61] V. & A., 1926, pp. 24, 25.
[62] V. & A., 1926, p. 24.   They are now in the Museum.
[63] Letter to L. R. Valpy, August 1864 : L. & L., p. 257.
[64] Letters to His Son Lucien, by Camille Pissarro, ed. John Rewald, 1944, p. 355.
[65] Walpole Society, xvi., 1927-1928.
[66] L. & L., p. 110.
[67] These monthly meetings were an early point of friction between Palmer and Linnell. Linnell wrote to Palmer in Rome on March 24, 1839 (Linnell MSS.) : " Surely had Mr. R. (i.e. Richmond) been as desirous of communicating what he believed to be his most valuable discoveries as I have been formerly when with you he was wont to visit the Hampstead Cottages I sh^d have received my own with usury.   I am out of the pale, I fear, too far to taste the salt of Art with such society—but I ought to remember that I was not one of the monthly meeting elite—when at the platonic feasts of reason & flow of souls only real Greeks from Hackney & Lisson Grove were admitted."   Hackney refers to Calvert and Lisson Grove to Palmer and his London house.
[68] i.e. his brother, William Palmer.
[69] Richmond MSS.
[70] Now in the National Portrait Gallery.
[71] Palmer, it must be remembered, was certainly known to a good many artists of the older generation.
[72] V. & A., 1926, p. 13.
[73] Richmond Account Books : Richmond MSS.
[74] See p. 100.
[75] I know nothing of Miss Sawkins : but the name is Sawkins, not Lawkins, as in L. & L., p. 179.
[76] It hung next to Constable's " Jacques and the Wounded Stag " in the Academy.
[77] There was much revival of interest about now in Sir Thomas More.   Cresacre-More's life of his grandfather was published ; and Palmer was no doubt acquainted with Southey's Sir Thomas More, or Colloquies on the Progress and Prospects of Society, 1829, which is full of sentiments about industry, Catholic emancipation, primitive cottages, the peasantry, etc., in tune with Palmer's anti-modernism.   This is the book so savagely reviewed, upon laisser-faire principles, by Macaulay, in his Essays.   Southey contrasts country cottages, their " weather stains, lichens and moss " and rose bushes, with the offensive temples and hovels of manufacturing Mammon, which cannot be mellowed by time.   " Here is wisdom," sneers Macaulay.   " Here are the principles on which nations are to be governed.   Rose-bushes and poor rates, rather than steam-engines and independence.   Mortality and cottages with weather-stains, rather than health and long life with edifices which time cannot mellow."   Southey makes More say " The spirit which built and endowed monasteries is gone.   Are you one of those persons who think it has been superseded for the better by that which erects steam engines and cotton mills ? "—Vol. i. p. 158.
[78] Richmond MSS.

CHAPTER VI (pages 103-122)

[1] See p. 74.
[2] Nothing better reveals the feelings inspired by Irving than the extraordinary portrait of him preaching in the open air by his follower, Faithful Pack, which now belongs to the Presbyterian Historical Society and is reproduced in A. L. Drummond's Edward Irving and His Circle.   One hand is raised in the air, and the tall figure in black stands against what I take to be the smoke of the wrath to come.   Beneath the Bible held low in the other hand crowd the caricatured, grotesque faces, in miniature, of his leading followers.
[3] Stanley's Life of Arnold, 12th ed., vol. i. p. 266.
[4] Letter to Rev. J. P. Wright, Sept. 24, 1878.
[5] No. 1810, Dec. 11, 1832.
[6] In the List of Voters for 1832-1833, under Shoreham : " Samuel Palmer of No. 4 Lisson Grove North, Marylebone.   Qualification.   Freehold houses and garden. Occupied by John Tooth and others."—Information from the Clerk of Kent County

Council. A letter from Henry Walter to George Richmond, from Shoreham, March 24, 1831, makes it clear that Palmer was already intending to buy two houses in the village.—Richmond MSS.

[7] Arthur Thistlewood, one of the Cato Street conspirators, hanged in 1820 ; Jeremiah Brandreth, hanged in 1817 for heading an insurrection in the Midlands.

[8] Like much else written and believed by Palmer, this pamphlet stuck in Linnell's gizzard. He refers to it in his prickly correspondence with Palmer while Palmer and Linnell's daughter were on their honeymoon in Italy : " Palmer writes me a very pretty letter about Art in Florence & in his usual way [says ?] how pleasant it will be for us to converse only upon points wherein we agree & while he writes the sentences, digs his elbow in poor Locke's face & plasters it over with his hand in which he always keeps a [pitch ?] plaster to burke any friend to liberty who may be within his reach. Who however can expect to escape his sting when the divine Milton occasionally comes in for a wound in any part which he may deem most vulnerable. As a schoolmaster he is treated as a fool miscalculating all the material he had to work upon to such a degree as to render all his schemes for teaching youth quite unpracticable unless every boy was another Milton. Poor Idiot. Can you who read his poetry with such delight believe it—I do not think you can or if you read his prose & try to imitate his style therein (as a certain gent did when he wrote an address to the Electors of Kent) can you help feeling the power of his words inspired by that sincere & hearty love of truth, which as he said is the only source of true eloquence. . . . The same fountain does not send forth sweet water & bitter. . . ."—Letter to Hannah Palmer, Sept. 30, 1839 : Linnell MSS.

[9] L. & L., p. 54. I have not been able to trace this in any of the Giles wills.

[10] In 1832, not in 1833, as A. H. Palmer states (V. & A., 1926, p. 9). No. 4 Grove St., Lisson Grove is given as his address in the Royal Academy catalogue for 1832.

[11] A. H. Palmer wrote to F. L. Griggs, Nov. 25, 1924, that he was sending him a Shoreham oil, bearing on the back " the original signed label, when he was living at Shoreham, but used his little London house for teaching headquarters."

[12] See p. 13.

[13] Now in possession of Mrs. Walter Medlicott.

[14] See p. 25.

[15] Bulletin of the Metropolitan Museum of Art, vol. xvi., No. 5, 1921, p. 96 seq.

[16] L. & L., pp. 46, 47.

[17] See Catalogue, No. 146.

[18] L. & L., p. 54.

[19] See p. 124.

[20] Royal Academy Catalogues, 1833, 1834.

[21] Richmond MSS.

[22] L. & L., pp. 54, 55.

[23] From a letter to George Richmond, June 3, 1838 (Richmond MSS.). A later view of Palmer's on landscape is given in a letter to his wife : ." Landscape is of little value, but as it hints or expresses the haunts or doings of man. However gorgeous, it can be but Paradise without an Adam. Take away its churches . . . and you have a frightful kind of Paradise left—a Paradise without a God " (1856).—L. & L., p. 115. Landscapes also, for him, needed vivifying by the glint of water (see p. 50).

[24] Letter to Sir William Blake Richmond, May 10, 1879 : Richmond Papers, p. 291.

[25] See p. 72.

[26] From the chapter on " The Influence of Solitude on the Imagination." New ed. 1827, p. 281 ; Zimmerman, 1827 ed., p. 293.

[27] Letter to L. R. Valpy (undated) : L. & L., p. 399. The essay on " Decision " was also a powerful, even fatal influence on another painter, Benjamin Robert Haydon.

[28] The Essays were published in 1805. The quotations are from the 3rd edition, 1806. The Essays reached their 24th edition in 1851.

[29] i.e. Edward Calvert. See p. 41.

[30] Richmond MSS.

[31] See p. 92.

[32] Palmer, as one might expect, admired the Port Royalists.

[33] Richmond's first child Harriet, who died in 1835.

[34] Richmond MSS.

[35] V. & A., 1926, p. 24.

[36] Note on a watercolour by Richmond, now in possession of his grandson, Rev. H. Kennedy

CHAPTER VII (pages 123-140)

[1] A. H. Palmer's statement (*L. & L.*, p. 56) that Calvert was with them was an error based on a confusion of dates.

[2] Richmond MSS.

[3] In the British Museum. Reproduced in Binyon's *Followers of William Blake*, where the assumption is made.

[4] Bishop Jebb (1775-1833) and Alexander Knox (1757-1831), forerunners of the Oxford Movement. Jebb had some, probably slight, interest in Blake. He sent Mrs. Blake twenty guineas after Blake's death, Mrs. Blake sending him in return a copy of the *Songs of Innocence and Experience* (Gilchrist, vol. i. p. 365). Palmer is probably referring to *Thirty Years' Correspondence Between Bishop Jebb and Alexander Knox*, 1834.

[5] Richmond MSS. A different version of this letter, with a different address, and wrongly dated 1835, is given by A. H. Palmer, presumably from a draft : *L. & L.*, pp. 184-188.

[6] See pp. 14-15.

[7] Jakob Götzenberger (1800-1866), a follower and pupil of Cornelius. He did decorations in Bridgewater House. Crabb Robinson introduced him to Blake, about whom he was enthusiastic. Mona Wilson's *Life of William Blake*, p. 297 ; Edith Morley, *Crabb Robinson*, p. 19.

[8] A. H. Palmer, somewhat biassed as he was against his grandfather, took the same view as Crabb Robinson, after a scrutiny of all the Linnell family MSS., including many no doubt which have not been seen by various authorities on Blake—MSS. covering all Linnell's transactions down to his dealings with Tatham over Blake and Mrs. Blake (" no wonder they fell out ") and the undertaker's bill for Blake's funeral (Letter to F. L. Griggs, March 18, 1923). He declared that it was Butts " to whom and not to Linnell were chiefly due Blake's life and his ability to produce the *Job* and *Dante* drawings." And certainly what is known of Linnell's character, of his worship, as A. H. Palmer put it, of God and Mammon, of his devoted self-interest, and of the loathing which other artists had for him, makes one doubt if the compliments which Blake scholars down to Geoffrey Keynes hand out to him, are really well founded.

[9] MS. Note-book: Dr. Williams' Library. Crabb Robinson's friend, J. J. Masquerier (1778-1855), was a mediocre painter of portraits in a conventional style based on eighteenth-century practice—not the kind of artist who would see any value in Palmer.

[10] *E. T. Daniell : A Memoir*, by F. B. Beecheno, 1899, pp. 7, 8.

[11] Journal (Dr. Williams' Library), Dec. 17, 1836.

[12] In the Collection of Mr. Leonard Duke.

[13] The " Mount Siabod " belongs to Mr. Martin Hardie, and the " Llyn Gwinedd " is in the Collection of Mrs. Walter Medlicott. Other examples, besides those I have mentioned, are in the Collections of Mr. Martin Hardie, Sir Frank Short, R.A., and Colonel Buchanan.

[14] Journal (Dr. Williams' Library), Jan. 23, 1837.

[15] *L. & L.*, p. 57. Unfortunately, the correspondent is not named.

[16] MS. now in the Victoria and Albert Museum : *V. & A.*, 1926, p. 25.

[17] Information from the Secretary. In a letter to Miss Mona Wilson, Nov. 16, 1925, A. H. Palmer referred to his uncle William Palmer as " that curiosity of weakness, ineptitude, and foolishness . . . the man's singular character and baleful activities " and " his connection with Frederick Tatham." The subject is the disposal of the Rossetti MS.

[18] Story's *Life of John Linnell*, vol. i. p. 199.

[19] It is interesting to compare Friedrich's conception of art with Palmer's. Friedrich wrote : " Schliesse Dein leiblichs Auge damit Du mit dem geistigen Auge zuerst siehest Dein Bild ; Dann fördere zutage, was Du im Dunkeln gesehen, dass es zurück wirke auf die Andern von aussen nach innen."—" Shut your bodily eye, so that you see your painting with your spiritual eye. Then bring to light what you have seen in darkness so that it may influence others from without inwards."—C. D. Friedrich, *Bekenntnisse*, ed. K. K. Eberlein, 1922, p. 121. Quoted by Hermann Beenken, *Burlington Magazine*, vol. lxxii., 1938, pp. 171-175. Friedrich also said : " Der Edle Mensch erkennt in allem Gott, der gemeine Geist."—" The noble man recognizes God in everything, the ordinary man sees only the form, not the spirit."

[20] Richmond MSS. Linnell had been put out by Palmer's new interest in Titian and the Venetians ; his view seems to have been that his son-in-law and daughter were merely in Rome as emissaries of John Linnell, to bring him back coloured copies of the Vatican Raphaels and Michelangelos, but he suspected Palmer's interest in the Venetians was getting in the way.—Linnell MSS.

[21] The Italian correspondence went from bad to worse. Linnell to Palmer, June 30, 1839 : " You know I have prophesied that our differences of opinion upon some subjects will one day cause a separation & I fear now that the latent qualities are about to be develloped (sic) which will prove one a true prophet—one of the first signs of the disappearance of the crutch is always a disallowance of those familiar expressions which accompany friendship & sincerity."

His letter to Hannah Palmer on Milton and Palmer's politics has already been quoted (Note 8, to Chapter VI). The question of Hannah staying with her parents on their return and the question of the date of the return, were also laboured. The letters' reproofs, bitternesses and all, whether to Palmer or his wife, were all crowded on to one sheet ; and a more egregious example of a father-in-law's interference on a honeymoon would be hard to find. The climax is in a letter from Linnell to Palmer, Oct. 16, 1839 : " Dear Palmer,—You say you are related to the Fox family. I thought so. It is a pity you were not named Fox Palmer instead of Samuel. It w^d be so characteristic of your doubles & turns in argument—Why you are like Mrs. Quickly— a man knows not where to have you—here in the last letter received only yesterday you pretend to be innocent of all provoking language & take great praise to yourself for not roaring like a Lion. Whoever heard a Fox do so ? No, he gains his point by secret sly means. . . ."—Linnell MSS.

[22] Linnell MSS.

[23] A. H. Palmer to Martin Hardie, March 1, 1929.

[24] A. H. Palmer to F. L. Griggs, March 18, 1923.

[25] A. H. Palmer to F. L. Griggs, Aug. 28, 1924.

[26] A. H. Palmer to F. L. Griggs, Oct. 22, 1925.

[27] A. H. Palmer to F. L. Griggs, Nov. 13, 1925.

[28] A. H. Palmer to F. L. Griggs, 1925.

[29] Linnell MSS. Partly quoted in *V. &. A.*, 1926, p. 10.

[30] Calvert's " Chamber Idyll " (with other Calverts) hid in this portfolio, kept " in a little envelope, for fear of Victorian blushes."—A. H. Palmer to F. L. Griggs, July 27, 1923.

[31] *Notes Taken During the Lessons in Watercolour Painting from Samuel Palmer to Louisa Twining*, 1856.—Ashmolean Museum.

[32] See pp. 52-53.

[33] *L. & L.*, p. 37.

[34] One could draw up a curious list of poets and painters born on either flank of 1800—it would include not only Clare and Palmer, but Beddoes, von Holst, Darley, Hartley Coleridge, A. W. Pugin, C. J. Wells—who managed to make no satisfactory bridge from the old world into the new.

BIBLIOGRAPHY

A. H. PALMER). . . *Notes on a Collection of Drawings, Paintings and Etchings by the late Samuel Palmer.* (By F. G. Stephens, L. R. Valpy, and A. H. Palmer.) Fine Art Society, 1881.

A. H. PALMER . . *Samuel Palmer: A Memoir*, 1882.
The Story of an Imaginative Painter, in *The Portfolio*, 1884, pp. 145-151.
The Life and Letters of Samuel Palmer, 1892.
Catalogue of An Exhibition of Drawings, Etchings and Woodcuts by Samuel Palmer & other Disciples of William Blake. (At the Victoria and Albert Museum.) *Introduction and Notes by A. H. Palmer.* 1926.

SAMUEL PALMER) . . *An Address to the Electors of West Kent, by an Elector*, 1832. (No copy known. Extracts in *The Maidstone Gazette*, No. 1810, Dec. 11, 1832.)

SAMUEL PALMER. . *Autobiographical Letter*, in *The Portfolio*, 1872, p. 163.
An English Version of The Eclogues of Virgil, 1883.
The Shorter Poems of John Milton, with Twelve Illustrations by Samuel Palmer, 1889.

GEORGE RICHMOND . . Notes on Edward Calvert, in *The Athenæum*, Aug. 25, 1883, p. 251.

A. M. W. STIRLING . *The Richmond Papers*, 1926.

SAMUEL CALVERT) . *A Memoir of Edward Calvert, by His Third Son*, 1893.

A. J. FINBERG . . *The Engravings of Edward Calvert*, in *The Print Collector's Quarterly*, vol. xvii., No. 4, 1930.

W. B. YEATS. . . *A Book of Images, Drawn by W. B. Horton & Introduced by W. B. Yeats*, 1897 (on Calvert).

L. BINYON. . . *The Engravings of William Blake and Edward Calvert*, in *The Print Collector's Quarterly*, vol. vii., No. 4, 1917.
The Followers of William Blake, 1925.

ELIZA FINCH) . . *Memorials of Francis Oliver Finch, Edited by his Wife*, 1865.

A. G. B. RUSSELL . *The Letters of William Blake, together with a Life by Frederick Tatham*, 1906.

CAMPBELL DODGSON . *The Engravings of George Richmond and Welby Sherman*, in *The Print Collector's Quarterly*, vol. xvii., No. 2, 1930.

A. T. STORY . . *The Life of John Linnell*, 1892.

ALEXANDER GILCHRIST. *The Life of William Blake, "Pictor Ignotus,"* 2 vols. 1863. *Everyman Edition*, ed. Ruthven Todd, 1942.

MONA WILSON . . *The Life of William Blake*, 1927.

MARTIN HARDIE	.	*Samuel Palmer*, in the annual volume of the Ol Watercolour Society's Club, 1926-1927.
		Samuel Palmer, Publication No. 7 of The Prin Collector's Club, 1927.
R. G. ALEXANDER	.	*A Catalogue of the Etchings of Samuel Palmer* Publication No. 16 of The Print Collector's Club, 193?
T. STURGE MOORE	.	*Samuel Palmer's Happiest Designs*, in *Apollo*, Dec 1936.
GEOFFREY KEYNES	.	*A Bibliography of William Blake*, 1921. New York 1921.
J. L. ROGET	. .	*A History of the Old Watercolour Society*, 1891.
ALEXANDER BRODIE (ed.)		*Reminiscences of Solomon Alexander Hart, R.A* (privately printed), 1882.
F. B. BEECHENO	. .	*E. T. Daniell: A Memoir*, 1889.
T. S. COOPER	. .	*My Life*, 1890.
F. G. STEPHENS	. .	*Memorials of Mulready*, 1890.

CATALOGUE OF SAMUEL PALMER'S WORK,
1812–1835

PAINTINGS, watercolours, drawings, and engravings are included together, as far as can be judged in chronological order. Works I have not seen, or of which reproductions are not available, are described between quotation marks, and works which can no longer be traced are printed in smaller type. Several Palmers now (1945) are inaccessible, which accounts for the meagreness of some descriptions. An asterisk against a title denotes that I have invented a new and, I think, a more appropriate name. The point will usually be obvious, *e.g.* in relating drawings to a final painting.

Abbreviations: B.I.=*British Institution*; L. & L.=*"The Life and Letters of Samuel Palmer, Painter & Etcher"*: A. H. Palmer, 1892; Memoir=*"Samuel Palmer: A Memoir"*: A. H. Palmer, 1882; F. G. Stephens=*"Notes on a Collection of Drawings, Paintings and Etchings by the late Samuel Palmer,"* by A. H. Palmer, L. R. Valpy and F. G. Stephens, 1881; R.A.=*Royal Academy*; R.A., British Art, 1934=*Exhibition of British Art, Royal Academy, London,* 1934; V. & A., 1926=*"Catalogue of an Exhibition of Drawings, Etchings and Woodcuts, by Samuel Palmer & Other Disciples of William Blake,"* with an introduction & notes by A. H. Palmer, *Victoria and Albert Museum,* 1926; Binyon=*"The Followers of William Blake, Edward Calvert, Samuel Palmer, George Richmond & Their Circle"* : Lawrence Binyon, 1925.

Left and right mean left and right of the spectator. Sizes are in inches, height being given first.

Palmer's early watercolours and pictures are not always in a good state—but less from the employment of sound colours than from their preparation. The brilliance of his colour, and its freshness, are unchanged. A. H. Palmer states: "Although purchased with difficulty out of the most scanty means, none but the very choicest materials were used, even to pure gold and ultramarine; for brilliancy and durability were considered as above all things imperative." He ground his colours himself (*L. & L.*, p. 51). "He indulged in pure ultramarine for his skies and distances, with madder carmine and other costly pigments. . . . To save time he used a good deal of warmish middle-tint paper, and heightened with body colour,—a practice he utterly eschewed in his finished drawings" A. H. Palmer, *Portfolio*, 1884, p. 149). It is the body-colour, the thick paste of several of these studies, which, it should be remembered, were meant only as studies, which is now liable to break and flake off.

Round about 1825, he was making experiments which are not standing up well. For instance, his series of 1825 monochromes (Nos. 38-43) appear to be drawn in sepia mixed with gum, and then glazed. The drawings have not only darkened, but pieces are inclining to break away.

The early oils need careful treatment. Towards the end of his Shoreham years he recorded "many and elaborate experiments in oil vehicles which evidently consumed a large amount of time" (*L. & L.*, p. 55), and he "largely experimented in egg vehicles" (*L. & L.*, p. 67).

Oils and watercolours "were often begun in tempera" (*L. & L.*, p. 51); and the oils were painted on white grounds, "laid with 'Blake's white,' a pigment for making which Blake gave my father the recipe." (Palmer refers to this in letters as "Mrs. Blake's white"), or else the picture was done on paper glued to the panel. None of the pictures have suffered disastrously like some of Blake's; but often they appear to be finished with specklings and touches of tempera, less durable than the pigment beneath, and too easily removable. "Like Blake and Linnell, Palmer and his friends were well acquainted with Cennini's *Treatise on Painting*. (See p. 194, No. 169; and *Gilchrist*, vol. i. p. 369.")

1. SKETCH OF A WINDMILL. (1812.)

On the back, in ink, "Dec 19 1812"; in pencil, "The date is my dear Mother's writing. I gave this to dear Herbert Sept. 5 1862. S. Palmer."

Watercolour ($1\frac{5}{8} \times 2\frac{1}{16}$).

Exh. V. & A. 1926, No. 45. Coll. Samuel Palmer; A. H. Palmer.

2. POLLARD WILLOW, TOTTENHAM MARSHES. (*c.* 1819.)

On the back, in ink, "Tottenham Marshes—This pollard willow was enriched with a great variety of tints some of rich olive green and others where the mosses had not prevailed of a silvery grey— The foliage was of a light green not very warm—S. Palmer."

Pencil ($7\frac{3}{8} \times 4\frac{7}{16}$).

Dated by A. H. Palmer "about 1819." Cf. Pollard Willow, Plate 18, David Cox's *Treatise on Landscape Painting & Effect in Watercolours*, 1813. See also No. 16. Exh. V. & A., 1926, No. 46. Coll. Samuel Palmer; A. H. Palmer; Christie's, March 4, 1929, No. 52. Thomas Lowinsky, Esq.

3. POTATO SHED, TOTTENHAM MARSHES. (*c.* 1819.)

A tumble-down shed, with a thatched roof, out of which branches are growing. On the right, a cart wheel. On the back, in the

artist's hand, in ink, "Potatoe Shed, Tottenham Marshes—S. Palmer."
Pencil ($4\frac{7}{16} \times 7\frac{5}{16}$).

Dated by A. H. Palmer "about 1819." Exh. V. & A., 1926, No. 47. Coll. Samuel Palmer; A. H. Palmer; Christie's, March 4, 1929, No. 52.   Thomas Lowinsky, Esq.

4. LANDSCAPE WITH RUINS. (*c.* 1819.)
   Exh. R.A., 1819, No. 257.

5. COTTAGE SCENE: BANKS OF THE THAMES, BATTERSEA. (*c.* 1819.)
   Exh. R.A., 1819, No. 259.

6. A STUDY. (*c.* 1819.)
   Exh. R.A., 1819, No. 414.

7. BRIDGE SCENE: COMPOSITION. (*c.* 1819.)
   (*Frame size:* 25×21.) Exh. B.I., 1819, No. 141.

8. LANDSCAPE: COMPOSITION. (*c.* 1819.)
   (*Frame size:* 39×34.) Exh. B.I., 1819, No. 169. Purchased for 7 guineas by "Mr. Wilkinson. No. 4 Beaumont St., Marylebone" (*L. & L.,* p. 7).

9. WOOD SCENE: A STUDY FROM NATURE. (*c.* 1820.)
   Exh. R.A., 1820, No. 185.

10. A STUDY FROM NATURE: BATTERSEA. (*c.* 1821.)
    Exh. R.A., 1821, No. 49.

11. LANGLEY LOCKS, HERTS. (*c.* 1821.)
    (*Frame size:* 24×31.) Exh. B.I., 1821, No. 278.

12. STUDY FROM NATURE, AT BATTERSEA. (*c.* 1821.)
    (*Frame size:* 24×20.) Exh. B.I., 1821, No. 156.

13. MAIDSTONE BRIDGE. (1821.)
    "Scene on the river, with figures fishing in foreground . . . signed and dated 1821."
    "*In pen & bistre wash.*" ($7\frac{1}{2} \times 10\frac{1}{2}$.)
                                          Formerly E. Parsons & Sons, London.

14. EVENING. (1821.)
    "A reposeful village scene on the banks of a stream, with bridge across, a horse feeding by the side of a road, figures seated on a walk in front of a cottage. Signed and dated 1821."
    "*In pen & bistre.*" ($7\frac{1}{2} \times 10\frac{1}{2}$.)
    Possibly a study for "On the Thames: Evening" (See No. 22).
                                          Formerly E. Parsons & Sons, London.
                                          Victoria and Albert Museum, London.

15. STUDIES OF COTTAGE SCENERY. (*c.* 1821.)
    Two on one sheet.
    Sepia (size of drawings, each $2\frac{3}{8} \times 4$).
                                          Sir Frank Short, R.A.

16. OLD COTTAGE AND ELMS. (*c.* 1821.)

A thatched cottage, with half-timbered gable, in front of trees in leaf. On the back in pencil in S. Palmer's hand:

> "Wretch even then, life's journey just begun
> (Cowper's Poem, 'On The Receipt of My Mother's Picture')
>
> O blindness to the future wisely given,
> That man may fill the station marked by Heaven."

Sepia ($2\frac{3}{4} \times 4\frac{5}{8}$).

Dated by A. H. Palmer "before 1822." Compare Plate 8, "Lane at Edgebaston," aquatint in sepia-colour, David Cox's *Treatise on Landscape Painting & Effect in Watercolours*, 1813. See also No. 2. Exh. V. & A., 1926, No. 8. Repro. Binyon, Plate XVIII. Coll. Samuel Palmer; A. H. Palmer.

Victoria & Albert Museum, London.

17. STUDY OF OLD BUILDINGS. (1821.) Plate 5.

A rutted road leading to a river. A bridge in the middle distance. Left, a tall tree in front of houses, and a man on horseback by an archway. Right, houses, with a ladder against a window. Background of clouds. Signed "S. Palmer," and dated 1821.

Pen and sepia wash ($7\frac{1}{2} \times 10$). The late Sir Michael Sadler.

18. *SUSSEX: STORM APPROACHING. (1821.) Plate 6.

In the foreground, a green sea, slashed with dark green. A yellow clump of land, left, with green bushes; and beyond it red-brown houses, which lead into a narrow strip of yellow and white between green water touched with purple and grey-blue land. Above a heavy sky of dark-lead blue cloud, with white and grey clouds, right, under a clear sky of pale blue. Inscribed, foreground left, "At Hailsham SP" (monogram); top, right, "1821 Sussex 7.17."

Watercolour ($8\frac{5}{16} \times 12\frac{1}{2}$).

Possibly a study for "Hailsham, Sussex; Storm Coming On" (see No. 20). The inscription "at Hailsham" is puzzling, since it i a sea drawing, and is clearly based on the engraving of Rye, i Turner's *Southern Coast of England*. Exh. V. & A., 1926, No 49 (Plate XV); repro. *Old Water-Colour Society Club Annua Volume*, No. IV. Plate X. Coll. Samuel Palmer; A. H. Palmer Christie's, March 4, 1929, No. 40. Leonard Duke, Esq.

19. A STUDY FROM NATURE. STORM APPROACHING (1821.)

Middle distance, left, a white tower. Foreground, right, a log left, a tree. In the background, clouds and a wall of rain, over th

ea.   Signed "S Palmer," inscribed on back "A Study from Nature.
torm Approaching   1821."
  Pen & sepia wash (7¾× 10¾).
  Similar in composition and viewpoint to preceding watercolour.
Henry Reitlinger, Esq.

0. HAILSHAM, SUSSEX: STORM COMING ON.   (*c.* 1822.)
  (*Frame size:* 40×36.)   Exh. B.I., 1822, No. 106.   See Nos. 18 and 19.

1. A LANE SCENE, BATTERSEA.   (*c.* 1822.)
  (*Frame size:* 24×20.)   Exh. B.I., 1822, No. 101.

2. ON THE THAMES: EVENING.   (*c.* 1822.)
  (*Frame size:* 30×25.)   Exh. B.I., 1822, No. 195.

3. VIEW.   (*c.* 1823.)
  Exh. R.A., 1823, No. 32.

4. LEAVES FROM A SKETCH-BOOK.   (1824.)
  (1) "Above, in a straight row, twenty-three kinds of trees, with a river and
stant hilly landscape.   Beneath a row of heads.   In lower left hand corner, a
wer (inscribed 'A very old tower, Lambeth Palace'), drawn with great minute-
ess.   To the right, a cottage with vine, Bishop's Walk."   (Page 4 of the original
ok.)

  (2) A woman reclines across the page from right to left, with her left hand
a Bible, on the side of which is written "The earth is full of Thy richness."
the middle distance, a church spire against a field of hop-poles.   To the left
vo men with scythes, and woman with buckets on a yoke.   Above, sheep.   To
e right, poplar trees and five birds in the sky.   In the background, a vast
yed sun sinking behind hills.   (Page 9 of the original book.)
  Repro. *V. & A.*, 1926, Plate V.

  (3) (Plate 7.)   In the centre, design for a drawing—a shepherd
ith a crook under a horse-chestnut tree, with another shepherd
d sheep under a squat tree.   Various studies of trees, left, right,
d below.   Right, leaves in a stone window, near which is written
The angle of the palace . . ."   Against the trees, left, "Somtimes
wall of trees crude & lumpy with the light nowhere seen through
xcept at the edges of the mass."   The mount covers some of the
rawing and writing.   On the reverse, "The earth is full of thy
chness."   (Page 10 of the original book.)
Victoria and Albert Museum, E 2359—1928.

  (4) Right, a battlemented city, with trees under a crescent moon, and large
rs.   Left, a tower and trees.   For the inscription written above in Palmer's
nd, see Chapter III, p. 26.   (Page 21 of the original book.)
  Repro. *V. & A.*, 1926, Plate V.

  (5) "Landscape, with row of distant trees, standing corn, and deep down
ong the trees to the right a cottage with a semi-circular thatched roof.   On
e horizon, a great crescent moon 'with the old moon in her arms.'"   (Page 26
the original book.)

(6) "Two studies of a lion, showing with elaborate minuteness the insertion of each whisker." (Page 31 of the original book.)

(7) A valley, church spire, cornfields, and trees. For the inscription, in Palmer's hand, see Chapter III, p. 27. Reverse: Sketch of sloping ploughland, and a hedge. For the inscription, in Palmer's hand, see Chapter III, p. 27.

Victoria and Albert Museum, E 3513—1928.

(8) (Plate 8.) Two delicate tree trunks, a stile, and a house. And a bit of landscape with articulate, formalized plants and grasses distinct in stem and leaf. Reverse: Woodland, studies of tree trunks, a spire in a landscape. (Page 93 of the original book.)

Victoria and Albert Museum, E 3512—1928.

(9) In foreground, a corn sheaf. Right, a man piping under bough of apples. Left, a woman seated, under a tree. Middle distance, a shepherd and sheep, under a round sun.

Victoria and Albert Museum, E 3514—1928.

(10) Women dance to a piper round corn-sheafs before a harvest moon with an outer ring. Blake-like figures framing the page in the foreground. Fragments of minute landscape, including a church spire and large stars. Inscribed in Palmer's hand, "The moon also to rule by night for his mercy endureth for ever." (Page 39 of the original book.)   Victoria and Albert Museum, E 2358—1928.

All drawn in pen, some with wash ($4\frac{5}{8} \times 7\frac{1}{2}$).

Nos. 1 and 2, 4, 5, 6, and 10 exh. V. & A., 1926, No. 50. The present whereabouts of Nos. 1, 2, 4, 5, and 6 unknown.

These ten pages come from an oblong Whatman sketch-book bequeathed by George Richmond, R.A., to A. H. Palmer, who destroyed all his father's other sketch-books. For a description of this sketch-book, see A. H. Palmer's introduction, *V. & A. Catalogue*, 1926, p. 3.

25. LANDSCAPE: TWILIGHT. (*c.* 1824.)
Exh. R.A., 1824. No. 504.

26. TWILIGHT. (1824 or 1825.)
A picture sold to Mr. Bennett for £3, 3s. (see No. 31) in 1825. Palmer mentions work on a painting of this name in 1824 in his note-book. January 2nd 1825.—*L. & L.*, p. 13.

27. JOSEPH'S DREAM. (1824.)
A painting of this name mentioned by Palmer in his sketch-book for Jan. 2 1825.—*L. & L.*, p. 13.

28. STUDY OF A HEAD. (*c.* 1824.)
Exh. R.A., 1824, No. 706.

29. STUDY OF A HAND HOLDING A KNOBBED STICK.   (1825.)
Signed "S. Palmer, 1825."
Pen and chalk (4× 2¾).
Coll. Lady Kennedy, a daughter of George Richmond.
Victoria and Albert Museum, London.

30. THE REPOSE OF THE HOLY FAMILY.   (*c.* 1824-1825.)
Plate 9.
The Holy Family—the Virgin in a red robe—repose between a palm tree and a field of heavy-eared corn which slopes steeply past a roof into a dark valley. The donkey feeds beside them. Swelling land with trees in the background, under a blue-green sky. The text for this picture was, "The foxes have holes and the birds of the air have nests, but the Son of Man hath not where to lay His Head."
Oil and tempera, on panel (12¾× 15½).
Now known as "The Rest on the Flight to Egypt." Probably it is the "Holy Family" Palmer was working on round about July 15, 1824 (Note-book, Jan. 2nd, 1825: *L. & L.*, p. 13). The donkey is from Blake's "Flight into Egypt" (Metropolitan Museum) or his colour-printed drawing, "Triple Hecate"; and soon after July 15, 1824, Palmer was in contact with Blake.
Exh. Tate, Blake Exhib., 1913, No. 137; R.A., British Art, 1934, No. 558.   Coll. John Giles; Christie's, Feb. 2, 1881, No. 622; John Richmond; Christie's, March 4, 1929, No. 81.
Ashmolean Museum, Oxford.

31. A SCENE FROM KENT.   (*c.* 1825.)
Lit. *European Magazine*, 1825, quoted Whitley, *Art in England*, 1821-1837, pp. 90-91: An Academy notice—". ... two pictures by a Mr. Palmer so amazing that we feel the most intense curiosity to see what manner of man it was who produced such performances. We think if he would show himself with a label round his neck, 'The Painter of *A View in Kent*,' he would make something of it at a shilling a head. What the Hanging Committee means by hanging these pictures without the painter to explain them is past our conjecture."
Exh. R.A., 1825, No. 384.   Possibly "The Scene from Kent," sold in 1825 to Mr. Bennett (? Hon. Henry Grey Bennet, M.P.), *L. & L.*, p. 17.

32. A RUSTIC SCENE.   (*c.* 1825.)
Exh. R.A., 1825, No. 410.   Possibly the "Rustic Scene," sold for £7, 7s. to Mr. Bennett in 1825. (See No. 31.)   Untraced.

33. WINDSOR.   (1825.)
A picture sold to Mr. Bennett in 1825 for £5, 5s. (See No. 31.)   Untraced.

34. HARVEST MOON.   (1825.)
A picture sold to Mr. Bennett (see No. 31) in 1825 for £7, 7s.   Untraced.

35. SIX DRAWINGS.   (1825.)
Six drawings were sold to Mr. Bennett (see No. 31) in 1825 for £1, 10s. Untraced.

36. YOUNG MAN YOKING AN OX.   (1825.)

In the foreground, a plough, a smocked man in a straw hat treading on delicate herbage, puts a yoke on to an ox. Right, a thatched cottage with diamond-paned window under trees in leaf. Left, two oxen moving down hill against field of heavy eared corn, a tree against a dark wooded hill on which there is ploughland and corn in stooks against the hill brow, a full glowing sun. Six rooks fly over the corn. Beyond, a hill with faintly drawn hop-poles. Inscribed on back, "'Young Man Yoking an Ox' bought by me at George Richmond's sale 1897."

Indian ink ($5\frac{9}{10} \times 7$).

A study for No. 36. Coll. George Richmond, R.A.; Christie's, April 29, 1897 (168); Coll. Hon. Mrs. Arthur Davey; Christie's, June 28, 1940 (47).   Ashmolean Museum, Oxford.

37. SKETCH-BOOK PAGE.   (*c.* 1825.)   Plate 10.

At the top, a solid crescent moon in its first quarter, against a dark wooded hill. Left, a church spire lightly sketched. Below the hill, a stippled cornfield (?), sheep, a log, and a group of figures seated on the ground. Three more formalized versions of the same moon-and-hill theme below. On the reverse, a slight pencil sketch of wooded hilly country.

Pen and pencil ($7\frac{1}{8} \times 4\frac{9}{16}$).

Related to "Late Twilight" (No. 41).

Coll. Howard Wright.

Col. Bertram Buchanan.

38. A RUSTIC SCENE.   (1825.)   Plate 11.

In the foreground, a smocked man, stepping on delicate herbage by a plough, places a yoke on one of the oxen. Left, a bare tree trunk, fruit on a branch, a man with oxen ploughing under a hill. Centre, under the hills, heavy-eared corn. Right, thatched roof of cottage. On skyline between two hills, a blunt, turreted church spire. Over hill a crescent moon. Signed "Samuel Palmer 1825."

Sepia mixed with gum, and varnished ($6\frac{9}{10} \times 9\frac{3}{10}$).

Written on the original mount was:

> "Libra die somnique pares ubi fecerit horas
> Et medium luci atque umbris jam dividit orbem;
> Exercete, viri, tauros, serite hordea campis
> Usque sub extremum brumae intractabilis imbrem.
> VIRGIL, *Georgics I.*"

See also No. 36. Exh. R.A., 1826, No. 849 (?), Burlington House, Winter Exhib., 1893, No. 116. Lit. : *Apollo*, Dec. 1936,

p. 331, T. Sturge Moore (repro.).   Coll. Samuel Palmer; J. W.
Overbury; Giles Overbury.   Ashmolean Museum, Oxford.

39. *VALLEY WITH A BRIGHT CLOUD. (1825.)   Plate 12.
    In the foreground, two birds.   Left, a huge section of tree
trunk, a lane rising up hill under trees.   Right, clotted trees.
Centre, a stream; church spire under a hill.   Above, a piled mass
of cloud.   Signed in printed letters, "SAMUEL PALMER   1825."

Sepia mixed with gum, and varnished ($7\frac{1}{8} \times 10\frac{15}{16}$).
On the original mount was:

> "And this our life, exempt from publike haunt,
>   Findes tongues in trees, bookes in the running brookes,
>   Sermons in stones, and good in everything.
> *As You Like It.*"

    Exh. Burlington House, Winter Exhib., 1893, No. 116.   Lit.:
Apollo, Dec. 1936, p. 335, T. Sturge Moore (repro.).   Coll. Samuel
Palmer; J. W. Overbury; Giles Overbury.
                    Ashmolean Museum, Oxford.

40. *EARLY MORNING. (1825.)   Plate 13.
    Foreground, a rabbit, throwing a shadow on a woodland track.
Left, a log between minutely drawn grass and leaves, above it a
thick tree on a branch of which are two birds.   Centre, a group of
persons, seated in a valley in front of a field of heavy-eared corn.
Above the corn the chimney and thatched roofs of a cottage.   Objects
cast their shadows across to the right.   Signed in printed letters,
"SAMUEL PALMER   1825."

Sepia mixed with gum, and varnished ($7\frac{7}{16} \times 9\frac{3}{16}$).
On the original mount was:

> "I rose anone and thought I would gone
> Into the woodes to hear the birdes singe
> When that the misty vapour was agone
> And cleare and faire was the morninge.
> CHAUCER."

(though the quotation comes from Lydgate's *Complaint of The
Black Knight*, then given to Chaucer).
    Exh. Burlington House, Winter Exhib., 1893, No. 116.   Lit.:
Apollo, Dec. 1936, p. 329, T. Sturge Moore (repro.).   Coll. Samuel
Palmer; J. W. Overbury; Giles Overbury.
                    Ashmolean Museum, Oxford.

41. LATE TWILIGHT. (1825.)   Plate 14.
    Foreground, centre, a stile; left, a man asleep across two sheep;
right, a rabbit, a pool of water and a log.   Beyond, a partly harvested

cornfield with standing sheaves, unreaped heavy-eared corn on the right; behind the field, a thatched cottage and a church spire among trees. Above the trees, nearly touching a long, curled band of pale cloud, a crescent moon, partly ringed around.

Sepia mixed with gum, and varnished ($7\frac{1}{16} \times 9\frac{3}{16}$).

On the original mount was:

"The west yet glimmers with some streaks of day. MILTON."

Cf. No. 37. Exh. R.A., 1826, No. 570; Burlington House, Winter Exhib., 1893, No. 116. Lit.: *Apollo*, Dec. 1936, p. 332, T. Sturge Moore (repro.). Coll. Samuel Palmer; J. W. Overbury; Giles Overbury.　　　　　　　　　　　Ashmolean Museum, Oxford.

42. THE SKIRTS OF A WOOD. (1825.) Plate 15.

Foreground, centre, a flock of sheep. Piping shepherd, and shepherdess, seated above them under a twisted horse-chestnut in leaf, in the fork of which is a bird's nest, bird, young birds, and eggs. Extreme right, a bare tree trunk. Beyond, a stream and a cottage, surmounted by a cliff near the edge of which leans, in front of his flock, a shepherd on his crook. On left of chestnut tree, a distant vista to a signpost and a cottage. Dated 1825.

Sepia mixed with gum, and varnished ($6\frac{13}{16} \times 10\frac{11}{16}$).

Exh. R.A., 1826, No. 714; Burlington House, Winter Exhib., 1893, No. 116. Lit.: *Apollo*, Dec. 1936, p. 334, T. Sturge Moore (repro.). Coll. Samuel Palmer; J. W. Overbury; Giles Overbury.

Ashmolean Museum, Oxford.

43. *THE VALLEY THICK WITH CORN. 1825. Plate 16.

Foreground, a bearded man lies on the ground reading from a book. He is half-surrounded by heavy-eared corn. Right, a stile. Beyond it, cattle standing under a wall of corn below a steep hill. Left, standing sheaves, sheep, a piping shepherd. Over the valley, behind a church spire, a full moon, an owl flying across its face. Signed in printed letters, "SAMUEL PALMER 1825."

Sepia mixed with gum, varnished ($7\frac{1}{8} \times 10\frac{7}{8}$).

On the original mount was: "Thou crownest the year with thy goodness; and thy clouds drop fatness. They shall drop upon the dwellings of the wilderness; and the little hills shall rejoice on every side. The folds shall be full of sheep, the valleys also shall stand so thick with corn that they shall laugh and sing. Ps. lxv."

Exh. Burlington House, Winter Exhib., 1893, No. 116. Lit.: *Apollo*, Dec. 1936, p. 330, T. Sturge Moore (repro.). Coll. Samuel Palmer; J. W. Overbury; Giles Overbury.

Ashmolean Museum, Oxford.

44. THE HAUNTED STREAM. (*c.* 1826.) Plate 17.

Twilight: left, in the foreground, a man sits on the bank of a still stream, across which is a fretted, many-turreted Gothic chapel surmounted by a cross. Beyond distant mountains, and above a moon in its last quarter, and small flecks of white cloud.

Sepia ($3\frac{5}{8} \times 4\frac{3}{4}$).

A drawing to a text from Milton's *L'Allegro*, ii. 129-130:

> "Such sights as youthful poets dream
> On summer eves by haunted stream."

Reminiscent in design of the aquatint "Morning, Eton College," in David Cox's *Treatise on Landscape Painting & Effect in Water-colours*, 1813.

Exh. "One Hundred and One Drawings by English Artists": Cotswold Gallery, London, 1934, No. 67. (Repro. Plate IV in the catalogue, which quotes from a letter of A. H. Palmer's, May 17, 1930: "Propped up on my writing table . . . is the last but one of S. P.'s little Shoreham sepia drawings. It was the first version of a favourite Milton subject, the youthful poet on the banks of the Haunted Stream.")   Mrs. George A. Martin, Cleveland, Ohio.

45. BIBLICAL SUBJECT. (1826.)

For A. H. Palmer's description of this, see Chapter III, p. 32, quoted from *L. & L.*, p. 37.

Monochrome ($17 \times 11\frac{1}{2}$).

Coll. Samuel Palmer; A. H. Palmer.

46. *A SHEPHERD AND HIS FLOCK UNDER THE MOON AND STARS. (*c.* 1826.) Plate 18.

A crescent moon lies on its back, accompanied by huge stars, above a hill-top. On the right a castle, on the left a Gothic building. Dark clotted trees below the moon, and in the foreground, a shepherd with his crook, and his sheep, all lit by the moon.

Sepia and Chinese white ($4\frac{1}{4} \times 5\frac{1}{8}$).

Cf. description of "Naomi before Bethlehem" (1826), No. 47. Exh. V. & A., 1926, No. 71 (Plate IX). Coll. Samuel Palmer; A. H. Palmer.   Martin Hardie, Esq.

47. NAOMI BEFORE BETHLEHEM. (1826.)

For A. H. Palmer's description of this, see Chapter III, p. 31, quoted from *L. & L.*, p. 38.

Monochrome ($17 \times 11\frac{1}{2}$).

Coll. Samuel Palmer; A. H. Palmer.

48. ARTIST'S HOME. (1826.)

"(Aug. 31. 1826) . . . this day, I believe, I took out my *Artist's Home*, have through a change in my visions got displeased with it; but I saw that in it which resolved me to finish it. Began this day with scripture." *L. & L.*, p. 34.

49. LANDSCAPE: GIRL STANDING. (*c.* 1826.)

In the foreground, a girl standing by a plough on a steep ploughed field. She looks across two oxen and the thatched roof of a barn below into a valley with a shining river below dark hills. Trees, centre, left and right. Extreme left, a cottage.

Sepia ($4\frac{1}{2} \times 5\frac{1}{4}$).

Lit.: *Tate, Catalogue British School,* 1929, No. 3701. Repro. Binyon, Plate 27. Coll. George Richmond, R.A.; John Richmond.

Tate Gallery, London.

50. *HARVEST UNDER A CRESCENT MOON. (*c.* 1826.) Plate 19.

A crescent moon in its first quarter hangs under the end of a wooded hill, lighting the line of standing corn below, stretching along beneath the dark hill. Left, a cottage; right, in foreground, stooks of corn. Two men busy with sickles in their left hands; a third man stooks up the corn.

Wood engraving ($1\frac{1}{16} \times 3\frac{1}{32} \times 1\frac{1}{32}$).

Palmer wrote on January 3, 1827 (from Calvert's house in Russell St., North Brixton) to George Richmond:

" Would you do me the favour to give my best respects to Mr. Sherman & tell him I rather wish that my block should not be proved & retouch'd—the getting a bad proof such as they give at the shops inclining artists to retouch & Mr. Calvert says no wood engravers can with advantage retouch after prooving & that they all have regretted it when they have so done. Therefore I should be obliged to Mr. Sherman if he would complete the cutting without obliterating the drawings."—(Richmond MSS.)

Possibly he is referring to this engraving, or to a later version of it cut from his drawing by Welby Sherman, who also did an engraving on the wood after Calvert, as well as other engravings (Nos. 60 and 142) after Palmer. But Dr. Campbell Dodgson believes this was cut directly by Palmer—"there are no lines cut in facsimile, but only white lines made with the graver as the engraver went along, in the way that an original wood engraver works" (*in lit.*).

No early proofs were known to A. H. Palmer, who sent the block to Martin Hardie in May 1920. The block was cut on a rough piece of boxwood, with only its face levelled. A. K. Sabin took five impressions from it in this state on China paper. Of these one is in the Victoria and Albert Museum, two went to A. H. Palmer, one belongs to Martin Hardie, and one to Geoffrey Grigson. The block (which was destroyed in an air-raid on East London in 1940) was subsequently squared and built up to type height. In 1932 fifty impressions were printed on Japon vellum. One of these is in the Ashmolean Museum, another in the British Museum.

51. A WINDMILL AND CORNFIELD. (*c.* 1826.) Plate 20.

Headed plants, and tree stumps, in the foreground. Beyond, corn lying reaped in swathes: then a wall of corn cut into by a path: two persons in the corn. Beyond again, right, a windmill, flanked left, by a house under trees with a square church tower, and, right, by a cottage from which rises a wisp of smoke. A landscape of fields and hills along the sky line, beneath piled-up cloud. Signed, left. On the back pencil drawing of a face in profile.

Sepia wash ($2\frac{21}{32} \times 4\frac{1}{8}$).

Exh. V. & A., 1926, No. 83; C.E.M.A., Art for the People, 1943, No. 38. Coll. John Giles; Christie's, Feb. 2, 1881, part of No. 611; John Richmond; Mrs. John Richmond; Christie's, March 4, 1929, No. 71.   Leonard Duke, Esq.

52. CORNFIELD, WINDMILL AND SPIRE. (*c.* 1826-1827.)

Twilight: between trees in leaf, left and right, a crescent moon in its first quarter hangs over a ploughed hill, to the right of which are a windmill and a slender spire. Delicate plants in the foreground. To the right a man driving a cart. Between cart and spire a cornfield, to the right of which a lane winds under trees towards the church.

Sepia.

Repro. Binyon, Plate. 18. Coll. Samuel Palmer; A. H. Palmer.

53. A HILLY SCENE. (*c.* 1826.) Plate 21.

Under a gothic arch of trees, framing the picture (one a horse-chestnut in flower), a jewelled landscape. A brown gate, open, in the foreground, and beyond, a lane leading by a green margin of grass through golden walls of enormous-headed corn. Down the path a figure with a white head approaches a gate. Beyond a grey church tower. Left, red-roofed houses. Right, a green hillside with sheep. Beyond, right, a windmill. Centre, a dark-green hillside with cattle, and a ring of hurdles. Above, hills again, touched, left, with yellow, green, and pale blue. More distant peaks, white touched with red. And, over all, in a blue-green sky a crescent moon on its back and a blazing star. Left, a fir tree; while in the foreground a tree springs up toward the moon, broken into by leaves. Written on the back: "No. 3 A Hilly Scene."

Watercolour, pen and tempera, heavily varnished, on panel (sight: $3\frac{1}{16} \times 5\frac{9}{32}$).

Cf. "Coming from Evening Church" (1830)—No. 83, Plate 38— and the 1825 drawing, "Late Twilight"—No. 41, Plate 14. This is intermediate. Lit.: S. P. to G. Richmond, Jan. 2, 1873: "I feel much pleased & much honoured that you should have found matter worthy of your attention in the 'Rustic Scene.' There was not quite the clearance you mention, only four, not five. I could not

help thinking as I turned them over, that had the picture fanciers
of that day given only a *little* encouragement, there need have been
no watercolours, but it was not to be." (Richmond MSS.)

Exh. R.A., Winter Exhib., 1893, No. 118, as "View near Sevenoaks"; Tate, Blake Exhib., 1913, No. 127, as " A Study, Shoreham."
Coll. G. Richmond, R.A. (who bought it from Samuel Palmer in
1873); Christie's, May 1, 1897, as "View near Sevenoaks"; Lady
Kennedy. Rev. H. Kennedy.

54. DARK TREES BY A POOL. (c. 1826-1827.)

Tall trees, delicately patterned, stand by a pool. Crops making
a pattern on the field, left; and on either side of the dark tree trunk,
right.

Sepia ($4\frac{1}{8} \times 2\frac{5}{8}$).

Exh. V. & A., 1926, No. 70. Repro. Binyon, Plate 34. Coll.
Samuel Palmer; A. H. Palmer. Martin Hardie, Esq.

55. MOONLIGHT: THE WINDING RIVER. (c. 1827.) Plate 22.

A night scene among trees, through the tops of which a full moon
is shining. Left, a fold of sheep, right, a cottage. The moon lights
up a winding river, beyond which are more woods and hills.

Sepia, touched with white ($10\frac{1}{2} \times 7\frac{3}{16}$).

Exh. V. & A., 1926, No. 60. R.A., British Art, 1934, No. 1126.
(Repro. *Commemorative Catalogue*, No. CLXXXIX.) Coll. Samuel
Palmer; A. H. Palmer; Christie's, March 4, 1929, No. 60.

Thomas Lowinsky, Esq.

56. GEORGE RICHMOND ENGRAVING "THE SHEPHERD." (1827.) Plate 23.

George Richmond in profile, wearing a tasselled nightcap,
intently at work at a desk, under a glass, beyond which is a lighted
candle. A burin and a scraper beside him. On the wall above his
head, a drawing or print: in right-hand corner: "Sept. 9 1827
W. S. from G. R." Below, in pencil in another hand: "Portrait of
Geo Richmond engraving the Shepherd."

Pen ($5\frac{1}{16} \times 4\frac{9}{16}$).

W. S. is no doubt Welby Sherman. Coll. George Richmond,
R.A.; Walter Richmond. Mrs. Walter Richmond.

57. *A YOUNG MAN IN A LANDSCAPE. (c. 1827-1828.)

"The head and shoulders of a very dark and heavy-browed young man who
gazes at us out of the picture. The intense colour of the flesh and hair is
heightened with real gold, and behind the red and green drapery that swathes
his shoulders—behind his long black locks is a small space into which are compressed a solemn, twilight sky; a landscape with a church, a castle, and a windmill; and, on a foreground knoll, a few Druidic remains brilliantly lighted from

the same source as the face itself. The painting is so thick that even the transparent tints stand up after the manner of bas-relief."—*L. & L.*, pp. 48-49.

On ivory (3½ *inches long*).

"(I) beg the favour that if in your ivory researches, you meet with 3 or 4 morsels of very fine ivory, size & proportion not very particular so they be from about 1 inch by 1½ inch up to about 3 inches by 2 inches, you would buy them for me. Some thoughts have concocted & condensed in my mind of what I have seen walking about in midsummer eves & I should not care if I got a few of the subjects on ivory now, to study upon with fresh recollections of similar appearances next midsumer if God spare me; I prefer doing them very small for they are not things by themselves but wings terraces or outbuildings to the great edifice of the divine human form—otherwise snares."—(S. P. to George Richmond, November, 14, 1827.   Richmond MSS.)

Coll. Samuel Palmer; A. H. Palmer.

58. PORTRAIT OF THE ARTIST.   (1828.)   Plate 24.

Full face, head and part of the shoulders. A white cravat.

Black and white chalk (11⅝× 9¹¹⁄₁₆).

This can be dated early in 1828 from the similar drawing of Samuel Palmer by George Richmond, done on Feb. 3, 1828, and now in the possession of Mrs. Walter Richmond, of Chester.

Exh. (? R.A., 1824, No. 706 "Study of a Head"). V. & A., 1926, No. 1 (Repro. Plate I); R.A., British Art, 1934, No. 1127; Paris, Louvre, La Peinture Anglaise XVIIIᵉ et XIXᵉ Siècles, 1938 (No. 216). Coll. Samuel Palmer; A. H. Palmer; Christie's, March 4, 1929, No. 41.   Ashmolean Museum, Oxford.

59. THE SHEPHERD.   (1828.)

An engraving after Samuel Palmer by Welby Sherman.

This is referred to in a letter from Samuel Palmer to George Richmond, June 24, 1828: "If Mr. Sherman have finish'd his print he needs not wait till I see it, but may bring it out directly if he please, as the more copies are sold the sooner the plate will be his own. Both with respect to finishing the shepherd & selling the impressions of the Samson I am sure he may freely apply to Mr. Linnell's kindness for advice." The letter is endorsed in George Richmond's hand: "Sherman's print of Mr. P's 'Shepherd' to be published immediately." (Richmond MSS.) (Richmond's own print of "The Shepherd" had been designed and engraved in 1827.) No impressions of this engraving are known.

60. OAK TREE AND BEECH: LULLINGSTONE PARK.   (1828.)
Plate 25.

In a wood in leaf: right, a wide-rooted, big-girthed oak rising to the point where its branches divide. The bark, lichen, etc., carefully detailed. Left, the tall smooth pillar of a beech. Signed, right, "S. Palmer fecᵗ."

Pen and ink, watercolour and gouache (11⅝× 18½).

Lit.: *V. & A.*, 1926, *Catalogue*, p. 8, where A. H. Palmer quotes an MS. letter from Samuel Palmer to George Richmond,

September 1828: "Mr. Linnell tells me that by making studies of the Shoreham scenery I could get a thousand a year directly. Tho' I am making studies for Mr. Linnell, I will, God help me, never be a naturalist by profession."—*L. & L.*, p. 45; and pp. 173-4 (letter from Samuel Palmer to John Linnell, Dec. 21, 1828): "Milton, by one epithet, draws an oak of the largest girth I ever saw, 'Pine and *monumental* oak': I have just been trying to draw a large one in Lullingstone; but the poet's tree is huger than any in the park: there, the moss, and rifts, and barky furrows, and the mouldering grey (tho' that adds majesty to the lord of forests) mostly catch the eye, before the grasp and grapple of the roots, the muscular belly and shoulders, the twisted sinews."

Exh. Walker Galleries, Early English Watercolours, July 1937, No. 87. Coll. John Linnell; Herbert Linnell.

Mrs. E. A. C. Druce.

61. ANCIENT TREES, LULLINGSTONE PARK. (1828.) Plate 26.

Left, a muscular tree trunk of great girth; centre, middle distance, a huge ancient oak, twisted, hollowed, and decaying. Grass in the foreground.

Pencil (10×14). See No. 60.

Repro. *L. & L.*, p. 44. Coll. Samuel Palmer; A. H. Palmer; Christie's, March 4, 1929, No. 56.   Sir Kenneth Clark.

62. OAK TREES IN LULLINGSTONE PARK. (1828.)

In a wood: left, a big-girthed, many-branched oak, sending out, right, a thick branch which stretches out across the drawing. The furrowed bark, lichen, etc., carefully detailed. A similar tree in the middle distance. Signed, right, "S. Palmer."

Pen and ink, watercolour and gouache on grey paper (11⅝×18½). (See No. 60.)

One of the studies made in 1828 for John Linnell. Lit.: Oppé, *Burlington Magazine*, August 1941, p. 56. Repro. *ibid.*; *Signature*, Nov. 1937; *Walker's Monthly*, June 1937. Exh. Walker Galleries, Early English Watercolours, July 1937, No. 88. Coll. John Linnell; Herbert Linnell.   National Gallery of Canada.

63. *CART-SHED AND LANE. (1828.)

Right, on rising ground, the hollow trunk of a tree, through which white cloud can be seen. Centre, a long thatched cart-shed, the thatch encrusted with moss, etc. Inside, five carts. Left, a lane leading away downhill under trees in leaf. Bright, piled clouds above the barn. Signed, right, "Sam! Palmer fect." On the back, an ink sketch of a turreted castle.

Pen and ink, watercolour and gouache ($10\frac{15}{16} \times 17\frac{11}{16}$).

One of the series of studies made in 1828 for John Linnell (see No. 60). Exh. Walker Galleries, Early English Watercolours, July 1937, No. 85. Repro. Binyon, Plate 22. Coll. John Linnell; Herbert Linnell.   Victoria and Albert Museum, London.

64. A TIMBERED COTTAGE.   (1828.)

An ivy-grown cottage, with two half-timbered gables on either side of a thin chimney. A woman stands at a door, right. Below, the gables, a top-hatted man leans over the fence. Left, a plaited fence. Signed, right, " S. Palmer."

Pen and ink and watercolour ($14 \times 17\frac{7}{8}$).

One of the series of studies made in 1828 for John Linnell (see No. 60). Exh. Walker Galleries, Early English Watercolours, July 1937, No. 84. Coll. John Linnell; Herbert Linnell.

Mrs. E. A. C. Druce.

65. *BARN IN A VALLEY.   (1828.)   Plate 27.

Under a dark-shaded hill, a barn, and a circular corn-stack. Right, a thatched shed, seen through trees. Left, a plough. Signed, right, "S. Palmer."

Pen and brush in bistre, indian ink and gouache over pencil on brownish paper ($11\frac{1}{8} \times 17\frac{5}{8}$).

One of the series of studies made in 1828 for John Linnell (see No. 60). Exh. Walker Galleries, Early English Watercolours, July, 1937, No. 86. Lit.: *Ashmolean Museum Report*, 1938, p. 36; Plate XII (as "The Valley of Vision"). Coll. John Linnell; Herbert Linnell.   Ashmolean Museum, Oxford.

66. THE VILLAGE OF SHOREHAM, NEAR SEVENOAKS.   (? 1828.)

A sketch from a hillside above Shoreham, showing a glimpse of Palmer's home, Waterhouse.

Sepia, touched with white ($9 \times 11\frac{3}{4}$).

Judging from size and A. H. Palmer's note (*V. & A.*, 1926, p. 34) probably one of the direct sketches made about 1828 (cf. Nos. 60–66). Exh. V. & A., 1926, No. 52. Coll. Samuel Palmer; A. H. Palmer; Christie's, Feb. 20, 1829, No. 42; Messrs. Rinder.

67. THE VALLEY FARM.   (c. 1828.)

In the foreground, right, a swirl of bushes, a shepherd and flock in a lane. Middle distance, a group of farm buildings under the wall of a valley. A side valley winds back above the farm. Sheep on the field above the farm. Pale clouds faintly shown above the hills by white chalk on the grey paper and Chinese white outlining points on the valley edge. In a foreground field, indications of a man ploughing with a team.

Pen, pencil, chalk and Chinese white on grey paper (sight:
$8\frac{7}{16} \times \frac{11}{16}$).

Coll. Samuel Palmer; A. H. Palmer; Christie's, March 4, 1929,
No. 44; Sir Kenneth Clark.   Graham Sutherland, Esq.

68. THE BRIDGE AT SHOREHAM. (*c.* 1828.) Plate 28.

A bridge casting a dark line of shadow. Bits of tree trunk and
large stones in the foreground, left. Two figures and children on
the bridge, beyond which a white river winds away through meadows
towards a white-touched house among trees. Pollard trees beyond
the bridge, and white sheep in the meadow beyond them. A tree
on the right. In the distance, tufted trees, another bridge, and hills.
Inscribed in Palmer's hand: "From Waterhouse—The Groombridge
house over the pollards."

Watercolour, pen and pencil on grey paper (sight: $8\frac{7}{10} \times 10\frac{7}{10}$).

Coll. John Giles; Christie's, Feb. 2, 1881, No. 610; John
Richmond; Mrs. John Richmond.   Eardley Knollys, Esq.

69. RUTH RETURNED FROM THE GLEANING. (*c.* 1828?.)
Plate 29.

The large figure of Ruth, carrying a sack under her left arm,
and holding a staff in her right hand, strides from a cornfield over the
lip of ground into a valley between steep hills. By a latticed window
below her a figure reads by candlelight. Beyond, left, a fruit tree;
and in the valley, winds a stream, under a sheep-speckled hill. Right,
a stook of corn below a branch of fruit.

Chalk and wash (size of sheet: $11\frac{9}{16} \times 11\frac{1}{2}$).

Exh. R.A., 1829, No. 641; V. & A., 1926, No. 58. Repro. in
catalogue, Plate VII (also *L. & L.*, p. 48; Binyon, Plate XIX).
Lit.: *V. & A. Catalogue*, p. 35; *L. & L.*, pp. 49 and 178. Coll.
Samuel Palmer; A. H. Palmer.

Victoria and Albert Museum, London.

70. THE DELUGE: A SKETCH. (*c.* 1828?.)

"Beneath a dark lowering sky, an illimitable waste of waters bears the distant
ark, and surges round a few isolated foreground rocks which it will soon cover.
Stretched supine upon them dead or dying lies at full length a tall and beautiful
undraped woman. One arm rests on her dead child, the other falls, together
with her long hair, into the waves."—*L. & L.*, pp. 49-50; see also pp. 33-34
and 178.

A monochrome.

Exh. R.A., 1829, No. 516. Coll. Samuel Palmer; A. H. Palmer.

71. A BARN WITH A MOSSY ROOF. (*c.* 1828-1829.) Plate 30.

A barn of greyish-brown boards, with a blue lichenous growth,
and some green mould. The thatched roof, carefully drawn in

depth and detail, solidly moulded—pale brown, with a touch or two of pink, or pale red, interspersed with white. Deep growth of moss, dark olive-green, light green, pale yellow, with a few touches of golden yellow. Above, a sky, washed with a leaden blue, leaving much white. Brown earth and green plants in the foreground; and, left, the chimney and pinkish roof of a farmhouse.

Watercolour and pen ($10\frac{15}{16} \times 14\frac{3}{4}$ *across the top and* $14\frac{13}{16}$ *across the bottom*).

Exh. Tate Gallery, Blake Exhib. 1913, No. 128; V. & A., 1926, No. 85, Plate XI; Royal Society of British Artists, Winter 1943, No. 582. Repro. *Axis*, No. 7, 1936. Coll. Samuel Palmer; A. H. Palmer.   Martin Hardie, Esq.

72. A COW-LODGE WITH A MOSSY ROOF. (*c.* 1828-1829.)
    Plate 1.
    Golden straw in the foreground. Three cattle in the lodge, yellowish-red, red, and black. The grey uprights support a thatched roof heavy with moss and lichen, painted on thickly with light gold, dabs of green, spots of reddish-brown. A cloudy sky, watery-white with mauve shadows and touches of red. Right, foliage above two wooden fences.

Watercolour, gouache, and pen (*sight:* $10\frac{1}{16} \times 14\frac{5}{16}$).   Coll. Samuel Palmer; Howard Wright.

Colonel Bertram Buchanan.

73. COTTAGE AMONG TREES. (*c.* 1828.)
    A thatched cottage, or farmhouse, with tall chimneys, with a lichen roof alongside, bowered among trees in a valley. Hop-poles on the wooded hillside beyond.

Pen and wash (*size of sheet:* $11 \times 7\frac{1}{2}$).

Exh. V. & A., 1926, No. 75.   Coll Samuel Palmer; A. H. Palmer.   Martin Hardie, Esq.

74. THE PRIMITIVE COTTAGE. (*c.* 1828-1829.)
    A thatched cottage, centre, in a wooded valley; in the back-ground hills, on which is a long hop-field. Left, the chimney and roof-top of another cottage. Foreground, right, a stile.

Pen and sepia wash ($10\frac{3}{4} \times 14\frac{3}{4}$).

Exh. R.A., British Art, 1934, No. 1177, as "Shoreham." Coll. Samuel Palmer; A. H. Palmer; Christie's, March 4, 1929, No. 35, "best Shoreham period."   Thomas Lowinsky, Esq.

75. THE PRIMITIVE COTTAGE. (*c.* 1828-1829.) Plate 31.
    In a valley, below a hill sloping down from left to right, a thatched cottage, smoke coming from the chimney. Trees in leaf above the

cottage, left. On the hillside beyond, trees and shrubs. Written
on the back, in A. H. Palmer's hand, "The Primitive Cottage."

Pen and wash ($8\frac{7}{8} \times 10\frac{7}{8}$).

Exh. V. & A., 1926, No. 74, Plate VIII. Coll. Samuel Palmer
A. H. Palmer. Sir Frank Short, R.A.

76. AN ANCIENT BARN. (*c.* 1829.) Plate 32.

Nesting among tufted trees and bushes, a stolid thatched barn
with plank walls. Right, among the trees a roof and chimney, and
further right, fence and gate.

Pen and wash (*sight measurement:* $6 \times 10\frac{13}{16}$).

Coll. Samuel Palmer; A. H. Palmer; Christie's, March 4, 1929
Part of No. 55. Thomas Lowinsky, Esq.

77. *PEAR TREE IN A WALLED GARDEN. (*c.* 1829.) Plate 33

A cool coloured study of a pear tree against a garden wall of big
stones. Big clotted white blossom, and green leaves. Through
wall at right angles an arched doorway, and, right, another wall
tree. In the foreground, green plants twist and squirm. Above the
wall, hill-tops and white clouds.

Watercolour ($8\frac{3}{4} \times 11\frac{1}{8}$).

Lit.: *V. & A. Palmer Catalogue*, 1926, p. 35. Exh. V. &. A.
1926, No. 56; Amsterdam, 1936, No. 223; Paris, Bibliothèque
Nationale, 1937, No. 114; Louvre, La Peinture Anglaise XVIIIe &
XIXe Siècles, No. 216. Repro. *Signature*, Nov. 1937. Coll. Samuel
Palmer; A. H. Palmer ; Christie's, March 4, 1929, No. 45; Victor
Rienaeker. Mrs. K. T. Parker.

78. IN A SHOREHAM GARDEN. (*c.* 1829.) Plate 34.

A garden late in spring, and dominating it, an apple tree thickly
and roundly clotted with white, red-tinged blossom. The trunk
crusted with golden lichen. Beyond the tree walks a woman in a
flowing red skirt. Vegetables curling round stakes on the right
An eye'd and budded fertility of trees beyond the apple tree. Single
clots of apple blossom against the leaden-blue sky.

Watercolour and gouache ($11\frac{1}{16} \times 8\frac{3}{4}$).

Exh. V. & A., 1926, No. 62; R.A., British Art, 1934, No. 774
Lit.: *L. & L.*, p. 48. Repro. e.g. *Cat. Watercolour Paintings*
V. & A., 1927, Fig. 97; *Old Water-Colour Society*, *Annual Volume*
1927; in colour, *Burlington Magazine*, 49, 1926, p. 261; V. & A
postcard. Coll. Samuel Palmer; A. H. Palmer.

Victoria and Albert Museum, London.

79. A KENTISH IDYL. (*c.* 1829-1830.) Plate 35.

The full moon rises from behind a hill slope, into a sk

corrugated with white cloud. Under dark, moon-flecked trees on the right stands a man in a smock holding a stick in his left hand.

Sepia ($3\frac{3}{8} \times 4\frac{3}{16}$).

Repro. Plate 6, *Memoir*; Exh. V. & A., 1926, No. 80. Coll. Samuel Palmer; Mrs. S. Palmer; A. H. Palmer.

Sir Frank Short, R.A.

80. *A SHEPHERD LEADING HIS FLOCK UNDER THE FULL MOON. (*c.* 1829-1830.)   Plate 36.

A vast full moon has risen behind a wooded hill, gently sloping down from right to left. The sky is cloud-mottled, and the moon (there are leaves across its disc) shines over deep shade to touch on a shepherd and the flock he is leading across the foreground. A spotted, rocky hillside in the moonlight, left; and, right, a thatched barn under trees.

Sepia ($5\frac{13}{16} \times 7$).

Exh. V. & A., 1926, No. 72. Repro. *International Studio*, May 1927, p. 64. Coll. Samuel Palmer; A. H. Palmer; F. L. Griggs.

Leonard Duke, Esq.

81. *FULL MOON AND DEER. (*c.* 1829-1830.) Plate 37.

Moonlight: a vast full moon has risen into a mottled sky, above a cliff. Leaves black against the disc. Below, beyond the tufted background trees a woman stands left, and in the foreground three deer at rest.

Wash and body-colour ($5\frac{5}{16} \times 3\frac{11}{16}$).

Exh. V. & A., 1926, No. 71b.

Victoria and Albert Museum, London.

82. THE VALLEY OF VISION. (*c.* 1829-1830.)

"In the sunlit foreground, two shadowy figures, one a Christ-like shepherd driving some sheep. Behind them a woman and three children coming through a gateway. A meadow, barn, and track in the middle distance. In the background, the downs—their summit sunlit and sprinkled with snow, their base and the valley below in deep shadow, the trees bare. A beautiful and emotional landscape."

Pen and sepia, heightened in white ($11\frac{1}{16} \times 17\frac{1}{2}$).

Exh. V. & A., 1926, No. 59. Coll. Samuel Palmer; A. H. Palmer; Christie's, March 4, 1929, No. 30.

Leonard Duke, Esq.

. COMING FROM EVENING CHURCH. (1830.)   Plate 38.

Under an archway of trees in leaf, framing the picture, a full moon with a branch across it, hanging above hills on which there is a sheepcote. A church with a moonlit spire; and winding from it, to a cottage, right, above a winding moonlit stream, left, a procession of men and women and children, including the parson in cassock. Signed below, "PAINTED 1830 AT SHOREHAM KENT S. PALMER."

Oil and tempera on canvas (12× 7¾).

Exh. Tate, Blake Exhib., 1913, No. 133. Lit.: *Tate, Catalogue British School*, 1929, No. 3697. Coll. John Giles; Christie's, Feb. 2, 1881, No. 626; Dr. Richard Sisley; Mrs. John Richmond.

Tate Gallery, London.

84. A VILLAGE CHURCH AMONG TREES. (*c.* 1830.)

A church with a square tower and a spire, under tall clotted trees in full leaf. In the dark shade, a doorway or window lighted. In the foreground, sheep, and, right, seated figures. On the right, a tree, its leaves black and big against the sky.

Sepia (7³⁄₁₆× 6).

Exh. V. & A., 1926, No. 81 (Plate X). Coll. Samuel Palmer; A. H. Palmer. Sir Frank Short, R.A.

85. EVENING: A CHURCH AMONG TREES. (*c.* 1830.) Plate 39.

Twilight: in the foreground three figures driving sheep down a lane, below stooks of corn. A waggon visible in the deep shade below. Beyond the valley, among the trees, a church with spire rising above the hill. Right, a tree big and black against the evening light.

Sepia (6× 7¼).

Exh. Tate, Blake Exhib., 1913, No. 134. Lit.: *Tate, Catalogue British School*, 1929, No. 3698. Repro. Binyon, Plate 26. Coll. John Giles; Christie's, Feb. 2, 1881, Lot 612; Dr. Richard Sisley; Mrs. John Richmond. Tate Gallery, London.

86. *CORNFIELD BY MOONLIGHT, WITH THE EVENING STAR. (*c.* 1830.) Plate 40.

In the foreground stooks of corn. Right, a man in a smock holding a stick, walks along a wall of gold and orange corn. Beyond the corn, hills tufted with trees, under a young moon and the evening star.

Watercolour and gouache and pen (7¾× 11¾).

Exh. V. & A., 1926, No. 64; R.A., British Art, 1934, No. 769A; Manchester, British Art, 1934, No. 33. C.E.M.A.; Repro. (colour)

British Romantic Artists, John Piper, 1942.   Coll. Samuel Palmer;
A. H. Palmer; Christie's, March 4, 1929, No. 43.

Sir Kenneth Clark.

87. *SHEPHERDS, UNDER THE FULL MOON. (*c.* 1830.)
Plate 41.

A full moon rises behind a black slope, under a sky flecked with
white clouds. It lights up, left, a hillside, on which are hop poles
and a sheepfold. In the foreground, left, stands a shepherd, holding
a crook, among his sheep, and on the right, in front of trees (the
topmost with the white clouds showing between the branches), two
women. Under trees, below the black slope, the thatched roofs of
farm buildings.

Indian ink sepia and body-colour ($4\frac{1}{2} \times 5\frac{3}{16}$).

Exh. R.A., British Art, 1934, No. 1124 (2).   Repro. *Ashmolean
Report*, 1934, Plate VII.   Coll. Randall Davies.

Ashmolean Museum, Oxford.

88. *CORNFIELD AND CHURCH BY MOONLIGHT. (c. 1830.)

Figures, one carrying a sheaf of corn, walk in the moonlight
down a path with walls of corn towards dark, clotted trees, out of
which rises a church spire.   Beyond, the moonlit slopes of a
hill.

Indian ink wash ($5\frac{7}{8} \times 7\frac{1}{8}$).

Repro. Vasari Soc., 2nd series, xiv. 9; *Signature*, Nov. 7, 1937.
Exh. R.A., British Art, 1934, No. 1125.   Coll. Richard Redgrave,
R.A.; Sotheby's, June 29, 1932, No. 115.

Thomas Lowinsky, Esq.

89. *YELLOW TWILIGHT. (c. 1830.)   Plate 42.

A ridge, or headland, of wooded hill, stands against a lemon-
yellow sky, in which hangs a very pale crescent moon in its first
quarter.   Above the moon a band of pale blue.   Left, bands of orange
in the sky, above a sunset patch of red on yellow.   This red is
reflected on the tufted tree-tops, on the right.   The foreground is
warm brown, the trees are different shades of brown.   The hillside
below the moon is in deep purple shadow.

Watercolour and pen ($6\frac{1}{2} \times 10\frac{13}{16}$).

This drawing, luminous in a half-light, loses all its gentleness
and subtlety in half-tone reproduction.   The name by which it is
usually known, "Orange Twilight," is misleading.   Exh. V. & A.,
1926, No. 65 (Plate VIII); Amsterdam, 1936, No. 225; Paris,

M

Louvre: La Peinture Anglaise XVIIIe et XIXe Siècles, No. 217.
Coll. Samuel Palmer; A. H. Palmer.   Sir Eric Maclagan.

90. STUDY OF A BOUGH LOADED WITH APPLES. (1830.)
       Plate 43.
   (For the notes on this drawing see p. 95.)
   In left-hand corner, "1830 934."
   Chalk, touched with white (size of sheet: 11½× 17¾).
   Probably for No. 92—"The Magic Apple Tree." Lit.: *V. & A.,*
Palmer Catalogue, 1926, p. 36. Exh. V. & A., 1926, No. 63,
Coll. Samuel Palmer; A. H. Palmer; Christie's, Feb. 20, 1928,
with No. 38; Finberg.
                              Fitzwilliam Museum, Cambridge.

91. A COUNTRY ROAD LEADING TOWARDS A CHURCH.
       (1830.)   Plate 44.
   Between two banks, a road leads down to a church with a spire
and a yew tree. Trees, including on the right an apple tree, frame
the spire. On the bank, left, and in the foreground, sheep. Sitting
on the bank, right, two shepherds.
       Sepia (7¼× 5¹⁵⁄₁₆).
   A drawing related to No. 92, "The Magic Apple Tree." Exh.
V. & A., 1926, No. 82, Plate X. Coll. Samuel Palmer; A. H.
Palmer.   Sir Frank Short, R.A.

92. THE MAGIC APPLE TREE. (1830.)   Plate 45.
   From the right-hand bank of a steep lane leading down to a yew
tree and a church spire, hangs an apple tree, rich in apples, bright
red, touched, some of them, with white and yellow light. Beyond,
a great hillside of corn, varying from orange to the clearest, most
glowing yellow. The apple tree and spire are arched over with
trees in leaf. In the foreground, sheep, their backs lit up with
yellow and white. Beside them, left, a brown-faced shepherd
boy with a shepherd's pipe, in blue trousers. The sky above
the vivid hill a dark leaden mauve, which reflects mauve
shadows round the shepherd boy. "The whole is a conflagration
of colour."
       Watercolour and pen (13¾× 10¼).
   Lit.: *L. & L.*, p. 48; *V. & A.*, *Palmer Catalogue*, 1926, pp. 35-
36. Exh. V. & A., 1926, No. 61. Coll. Samuel Palmer; A. H.
Palmer; Christie's, Feb. 20, 1928, No. 38.
                              Fitzwilliam Museum, Cambridge.

93. THE HARVEST MOON. (*c.* 1830-1831.)   Plate 46.

"Under a huge golden moon, in a brownish madder sky, tinged with purple, a steep wooded hill. The moon is scarcely clear of the hill. A harvest field in the foreground, with gleaners dressed in rich, bright colours, one in a dress touched with crimson. Left, a loaded waggon. Right, under the hill a church spire. The prevailing colour a range of filmy variations on a dark rich umber."

Watercolour ($4\frac{7}{8} \times 5\frac{7}{8}$.)

Probably a drawing for the panel picture, No. 129. Exh. Cotswold Gallery, Second Annual Exhib. of Watercolours, March 1924, No. 32.   Dr. and Mrs. Gordon Bottomley.

94. A CHURCH WITH A BRIDGE AND A BOAT. (*c.* 1830.)

A square-towered church with a tall spire, below trees and hills. Right, a bridge. Top left, a bird. A yew tree below the tower, and in the foreground a man in a boat.

Sepia ($4\frac{1}{2} \times 3\frac{5}{8}$).

Coll. Samuel Palmer; A. H. Palmer.

Sir Frank Short, R.A.

95. A CHURCH WITH A BOAT AND SHEEP. (*c.* 1831-1832.)

A square-towered church with a tall thin spire, seen beyond two trees in leaf. Behind the spire, trees and hills. Left, the lighted windows of a house. Below the church, a stream, with a man poling a punt. In the foreground six sheep and two people.

Sepia.

Related to No. 94.   Mrs. George A. Martin, Cleveland, Ohio.

96. PASTORAL WITH HORSE-CHESTNUT. (c. 1831-1832.)

Under a horse-chestnut tree, a shepherd seated, with his flock in the foreground. Trees on the left.

Watercolour ($13 \times 10\frac{5}{16}$).

Exh. R.A., British Art, 1934, No. 784. Coll. (? John Giles; Christie's, Feb. 2, 1881, No. 607 or 609; W. F. Robinson, Q.C.); Rev. William Fothergill Robinson.

Ashmolean Museum, Oxford.

97. OLD HOUSE ON THE BANK OF THE DARENTH, SHORE-
     HAM, NEAR WATERHOUSE. (*c.* 1831-1832.)   Plate 47.

Autumn: in the foreground, a group of people, in blue and red and brown, seated, before cushioned grass, under a horse-chestnut.

Left, under trees, a red-roofed house, with yellow-leaved trees against its walls. Above, a lead-blue sky.

Watercolour and pen ($15\frac{7}{8} \times 12\frac{11}{16}$).

Exh. V. & A., 1926, No. 69. Coll. Samuel Palmer; A. H. Palmer; Christie's, March 4, 1929, No. 33.

Ashmolean Museum, Oxford.

98. *THE FLOCK AND THE STAR.   (*c*. 1831-1832.)   Plate 48.

A flock of sheep in the foreground, a few of them black. Left, trees against the light; right, on a grassy slope, a piping shepherd. Beyond the sheep a house with a lighted window, above which a rock-headed hill, with corn stooks, a hop garden, and tufted trees. Above the summit, five dark birds. To the right, the evening star. Note on the back: "No. 11 Flock of Sheep. S. Palmer bought by me at George Richmond's sale 1897. Tina Davey."

Indian ink ($5\frac{9}{16} \times 7$).

Possibly a drawing for "The Flock" (which was exh. R.A., 1834, see No. 146); and perhaps one of the "blacks" (see p. 99, and *L. & L.*, p. 179) exh. R.A., in 1832. Coll. George Richmond, R.A.; Christie's, April 29, 1897, No. 150. Coll. Hon. Mrs. Arthur Davey; Christie's, June 28, 1940, No. 47.   Ashmolean Museum, Oxford.

99. A CORNFIELD, SHOREHAM. (*c*. 1831-1832.)   Plate 49.

Twilight: in the foreground stooks of corn—to the right, a fence and stile; left, three figures, one a woman holding a sickle in her right hand. Beyond, trees against the evening light, a church spire above a shining river, a thatched cottage with a lighted window.

Sepia.

Cf. No. 130, "The Harvest Moon" in the National Gallery. Repro. by autotype, *Memoir*, 1882, p. 8. Possibly exh. R.A., 1832, "A Harvest Scene" (see No. 105) and one of the "blacks, which were in the exhibition " (Palmer to George Richmond, Sept. 21, 1832, p. 99, and *L. & L.*, p. 179). Coll. George Richmond, R.A.

100. THE FOLDED FLOCK. (*c*. 1831-1832.)   Plate 50.

Twilight: a shepherd with smock and hat and crook leans on a gate, before a fold filled with sheep, to the right and left of which is standing corn. Beyond, farm buildings under trees dark against the evening light. One window shines with light from within. Inscribed:

> "Where shepherds pen their flocks at eve
> In hurdled cotes amid the field secure.
>
> *Paradise Lost.*"

Indian ink ($5\frac{7}{8} \times 7\frac{1}{16}$).

Repro. by autotype, *Memoir*, 1882, p. 4. Possibly exh. R.A., 1832, as "The Sheep-Fold" (see No. 101) and one of the "blacks, which were in the exhibition" (Palmer to George Richmond, Sept. 21, 1832, p. 99, and *L. & L.*, p. 179). Exh. V. & A., 1926, No. 73 (as "The Sheep-Fold"). Coll. Samuel Palmer; Christie's, Feb. 20, 1928, No. 44. A. H. Palmer.   Vernon Wethered, Esq.

101. THE SHEEP-FOLD. (*c.* 1831-1832.)
Probably a drawing (*L. & L.*, p. 179), possibly identical with "The Folded Flock" (No. 100). Exh. R.A., 1832, No. 493.

102. SCENE NEAR SHOREHAM, KENT. (*c.* 1831-1832.)
Probably an indian ink drawing (*L. & L.*, p. 179). See also No. 159. Exh. R.A., 1832, No. 497.

103. A PASTORAL SCENE: TWILIGHT. (*c.* 1831-1832.)
Probably an indian ink drawing (*L. & L.*, p. 179). Exh. R.A., 1832, No. 547.

104. A PASTORAL LANDSCAPE. (*c.* 1831-1832.)
Probably an indian ink drawing (*L. & L.*, p. 179). Exh. R.A., 1832, No. 605.

105. A HARVEST SCENE. (*c.* 1831-1832.)
Probably an indian ink drawing (*L. & L.*, p. 179), and possibly identical with "A Cornfield, Shoreham" (No. 99). Exh. R.A., 1832, No. 614.

106. LANDSCAPE: TWILIGHT. (*c.* 1831-1832.)
Probably an indian ink drawing (*L. & L.*, p. 179). Exh. R.A., 1832, No. 816.

107. LATE TWILIGHT. (*c.* 1831-1832.)
Probably an indian ink drawing (*L. & L.*, p. 179). Exh. R.A., 1832, No. 818.

108. THATCHED COTTAGE AND CHURCH. (*c.* 1831-1832.)
    Plate 51.
A thatched cottage under trees, with a square-towered church beyond, and below, on the left. Hillside beyond.
    Sepia ($2\frac{5}{8} \times 4\frac{1}{8}$).
Exh. V. & A., 1926, No. 84; Coll. John Giles; Christie's, Feb. 2, 1881, part of No. 611; John Richmond, Mrs. John Richmond; Christie's, March 4, 1929, part of No. 71.

    Thomas Lowinsky, Esq.

109. DRAWING FOR "SCENE AT UNDERRIVER." (*c.* 1831-1832.)
    Plate 52.
A figure carrying buckets on a yoke walks down a lane through a hop-garden, under rocks muffled in foliage. Hop-wreathed poles, centre. A stack of hop-poles, right, and standing corn.
    Pen.
Study for No. 131. Repro. *L. & L.*, p. 405, as "A Kentish Hop-Garden, Shoreham." Coll. Samuel Palmer; ? A. H. Palmer.

110. THE SKYLARK. (*c.* 1831-1832.) Plate 53.
Early dawn: in the light that comes up through the clouds behind dark hills, a skylark rises in the clear sky—clear except for some tiny dapplings

of white cloud. A cottage, right. By the gateway in a fence, a figure, with face upturned and catching the light, watches the lark.

Sepia.

Probably one of the earliest drawings of a subject by which Palmer was always fascinated. The source is Milton's *L'Allegro*:

> "To hear the lark begin his flight,
> And, singing, startle the dull night,
> From his watch-tower in the skies,
> Till the dappled dawn doth rise."

Later versions are the painting "The Rising of The Lark" (Mrs. Medlicott, Newbury), which was done after his return from Italy, and "The Skylark," the etching of 1850. See *L. & L.*, p. 74. Repro. *Memoir*, Plate 8. Coll. Samuel Palmer; Mrs. S. Palmer.

111. *VALLEY WITH A CHURCH. (*c.* 1831-1832.)

A shepherd, right, carries a basket on his shoulder into a fold. In the valley below, a square church tower with a spire among trees; and houses below a large hill. Trees, left; distant hilly landscape, right.

Sepia.

Repro. *L. & L.*, p. 172, as one of two "Designs at Shoreham." Coll. Samuel Palmer; A. H. Palmer.

112. SHOREHAM, KENT. (*c.* 1831-1832.)   Plate 54.

In the shadowed foreground, sheep slightly drawn in pencil; trees, right. Below, a stream in the valley winding past clotted trees, under a bridge, past Lombardy poplars, and houses. A church above the stream, and above, a hillside divided into fields. Village, river, and hillside, shining in evening light.

Pen and wash (sight: $2\frac{13}{16} \times 4\frac{1}{4}$).

Coll. John Giles; Christie's, Feb. 2, 1881, part of No. 611; John Richmond; Howard Wright.

Col. Bertram Buchanan.

113. CRESCENT MOON WITH SHEEP. (*c.* 1831-1832.)

A moon in its first quarter, with the ring complete, shines between dark trees. Sheep in the foreground, and on the left, a shepherd reclining.

Sepia ($6\frac{3}{16} \times 7\frac{7}{16}$).

Coll. Richard Redgrave; Sotheby's, June 29, 1932, No. 116.

Henry Reitlinger, Esq.

114. MOONLIGHT: A LANDSCAPE WITH SHEEP. (*c.* 1821-
         1832.)

Foreground, a flock of sheep at rest, lit by the crescent moon in its first quarter, which hangs between dark trees, above a cornfield and against the steep sides of a hill. Between the corn and the sheep, two seated figures. Right, a deep vista under the trees.

Sepia (6× 7¼).

Related to the mezzotint, No. 142. Exh. Tate, Blake Exhibition, 1913, No. 136. Lit.: *Tate, Catalogue British School*, 1929, No. 3700. Repro. Binyon, Plate 29. Coll. John Giles; Christie's, Feb. 2, 1881, part of No. 444; Dr. Richard Sisley; Mrs. John Richmond.

·Tate Gallery, London.

115. BRIGHT CLOUD AND PLOUGHING.   (*c.* 1831–1832.)

Man and animals ploughing, right, on a hillside. Left, a valley with trees. Above, a huge thunder-cloud, with dark stratus across it.

Sepia (3⅝× 4¼).

Probably one of the first drawings from which "The Bright Cloud" (No. 136) and "The White Cloud" (No. 135) were elaborated. Coll. Mrs. Louisa Mary Garrett.

Manchester City Art Gallery.

116. *BRIGHT CLOUD, SHEPHERD, AND WINDMILL.   (*c.* 1831–1832.)

A shepherd leans on his staff, looking down a slope on which his sheep are lying. On the heath beyond, a windmill. Above it, a thunder-cumulus cloud, with bars of dark stratus below. Right, a tree.

Sepia (*sight:* 3½× 4⅜).

Probably one of the first drawings from which "The Bright Cloud" (No. 136) and "The White Cloud" (No. 135) were elaborated. Repro. *Memoir*, p. 82, as "The Windmill." Exh. V. & A., 1926, No. 78, as "A Heath with a Shepherd and his Flock." Coll. Samuel Palmer; Mrs. Samuel Palmer.   Mrs. Bryan Hook.

117. BRIGHT CLOUD: SUNSHINE AND SHADOW.   (*c.* 1831–1832.)

A woman with a pail on her head, and a man with a stick drive cattle down into a hollow under clotted trees. Left, farm buildings. White thunder-clouds in the sky, barred with dark stratus, over distant hills.

Sepia (3¹¹⁄₁₆× 4¹¹⁄₁₆).

One of the "Bright Cloud" series. Cf. composition of "The Bright Cloud" (No. 136); cf. also "The Golden Valley" (No. 134). Repro. *Memoir*, p. 16, as "Sunshine and Shadow"; Binyon, Plate 34. Exh. V. & A., 1926, No. 76 (Plate IX). Coll. Samuel Palmer; A. H. Palmer; Martin Hardie; the late F. L. Griggs.

118. DRAWING FOR "THE BRIGHT CLOUD."   (*c.* 1831–1832.)

Plate 55.

Under a solid pile of thunder-cloud, lightly barred with stratus, ground sloping up from left to right, on which lie a girl playing a pipe and a shepherd in smock and hat, and several sheep. Between sheep and cloud, a church spire. Under the trees, left, the ground slopes down to a building in the distance.

Indian ink (10× 10¾).

Exh. R.A., Winter Exhibition, 1893. Lit.: *L. & L.*, p. 49; *N.A.C.F. Annual Report*, 1917. Coll. Samuel Palmer; A. H. Palmer; F. G. Stephens. Presented by Hugh Blaker, through the N.A.C.F., to the Tate Gallery, 1917. Repro. *e.g.* Binyon, Plate 31.

Tate Gallery, London.

119. DRAWING FOR "THE BRIGHT CLOUD." (c. 1831-1832.)
     Plate 56.

Under a pile of thunder-cloud (more broadly realized than in No. 118), a hillside sloping up from left to right. Left, sitting under low trees, a shepherd, in a hat, playing a pipe, with a shepherdess. Beyond them, below the hill, a wide landscape. In the foreground, a flock of sheep.

Indian ink (6× 6).

Repro. *e.g.* Binyon, Plate 32. Purchased by the Museum from the Cotswold Gallery, 1927.   British Museum.

120. DRAWING FOR "THE WHITE CLOUD." (*c.* 1831-1832.)
     Plate 57.

Under a gleaming pile of thunder-cloud, barred below with dark stratus, trees above a stack, a thatched barn, and a church spire. In the foreground, a cornfield sloping up from left to right. From the right figures walk through the corn, some carrying sheaves. Centre, rooks flying over the corn.

Indian ink, sepia, and body-colour (5⅜× 6⁷⁄₂₅).

Exh. R.A. British Art, 1934, No. 1124 (1). Repro. *Ill. Souvenir of the Exhibition of British Art*, p. 89; *Ashmolean Report*, 1934, Plate VII. Coll. Randall Davies.

Ashmolean Museum, Oxford.

121. A MAN WITH A FAGGOT. (*c.* 1832-1833.) Plate 58.

A man in a smock carrying a faggot under one arm, and a basket in one hand, with a dog, walks towards a cottage below, left, with a smoking chimney and a lighted window. Tall tree, centre. Distant landscape below, left.

Sepia (4× 3⅜).

Possibly a drawing for "The Cottage Window," R.A., 1834 (No. 148). Cf. man with faggot and dog in drawing for "A Pastoral Scene" (No. 154). Coll. Mrs. Louisa Mary Garrett.

Manchester City Art Gallery.

122. STILL LIFE. (*c.* 1832-1834.)

A. H. Palmer to F. L. Griggs, Nov. 25, 1924: "I am DV about to send you a little Shoreham oil picture by S. P. It is a careful study of still life, and bears on the back the original signed label, when he was living at Shoreham, but used his little London house for teaching headquarters. It is the only picture of S. P.'s of this kind I ever saw. . . . The Shoreham oil pictures are very rare; and, as soon as I send you this little gift, I shall only have one left."

Oil.

This might be No. 149, "A Study from Nature," frame size, 14×16. Exh. B.I., 1834.

123. THE COTTAGER'S RETURN. (*c.* 1833.)

Twilight; a crescent moon in its first quarter hangs by trees in a lead-blue sky. Left and right, in the foreground, golden corn. A child pulling another child in a go-car, and a woman walking from the corn towards a cottage among the trees. Light shines from the window. Left, down below, a shining river winding in a distant landscape.

Watercolour and pen (size of paper: $6\frac{3}{8}\times8\frac{1}{8}$).

Coll. Sir Thomas Barlow; Sir T. D. Barlow.

Carl Winter, Esq.

124. A KENTISH SCENE. (*c.* 1833.)

Possibly identical with "The Shearers," No. 139. Exh. R.A., 1833, No. 657.

125. RUSTIC SCENE. (*c.* 1833.)

Possibly identical with No. 136, "The Bright Cloud." Exh. R.A., 1833, No. 356.

126. LANDSCAPE: TWILIGHT. (*c.* 1833.)

Oil and tempera.

Exh. R.A., 1833, No. 126; and possibly the "Twilight," exh. Fine Art Society, 1881-2, No. 7. Probably Coll. John Giles; Christie's, Feb. 2, 1881, No. 619; Fine Art Society. See also No. 141.

127. THE GLEANING FIELD. (*c.* 1833.)

Oil (and tempera?).

Exh. R.A., 1833, No. 48; Fine Art Society, 1881-2, No. 2. Possibly identical with No. 130, "The Harvest Moon," National Gallery. Coll. John Giles; Christie's, Feb. 2, 1881, No. 620; Fine Art Society.

128. *DRAWING FOR " LANDSCAPE, TWILIGHT."

Foreground, a knoll, speckled with plants; to the right, three figures, one with a bundle. Centre: a light breaks out of the darkness through a window between dark trees. Left, distant landscape.

Indian ink wash ($5\frac{5}{16}\times7$).

Similar in composition to No. 141, though, e.g., the disposition of the trees differs, and there is no waggon.

Exh. V. & A., 1926, No. 71*a* as " Landscape Sketch."

Victoria and Albert Museum, London.

129. THE HARVEST-MOON.   (c. 1833.)

"The moon has risen behind some lofty timber, driving back the mysterious shadows from the cornfield below, till all is bathed in rich amber light. Few other scenes would accord so well with the profound peacefulness of the deep azure sky, jewelled by a brilliant constellation—with the repose of the mysterious landscape threaded by a winding river. There is nothing out of place in the laden waggon with its team of oxen, or in the harvest labourers, for their dress proclaims them labourers of long ago."—*L. & L.*, pp. 46-47.

Oil (and tempera?) on panel ($8\frac{3}{4} \times 10\frac{3}{4}$).

Exh. R.A., 1833, No. 64.   Coll. Samuel Palmer; A. H. Palmer; Christie's, March 20, 1909, No. 84; sold to Eyre.

130. THE HARVEST MOON.   (c. 1833.)   Plate 59.

Twilight: a half-reaped field of corn, beneath high trees; women gleaning, and in the foreground, sheaves, a staff, a hat and a bottle. Two yoke of oxen pull a loaded waggon, left. A church spire visible among the trees, left centre. Right, a thatched cottage with a lighted, diamond-paned window Seen through a tree, extreme right, the full moon shows its rim above the hills. Signed, left, in capital letters, "S. PALMER."

Oil and tempera on mahogany (13×18).

Lit.: *National Gallery, Supplement to* 1929 *Catalogue*, 1939 (No. 4842), which suggests it may have been No. 129, "The Harvest-Moon," exh. R.A., 1833; but this picture does not tally with A. H. Palmer's description of "The Harvest Moon" (No. 129), *L & L.*, pp. 46-7, the dimensions of which (Christie's, March 20, 1909, No. 84) were $8\frac{1}{2} \times 10\frac{1}{2}$. Possibly identical with "The Gleaners," $11\frac{1}{2} \times 17\frac{1}{2}$ (Coll. A. H. Palmer; Christie's, May 24, 1909, No. 117; Vicars); or with No. 127, "The Gleaning Field" (Exh. R.A., 1833, No. 48).   Coll. Mrs. Louisa Mary Garrett.

National Gallery, London.

131. SCENE AT UNDERRIVER.   (c. 1833-1834.)   Plate 2.

Three figures, led by a fourth on horseback, move, from the left, by a lane which leads, between hop-poles twined with hops and golden corn, towards an autumnal, tree-muffled cliff. A stack, right, of dark grey and yellow hop-poles. On a label on the back, in Samuel Palmer's hand, "No. 4 Scene at Underriver Samuel Palmer. No. 4 Grove St. Lisson Grove Marylebone."

Oil and tempera on panel (*sight:* 7×10).

Cf. No. 109.   Exh. Fine Art Society, 1881-2, No. 1, as "The Hop Garden."   Lit.: F. G. Stephens, p. 13.   Coll. John Giles; Christie's, Feb. 2, 1881, No. 621; J. W. Overbury.   Mrs. Pilcher.

132. THE WEALD OF KENT.   (c. 1833-1834.)   Plate 60.

A tree, whose dark trunk has specks of red, stretches a branch across, from left to right.   Far below, seen from a glowing darkness through a window, a bright landscape of trees and fields stretching to a dark blue distance behind the branch and leaves.   Patches of pale blue in the landscape.   In the foreground, yellow, green, and reddish-brown grass, and left, below the tree, a warm patch of pale red.

Watercolour ($7\frac{3}{8} \times 10\frac{11}{16}$).

Exh. Tate Gallery, Blake Exhibition, 1913, No. 132; V. & A., 1926, No. 55 (Plate VI); repro. Binyon, Plate 24.   Coll. John Giles; Christie's, Feb. 2, 1881, No. 612; Dr. Richard Sisley; Mrs. John Richmond.   Eardley Knollys, Esq.

133. THE TIMBER WAGGON.   (*c.* 1833-1834.)

An oak tree, left, stretches out its autumnal leafy branches against a dark blue sky across to the right.   Below, in the foreground, oxen drag a timber waggon laden with a tree trunk.   A woman, in blue and red, and a man on the waggon.   Two men on the trunk.   Others follow behind, one in red, another in blue.   Beyond the waggon, far beneath, a lighted landscape of hedges and fields and farm buildings, seen as through a window.   Rock and a tree, right.

Watercolour (*sight:* $4\frac{15}{16} \times 6\frac{1}{8}$).

Compare " The Weald " (No. 132); and for the detail of the timber waggon, Turner's plate, " Poole," in the *Southern Coast of England*.   Exh. V. & A., 1926, No. 53, Plate VI.   Repro. also, *Print Collector's Bulletin* (Knoedler & Co., N.Y.), vol. i. No. 2, 1930, from which it appears that this quotation (*Paradise Lost*, ii. 488-491) was on the drawing on the mount:

> "As when from mountain tops the dusky clouds
> Ascending, while the north wind sleeps, o'er-spread
> Heaven's cheerful face, the lowring element
> Scowls o'er the darken'd landskip snow or shower."

Repro. colour, Binyon, Plate 23.   Coll. Samuel Palmer; A. H. Palmer; Christie's, Feb. 20, 1928, No. 46.   Messrs. Colnaghi; Messrs. Knoedler, N.Y., who sold it to the Alder Galleries, Kansas City, Mo., beyond which I have been unable to trace it.

134. THE GOLDEN VALLEY.   (*c.* 1833-1834.)

Golden corn in foreground, a ridge overlooking, below, golden and lemon-yellow cornfields, and a prospect of wooded hills.   Two women, one in red and blue, walk, right, after a waggon loaded with corn, which oxen pull downhill towards a farm.   The green top of a tall tree, left, catches the evening light. On the back, in Samuel Palmer's hand: "Old Paper, Unsized."

Watercolour (*sight:* $4\frac{15}{16} \times 6\frac{1}{8}$).

Cf. "Bright Cloud: Sunshine and Shadow" (No. 117), and "The Bright Cloud" (No. 136).   Repro. in colour, Binyon, Plate 33.   Exh. V. & A., 1926, No. 54 (as "Harvesting with Distant Prospect").   Coll. Samuel Palmer; A. H. Palmer; Christie's, Feb. 20, 1928, No. 47; Messrs. Dunthorne.

135. THE WHITE CLOUD.   (*c.* 1833-1834.)   Plate 61.

Composition as in the drawing (No. 120).   The thunder-clouds, white, touched with yellow and pink, gleaming against a white-touched blue sky, are less carefully defined; the same dark stratus stretches below. The trees are less thickly leaved, a ladder stands against the stack, and a white owl flies away, left, from the barn. The figure of a man against the barn and the two birds against the cloud, which appear in the drawing, have not been repeated. The corn, gold, touched with red and white. Red on the sheaves carried by the gleaners; and the woman's dress is blue over the shoulders and back. Vivid blue on the bundle carried by the last figure: a less intense, but light and clear blue of the sky, opposite, top left. Red roof, left. A green clotted yew tree against the barn. On the hill-top, left, green-clotted foliage. Deep blue edges the distant landscape. (The picture has been altered in cleaning since this photograph was taken, the owl and some of the foliage disappearing.)

Oil and tempera, transferred from millboard to canvas ($8\frac{3}{4} \times 10\frac{1}{2}$).

Coll. George Richmond, R.A.; Hon. Mrs. Arthur Davey (whose mother received it as a present from George Richmond on her twenty-fifth wedding anniversary); Christie's, June 28, 1940, No. 50.   Carl Winter, Esq.

136. THE BRIGHT CLOUD. (? 1834.)   Plate 62.

Above an autumnal, wooded valley, a great pile of white thundercloud in a pale, lead-blue sky. Purple shadows on the lower cloud-masses. Serene horizontal bars of stratus contrast with the cumulus. Left, cattle under trees, led by a procession of figures, one with a basket, one in red, one in green with a basket, one in white with a stick; at their head, one on horseback, in a green coat. In the valley below, right, a barn. A patch of red in the hillside trees above the barn, picking up the red of the walking figure. On a label on the back, in Samuel Palmer's hand, "No. 3 A Rustic Scene Samuel Palmer   No. 4 Grove Street Lisson Grove, Marylebone."

Oil and tempera on mahogany panel ($9\frac{1}{8} \times 12\frac{1}{2}$).

Compare the cumulus with horizontal bars in Plate 24 of David Cox's *Treatise on Landscape Painting & Effect in Watercolours*, 1813. Lit.: F. G. Stephens, 1881; *L. & L.*, pp. 20, 49, where it is called "an oil picture of the same subject" (as the Bright Cloud drawing, now in the Tate). Exh. R.A., either 1833, No. 356, "Rustic Scene"; or, probably, 1834, No. 517, "A Rustic Scene"; Fine Art Society, 1881-2, No. 6. Coll. John Giles; Christie's, Feb. 2, 1881, No. 625; W. F. Robinson, Q.C.; Richmond Robinson.
                                              Mrs. Richmond Robinson.

137. STUDY FOR "THE SHEARERS." (*c*. 1833-1834.)

A scythe, harvest barrel, stick, umbrella, coat, straw hat, and sheep-shears.

Wash and pencil (14× 10⅜).
Coll. George Richmond, R.A.; Walter Richmond.

Mrs. Walter Richmond.

138. STUDY FOR "THE SHEARERS."   (*c.* 1833-1834.)
Similar to No. 137, without the umbrella and the stick.   Straw is indicated and the tall beam of the picture.
Sepia.
Repro. *Memoir*, title-page.   ? Coll. A. H. Palmer.

139. THE SHEARERS.   (*c.* 1833-1834.)   Plate 63.
Framed by the wide doorway of a barn, on the edge of a hill, a group of three men and three women, one in red, sheep-shearing: trees above them.   On the right, a scythe, a basket, a small barrel, a straw hat, and a wooden fork.   Beyond the shearers, and below, a wide, hilly, golden landscape.
Oil and tempera on panel (20¼× 28).
Drawings for this picture are Nos. 137-8 and the latter is repro. *Memoir*, title-page.   Lit. (with repro.) S. Sitwell, *Narrative Pictures*, 1937, pp. 62-3.   Possibly identical with No. 124, " A Kentish Scene," R.A., No. 657, 1833.   Henry Walter exhibited (cf. foreground figure) a "Boy Shearing," B.I., 1833, from Shoreham.   Exh. Leger Galleries, Narrative Pictures of the Eighteenth and Nineteenth Centuries, 1937, No. 25.   Coll. Samuel Palmer ; A. H. Palmer; Christie's May 24, 1909, No. 118; May 25, 1936.

Henry Reitlinger, Esq.

140. THE SLEEPING SHEPHERD.   (*c.* 1833-1834.)   Plate 64.
Twilight: a young shepherd, in straw hat, smock, and blue trousers, asleep in golden light, in the doorway of a barn.   His dog leaps to the right, by his crook, a basket, and a bottle.   Beyond, a valley of clotted autumnal trees, under which is a cottage with a lighted window.   Beyond the trees the shoulder of a hill, outlined by afterglow.
Tempera with oil-colour glazes on paper affixed to panel (*sight:* 5× 20¼).
Lit.: T. Sturge Moore, *Apollo*, Dec. 1936 (repro. in colour).
Coll. Samuel Palmer; J. W. Overbury.

Giles Overbury, Esq.

141. LANDSCAPE, TWILIGHT.   (? 1834.)
In the foreground a knoll of yellow and green grass, with touches of brownish-red, some of the grass carefully detailed with its fruit. Below the edge of the knoll, two figures, one with a staff, stand in the glow from a diamond-paned window of a dark cottage, overhung with dark, autumnal trees.   Left, sheep at rest.   Right below the

knoll, oxen pull a loaded waggon.   Hills on the skyline: left, dark
blue-green hills, under blue-green clouds and an open, pale sky, the
light of which is deliciously reflected on the knoll.   Leaves "spotted"
on to the tree which hangs over the landscape from the right.   On
a label on the back, in Samuel Palmer's hand, "No. 6   Landscape
Twilight, Samuel Palmer, No. 4 Grove Street, Lisson Grove,
Marylebone."

Oil and tempera on panel $(8\frac{1}{2} \times 10\frac{1}{4})$.

Palmer exhibited two with this name at the R.A., one in 1833,
the other in 1834.   This is probably R.A., No. 419, 1834.   Coll.
Samuel Palmer; A. H. Palmer; Christie's, Feb. 20, 1928, No. 52.

Carl Winter, Esq.

142. EVENING.   (1834.)

A moon, in its last quarter, shines through trees on to a seated
shepherd and his flock.

*Mezzotint, after a painting (?) of Samuel Palmer's, by Welby
Sherman.   (Plate,* $8\frac{5}{8} \times 9\frac{9}{16}$ *subject,* $5\frac{7}{8} \times 7\frac{1}{16}$*.)*

State 1:—Before all letters.   Touched proof.   Dated in S.
Palmer's hand "March 21, 1834."   Exh. V. & A., 1926, No. 66.
Coll. A. H. Palmer.   Victoria and Albert Museum.

State 2:—Inscribed from Milton "EVENING LATE, BY THEN THE
CHEWING FLOCKS / HAD TA'EN THEIR SUPPERS OF THE SAVOURY HERB /
OF KNOT-GRASS DEW-BESPRENT."   PAINTED BY SAMUEL PALMER.
Published by Samuel Palmer, 4 *Grove Street, St. Marylebone* 1834.
Price 2/6.   ENGRAVED BY WELBY SHERMAN.   Exh. V. & A., 1926,
No. 67.   Coll. A. H. Palmer.   British Museum.

These impressions are described by Campbell Dodgson, *Print
Collector's Quarterly*, Vol. 17, No. 4, Oct. 1930, where the touched
proof is reproduced.   Another impression of the lettered state from
the collection of John Linnell is in the Tate Gallery.   Repro.
Binyon, Plate 30.   Palmer mentions this engraving in an MS. letter
to George Richmond (Oct. 14, 1834).   He refers to shortness of
money and would be "much obliged if as you kindly promised you
would let the little mezzotint flock hang up somewhere where i
can be seen as it might be of some service to Sherman or myself
who are both at present pinched by a most unpoetical & unpastoral
kind of poverty."

143. THE YOUNG TRAVELLER.   (*c.* 1834?.)

Sepia $(4\frac{1}{4} \times 3\frac{1}{4})$.

Exh. Cotswold Gallery: Samuel Palmer, March 1927, No.9.   Lit.
Catalogue, p. 7: "An early drawing made at the end of the Shoreham
period."   Coll. Bryan Hook.   Vernon Wethered, Esq.

144. LANDSCAPE, EVENING.   (c. 1834.)
    Exh. R.A., 1834, No. 49.

145. THE HARVEST FIELD.   (c. 1834.)
    Exh. R.A., 1834, No. 280.

146. THE FLOCK.   (c. 1834.)
    Exh. R.A., 1834, No. 119.   See No. 98.

147. STUDY OF A KENTISH HOP-BIN.   (1834.)
    A bin lying in a hop-field.   Notes in Samuel Palmer's hand:
'The younger (& smaller) hop leaves are of a lighter & yellower
green than the elder some of which are dark & cool & take very
gray lights from the sky & sometimes a pole clothed entirely with
the younger leaves is among the others quite a yellow green & not
only differs by colour from the rest but by being quite tender in
its reliefs and shadows—from being thinner of leaves (more slender
& regular in shape) without over-hanging masses & deep shades
under them.   The general colour of the ground excepting the flints
& chalk stones is decidedly warmer than the bin cloths & the latter
little warmer than the wood work but such of the stakes which
compose the bin as are rather brownish than greyish are very nearly
or quite as warm as the cloths & in some of their stains perhaps a
little warmer, but any part of the stakes where the dirty outside
has been chipped off would be warmer (yellower) & much lighter
than stakes or cloth.   It is hard to say whether cloth or bin stakes
are the lighter.   If the stakes appear so, it is because they take
more catching lights.
    "This bin in proportion & shapes was one of the best in the
garden.
    "A piece of white drapery is VERY much lighter than bin or
cloth—flesh unless very deep about the same lightness as the bin
cloth.
    "The colour of the lean earth which is about the centre of the
hop-hills is richer & warmer & darker than that of the trodden
ground.   There are four holes in hill within the shoots—out of
which the poles have been taken but they are only visible when
near the hill.   The ground much of it fine crumbly mould.   There
are a great many grey withered leaves about the ground & pieces
of bine about the poles are quite dark——   The hills are of fine
crumbled earth & all gradations from that up to bare lumps of the
stone—still of a crumbly texture with pieces of flint & chalk-stone
(Kent).   The touches of light gray and which [? white] are on
the ground of the garden not mixed with the mass but in spots
among stones—the earth is rich brown which is the mass.   Such of

the withered leaves grey as are scattered about are lighter & cooler
than the ground the green darker & warmer. The leaves (sentence
hidden by mount). The marly obliterated furrows of the plough
run in the direction of the line of hills." Dated 23.7.1834.

Watercolour and pencil. (Size of sheet: 11½ × 12.)

Possibly a study for No. 162, "The Hop Pickers." Exh. V. & A.,
1926, No. 57. Coll. Samuel Palmer; A. H. Palmer.

Victoria and Albert Museum, London.

148. THE COTTAGE WINDOW. (*c.* 1834.)
Unless A. H. Palmer was using this name for "Landscape, Twilight" (No
141) this picture was still in his possession in 1926. In a letter to F. L. Griggs
Feb. 2, 1926, he talks of "the last of my little Shoreham panel pictures, 'The
Cottage Window.'" See also No. 161. Exh. R.A., 1834, No. 1010.

149. A STUDY FROM NATURE. (*c.* 1834.)
(*Frame size:* 14 × 16.)
Exh. B.I., 1834, No. 315. Possibly identical with No. 122 ("Still Life").

150. LANDSCAPE. (*c.* 1834.)
(*Frame size:* 10 × 12.)
Exh. B.I., 1834, No. 10.

151. THE REAPER. (*c.* 1834.)
(*Frame size:* 15 × 17.)
Exh. B.I., 1834, No. 205.

152. EVENING. (*c.* 1834.)
(*Frame size:* 27 × 33.)
Exh. B.I., 1834, No. 342.

153. LANDSCAPE. (*c.* 1834.)
(*Frame size:* 9 × 11.)
Exh. B.I., 1834, No. 400.

154. DRAWING FOR "A PASTORAL SCENE." (1835.) Plate 6?
A crescent moon, barred with cloud, hangs over the sea.
headland and a rocky island, left. To the right of the moon, th
rocky crest of a hill, below which are hop-poles, then a half-reape
cornfield with harvesters. Up the valley from the sea, left, oxe
pull two waggons of corn. Right foreground, under trees, a ma
with a faggot of sticks, and a dog.
Bistre on Bristol board (7¾ × 4¹⁷⁄₃₂).
Repro. *L. & L.*, p. 172. Coll. Samuel Palmer; A. H. Palmer
Martin Hardie, Esq.

155. DRAWING FOR "A PASTORAL SCENE." (1835.)
In its last quarter, a crescent moon, of which the full circle
indicated, hangs over the sea, above a valley. To the right,
rocky, conical hill, ringed with trees and hop-poles. Below, ha

vesters in a half-reaped field.   Figures, one with a crook, right, foreground, below, a tree.

Sepia ($6 \times 7\frac{1}{4}$).

Nearer to the painting "A Pastoral Scene" (No. 156) than the preceding.   Exh. Tate, Blake Exhibition, 1913, No. 135.   Repro. Binyon, Plate 28.   Coll. John Giles; Christie's Feb. 2, 1881, No. 444 (as "The Harvest Moon," by which name it is given in *Tate Gallery: Catalogue British School*, 1929, p. 279);   Dr. Richard Sisley; Mrs. John Richmond.   Tate Gallery, London.

156. A PASTORAL SCENE.   (1835.)   Plate 66.

Twilight: a crescent moon in its first quarter, with bars of purple and blue cloud across its disc, hangs over blue sea.   To the right of the moon, a hill ending in rock, ringed about with hop-poles.   Below it a cornfield, and a group of men and women, touched with red, and blue, and pink.   From sheep, resting with light-tinged backs in the foreground, left, a valley winds deep down towards the sea, past a house.   In the foreground, right, two persons, one with a crook, under a tree.

Oil and tempera on panel (*sight:* $10\frac{3}{4} \times 15\frac{1}{2}$).

Palmer probably visited North Devon early in 1835; and this seems a blend of Devon coast and Shoreham vision.   Probably exh. R.A., 1835, as "Scene from Lee, N. Devon" or "The Cornfield"; also Fine Art Society, 1881-2, No. 8, as "The Harvest Field" (?)— (a "Harvest Field" was exh. R.A., 1834, see No. 145).   Coll. W. F. Robinson, Q.C.; Mrs. Abbott; Mrs. Walter Medlicott.

Ashmolean Museum, Oxford.

157. SCENE FROM LEE, NORTH DEVON.   (1835.)

Exh. R.A., 1835, No. 90.   ? identical with the preceding—No. 156— "A Pastoral Scene."

158. THE CORNFIELD.   (*c.* 1835.)

Exh. R.A., 1835, No. 153.   Possibly "A Pastoral Scene" (see No. 156).

159. A SCENE NEAR SHOREHAM, KENT.   (*c.* 1835.)

(*Frame size:* 18×21.)

Exh. B.I., 1835, No. 147.   An exhibit of the same name (see No. 102) was shown at R.A., 1832.

160. AT FILSTON FARM, KENT.   (*c.* 1835.)

(*Frame size:* 17×20.)

Exh. B.I., 1835, No. 154.

161. COTTAGE WINDOW.   (*c.* 1835.)

(*Frame size:* 16×17.)

Exh. B.I., 1835, No. 502.   Possibly identical with "The Cottage Window," ..A., 1834 (see No. 148).

N

162. THE LANE SIDE.   (*c.* 1835.)
   (*Frame size:* 25×31.)
   Exh. B.I., 1835, No. 341.

163. THE HOP PICKERS.   (*c.* 1835.)
   Oil.
   Exh. Soc. Brit. Artists, 1836, No. 45.

APPENDIX

It is not possible to give an approximate date to any of the following which cannot be traced, or else, because of the war, cannot be seen. Nos. 166-169 certainly belong to Palmer's Shoreham work.

164. THE MOWER'S RETURN.
   (*Oil?*)
   Picture in coll. John Giles; Christie's, Feb. 2, 1881, No. 623; sold to Warford.

165. A WINDMILL AMONG TREES.
   Sepia ($2\frac{7}{16} \times 4$).
   Coll. E. B. Jupp; M. B. Walker.
   British Museum (1913-5-28-55).

166. TREE AND SPIRE.
   A large bare tree; the spire of a village church on the right.
   Sepia (*sight:* $3\frac{1}{2} \times 4\frac{3}{8}$).
   Exh. V. & A., No. 79   Mrs. Bryan Hook.

167. A PATH THROUGH A CORNFIELD.
   A large tree on the right; a church in the hollow to the left.
   Sepia (*sight:* $3\frac{1}{2} \times 5$).
   Exh. V. & A., 1926, No. 77.   Mrs. Bryan Hook.

168. ON THE BANKS OF THE DARENT.
   Oil ($17 \times 11\frac{1}{4}$).
   Exh. V. & A., 1926, No. 68. Coll. Samuel Palmer; Mrs. A. H. Palmer; Christie's, March 4, 1929, No. 58; purchased by Crool.

169. SKETCH-BOOK PAGE.
   (*Page size:* $4\frac{1}{2} \times 7$.)
   In a sketch-book with 76 leaves with watermark *J. Whatman* 1824. Also in this book, "A Vision of Hercules" by Blake, inked over by G. Richmond, an extract in Blake's hand from Cennini's *Treatise on Painting*, Calvert's signature, notes and drawings by George Richmond, this one sketch by Palmer, and the book-plate of C. H. Tatham. Sotheby, July 28, 1920; lot 162.

INDEX

Aders, Charles, his collection of early German pictures, 14, 15, 142
Aegidiana, 141
Alison, Archibald, *Essays on Taste*, 54, 55, 87
Amberley, Lord and Lady, 20
" Ancients, The," 86
Arnold, Thomas, on the new and old ages, 103, 104

Baily, Mr., 115, 116, 120, 121
Baily, Mrs., 116, 117
Baptist Magazine, 1, 141
Barret, George, 15, 142
Barrow, Isaac, his *Sermons on the Creed*, 54, 58-9, 87
Barry, James, 143
Basire, James, 7
Bell, Clive, 52
Bennett, Mr. (? Hon. H. G. Bennet), 28, 29
Beulah, Land of, influence on S. P., 33, 144
Bird, Mr., 144
Blackwood's Magazine, 105
Blake, Catherine, 19, 61, 67, 151 ; and Frederick Tatham, 38 ; " Mrs. Blake's white," 75, 156 ; her funeral, 144
" Blake's white," 156
Blake, William, 15, 29, 51, 52, 56, 57, 82, 87, 134, 138 ; Rossetti MS., 3 ; meeting with S. P., 18 ; *Dante* designs, 19 ; as " The Interpreter," 19 ; visits Shoreham, 21 ; visits Calvert at Brixton, 21 ; promises to take S. P. to see Butts, 21 ; his funeral, 21 ; on St. Theresa, 22 ; on cathedral building, 22 ; advice to S. P. on imagination and vision, 22 ; on nature, 22, 23 ; on Claude, 22, 23 ; discusses *Marriage of Heaven and Hell* with S. P., 22 ; pictures, books, etc., of, owned by S. P., 23, 143 ; signs *Virgil* proofs for S. P., 23 ; influence of *Virgil* and *Dante* on S. P., 25 ; his *Dante* engravings given by Linnell to S. P.'s father, 80 ; S. P. on the *Dante*, 82 ; on the *Job*, 53 ; *Job* and E. T. Daniell, 131 ; his illustrations to Bunyan, 144 ; Blake-Linnell accounts (Yale University Library), 142, 143 ; influence on George Richmond, 43, 44 ; on nature and imagination, 148 ; entries in Richmond's (?) sketch-book, 194
Boconnoc, Cornwall, 39
Boddington, Mr., 131
Boehme, Jakob, 56-7, 147
Bonasone, 23, 29, 53, 94, 138, 146-7 ; Calvert on, 39-40, 147
Brandreth, Jeremiah, 105, 150

Breughel, 25 ; relation of " The White Cloud " to his " Corn Harvest," 109-110
Bridges, Robert, 44
Brinton, H. H., *The Mystic Will* (on Boehme), 147
Broad Stone of Honour, 47, 146
Brontës, The, 136
Brown, Ford Madox, 139
Browne, Sir Thomas, *Religio Medici*, 80 ; *Christian Morals*, 100
Buchanan, Col., 151
Bunyan, 19, 33, 34
Butts, Thomas, 21, 151
Byron, Lord, 40, 50

Calvert, Edward, 4, 23, 39-43, 52, 56, 67, 68, 97, 102, 108, 121, 134, 145, 149, 191 ; visited by Blake, 21 ; disapproves of destruction of Blake's MSS., 38 ; fondness for poetry of Wordsworth and Chapman and Landor, 40 ; on " The Ideal—the kingdom within," 47 ; his mysticism and paganism, 40-3, 65 ; sacrifices to the Gods, 42 ; his " Cyder Press," 81 ; on Rhineland skies, 119 ; his " Chamber Idyll," 152
Caravaggio, 22
Caroline, Queen, 46
Cat o' Nine Tails, 80, 148
Cato Street Conspiracy, 46, 150
Catterson Smith, P.R.H.A., 12, 43
Cennini's *Treatise on Painting*, 156, 194
Chalon, Alfred, admiration of Calvert, 39
Chapman, George, *Hymn to Pan*, 40
Chardin, 94
Chatham, Earl of, 105
Christopherus, Petrus, 14
Clare, John, 89, 139, 152 ; his admiration of Blake, 90
Claude, 36, 39, 94, 134, 138, 142 ; Blake on, 22, 23
Clay, Mr., 67
Coleridge, Berkeley, 100
Coleridge, Hartley, 100, 152
Coleridge, S. T., 54, 100, 118, 142, 145 ; on Pantheism, 42 ; his *Christabel*, 133 ; on Jakob Boehme, 147
Colour in the English School, 10, 141
Constable, John, 94, 132, 134, 149 ; animosity towards Linnell, 11, 135, 143
Cooke, George, the graver, 7
Cooper, Sidney, R.A., 43
Cooper, Thomas, on mysticism in England, 147
Corot, 94
Cotman, John Sell, 134

197

LIST OF ILLUSTRATIONS

33. Pear Tree in a Walled Garden (77).   *c.* 1829.

34. In a Shoreham Garden (78).   *c.* 1829.

35. A Kentish Idyl (79).   *c.* 1829-1830.

36. A Shepherd Leading His Flock under the Full Moon (80).   *c.* 1829-1830.

37. Full Moon and Deer (81).   *c.* 1829-1830.

38. Coming from Evening Church (83).   1830.

39. Evening: A Church among Trees (85).   *c.* 1830.

40. Cornfield by Moonlight, with the Evening Star (86).   *c.* 1830.

41. Shepherds under the Full Moon (87).   *c.* 1830.

42. Yellow Twilight (89).   *c.* 1830.

43. Study of a Bough Loaded with Apples (90).   1830.

44. A Country Road Leading towards a Church (91).   1830.

45. The Magic Apple Tree (92).   1830.

46. The Harvest Moon (93).   *c.* 1830-1831.

47. Old House on the Bank of the Darenth (97).   *c.* 1831-1832.

48. The Flock and the Star (98).   *c.* 1831-1832.

49. A Cornfield, Shoreham (99).   *c.* 1831-1832.

50. The Folded Flock (100).   *c.* 1831-1832.

51. Thatched Cottage and Church (108).   *c.* 1831-1832.

52. Drawing for "Scene at Underriver" (109).   *c.* 1831-1832.

53. The Skylark (110).   *c.* 1831-1832.

54. Shoreham, Kent (112).   *c.* 1831-1832.

55. Drawing for "The Bright Cloud" (118).   *c.* 1831-1832.

56. Drawing for "The Bright Cloud" (119).   *c.* 1831-1832.

57. Drawing for "The White Cloud" (120).   *c.* 1831-1832.

58. A Man with a Faggot (121).   *c.* 1832-1833.

59. The Harvest Moon (130).   *c.* 1833.

60. The Weald of Kent (132).   *c.* 1833-1834.

61. The White Cloud (135).   *c.* 1833-1834.

62. The Bright Cloud (136).   ? 1834.

63. The Shearers (139).   *c.* 1833-1834.

64. The Sleeping Shepherd (140).   *c.* 1833-1834.

65. Drawing for "A Pastoral Scene" (154).   1835.

66. A Pastoral Scene (156).   1835.

67. Mount Siabod (see p. 132).   1835 or 1836.

68. Study of a Garden at Tintern (see p. 132).   1835.

PLATES

Samuel Palmer assuming a Character. 1828. *Pen and pencil drawing by George Richmond (Private Collection).* $6 \times 4\frac{9}{10}$

4. Samuel Palmer. 1830.
*Miniature by George Richmond (National
Portrait Gallery)*

5. Study of Old Buildings (17). 1821.   *Pen and sepia wash.* $7\frac{1}{2} \times 10$

At Hailsham

July 9 1881

7.   Leaf from a Sketchbook (24).   1824.   Pen. $4\frac{5}{8} \times 7\frac{1}{2}$

8. Leaf from a Sketchbook (24). 1824. *Pen.* $7\frac{1}{2}\times4\frac{5}{8}$

9. The Repose of The Holy Family (30). *c.* 1824-5. *Oil and tempera.* $12\frac{3}{4} \times 15\frac{1}{2}$

10. Sketchbook Page (37). *c.* 1825. *Pen and pencil.* $7\frac{1}{8} \times 4\frac{9}{16}$

11. A Rustic Scene (38). 1825. *Sepia.* $6\frac{9}{10} \times 9\frac{3}{10}$

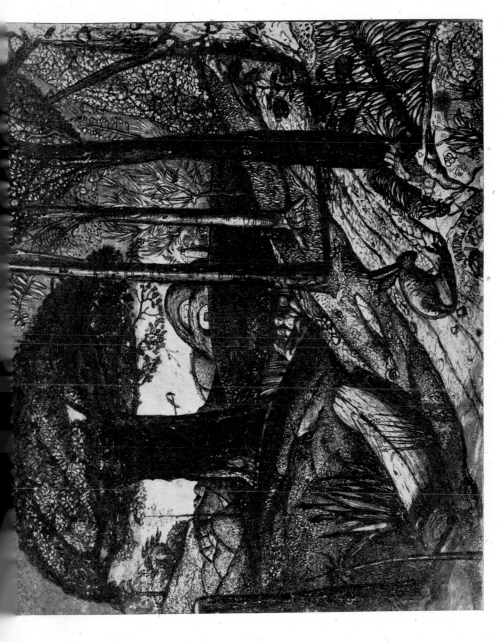

13. Early Morning (40). 1825.   *Sepia.* $7\frac{7}{16} \times 9\frac{3}{16}$

15.   The Skirts of a Wood (42).   1825.   *Sepia.* $6\frac{13}{16} \times 10\frac{11}{16}$

17.   The Haunted Stream (44).   *c.* 1826.   *Sepia.* $3\frac{5}{8} \times 4\frac{3}{4}$

18. A Shepherd and his Flock under the Moon and Stars (46). *c.* 1826.
Sepia and Chinese White. $4\frac{1}{4} \times 5\frac{1}{8}$

19.   Harvest under a Crescent Moon (50).   1826.
Wood engraving. $1\frac{1}{16} \times 3\frac{1}{32} \times 1\frac{1}{32}$

20.   A Windmill and Cornfield (51).   *c.* 1826.
Sepia. $2\frac{2}{3}\frac{1}{2} \times 4\frac{1}{8}$

21.　A Hilly Scene (53).　*c.* 1826.　*Tempera, watercolour and pen.*　$8\frac{1}{16} \times 5\frac{9}{32}$

2. Moonlight : The Winding River (55). *c.* 1827. *Sepia and white.* $10\frac{1}{2}\times 7\frac{3}{16}$

23.   George Richmond engraving " The Shepherd " (56).   1827.
Pen. $5\frac{1}{16} \times 4\frac{9}{16}$

24.   Portrait of the Artist (58).   1828.   *Chalk.* $11\frac{5}{8} \times 9\frac{11}{16}$

26.   Ancient Trees, Lullingstone Park (61).   1828.   *Pencil.*   10 × 14

28.   The Bridge at Shoreham (68).   *c.* 1828.   *Watercolour, pen and pencil.* $8\frac{7}{10} \times 10\frac{7}{10}$

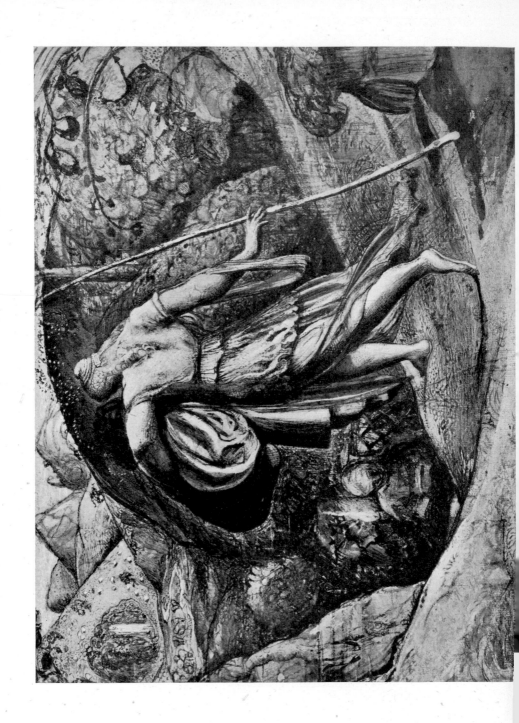

30. A Barn with a Mossy Roof (71). *c.* 1828-9. *Watercolour and pen.* $10\frac{15}{16} \times 14\frac{13}{16}$

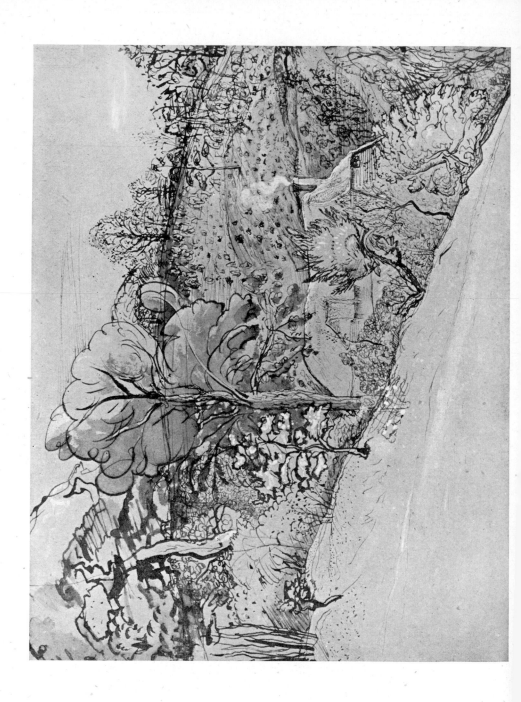

32. An Ancient Barn (76).   *c.* 1829.   *Pen and wash.* $6 \times 10\frac{3}{6}$

4.   In a Shoreham Garden (78). *c.* 1829.   *Watercolour and gouache.* $11\frac{1}{16} \times 8\frac{3}{4}$

35.   A Kentish Idyl (79).   *c.* 1829-30.   *Sepia.* $3\frac{3}{8} \times 4\frac{3}{16}$

A Shepherd leading his Flock under the Full Moon (80). *c.* 1829-30. *Sepia.* $5\frac{13}{16} \times 7$

37. Full Moon and Deer (81). *c.* 1829-30.
Wash and body-colour. $5\frac{5}{16} \times 3\frac{11}{16}$

Coming from Evening Church (83).   1830.   *Oil and tempera.* $12 \times 7\frac{3}{4}$

40. Cornfield by Moonlight, with the Evening Star (86). *c.* 1830. *Watercolour, gouache and pen.* $7\frac{3}{4} \times 11\frac{3}{4}$

41.   Shepherds, under the Full Moon (87).   *c.* 1830.
Indian ink, sepia and body-colour. $4\frac{1}{2} \times 5\frac{3}{16}$

42. Yellow Twilight (89). *c.* 1830. *Watercolour and pen.* $6\frac{1}{2} \times 10\frac{13}{16}$

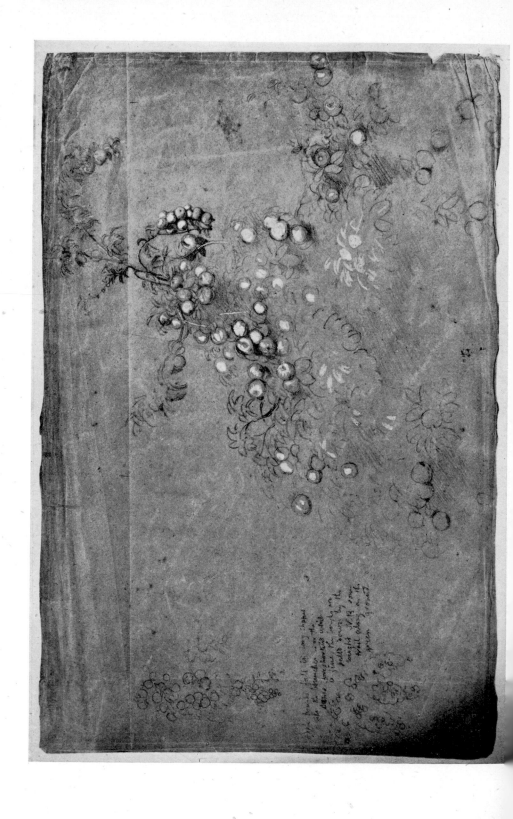

44.　A Country Road leading towards a Church (91).　1830.　*Sepia*.　$7\frac{1}{4} \times 5\frac{15}{16}$

45.   The Magic Apple Tree (92).   1830.   *Watercolour and pen.* $13\frac{3}{4} \times 10\frac{1}{4}$

46. The Harvest Moon (93). *c.* 1830-1. *Watercolour* $4\frac{7}{8} \times 5\frac{7}{8}$

47.　Old House on the Bank of the Darenth, Shoreham, near Waterhouse (97).
c. 1831-2.　*Watercolour and pen.*　$15\frac{7}{8} \times 12\frac{11}{16}$

8. The Flock and the Star (98). *c.* 1831-2. *Indian ink.* $5\frac{9}{10} \times 7$

A Cornfield, Shoreham (99). c. 1821-2.

50.   The Folded Flock (100).   *c.* 1831-2.   *Indian ink.* $5\frac{7}{8} \times 7\frac{1}{16}$

51. Thatched Cottage and Church (108).   c. 1831-2.
Sepia. $2\frac{5}{8} \times 4\frac{1}{8}$

53.   The Skylark (110).   c. 1831-2.   Sepia.

52. Drawing for " Scene at Underriver " (109). *c.* 1831-2. *Pen.*

54. Shoreham, Kent (112). *c.* 1831-2. *Pen and wash.* $2\frac{13}{16} \times 4\frac{1}{4}$

56.   Drawing for "The Bright Cloud" (119).   *c.* 1831-2.   *Indian ink.*   6 × 6

57.   Drawing for " The White Cloud " (120).   *c.* 1831-2.
Indian ink, sepia and body-colour. $5\frac{3}{5} \times 6\frac{7}{25}$

58.   A Man with a Faggot (121).   *c.* 1832-3.   *Sepia.*   4 × 3⅜

60. The Weald of Kent (132). *c.* 1833-4. *Watercolour.* $7\frac{3}{8} \times 10\frac{11}{16}$

62.   The Bright Cloud (136).   *Oil and tempera.* $9\frac{1}{8} \times 12\frac{1}{2}$

Oil and tempera. 20¼ × 28

64. The Sleeping Shepherd (140). *c.* 1833-4. *Oil and tempera.* 15 × 20¼

65. Drawing for " A Pastoral Scene " (154). 1835. *Bistre.* $7\frac{3}{4} \times 4\frac{17}{32}$

66.   A Pastoral Scene (156).   1835.   *Oil and tempera.* $10\frac{3}{4} \times 15\frac{1}{2}$

68. Study of A Garden at Tintern (p. 132). 1835. *Watercolour and pen.* $14\frac{3}{4} \times 18\frac{3}{4}$